Harry E. Lutz

A Student's Views Abroad

Harry E. Lutz

A Student's Views Abroad

ISBN/EAN: 9783337419899

Printed in Europe, USA, Canada, Australia, Japan

Cover: Foto ©Andreas Hilbeck / pixelio.de

More available books at **www.hansebooks.com**

VIEWS ABROAD.

CIRCLEVILLE, OHIO:
UNION-HERALD PUBLISHING HOUSE.
1888.

TO MY WIFE
THIS VOLUME
IS INSCRIBED.

PREFACE.

This volume consists of extracts from my journals and published letters concerning a two years' tour through Holland, Belgium, Germany, Austria, Italy, Sweden, Finland, Russia, Denmark, Switzerland, France, Malta, Egypt, Palestine, Asia Minor, Turkey, Greece, England, Scotland and Ireland. The entire book was written amid the scenes described. I was fresh from college when the trip was begun and was not yet twenty-one years of age when I returned home. The book records the impressions of a student and I have made no effort to change any part of it to correspond with subsequent opinions which I may have formed.

The entire trip was made at an expenditure of only $750 and may therefore demonstrate to the Ohio student how easy it is to make a tour through Europe and the East without possessing the vast bank account which some people think necessary.

HARRY E. LUTZ.

CIRCLEVILLE, OHIO, December 1st, 1887.

CONTENTS.

CHAPTER I.

The voyage.—Landing at Rotterdam.—Trip on a Dutch canal.—Historical scenes at Delft and Ryswick. . 13

CHAPTER II.

The Hague.—Famous scenes in Holland's history.—Leyden and its University.—Amsterdam.—Zaandam.—Peter the Great as ship carpenter. 25

CHAPTER III.

Battle-field of Waterloo.—Brussels.— Up the Rhine.—The castled crags.—Arrival at Stuttgart. . . 42

CHAPTER IV.

Winter at Stuttgart.—Study of the German language.—Fatherland customs.—Christmas in a country village 62

CHAPTER V.

Beginning of the summer's tour.—Hohenstaufen Castle.—Ulm and Augsburg.—The art treasures of Munich.—Innspruck.—Over the Brenner Pass into Italy. . 86

CHAPTER VI.

Verona.—Venice.—First Gondola Ride.—St. Mark's and the Palace of the Doges.—Ravenna.—Arrival at Naples. 103

CHAPTER VII.

Naples.—The filthiest city in the world.—The charming Bay of Naples.—Ascent of Mt. Vesuvius.—Pompeii. 123

CHAPTER VIII.

From Naples to Rome.—First Impressions of the Eternal City.—The Forum.—Coliseum and St. Peter's.—The Ruins in and about Rome.—Excursions in the vicinity. 138

CHAPTER IX.

Farewell to Rome.—Up the coast to Leghorn.—Arrival at Florence.—The Art Treasures, Churches and Tombs of the Tuscan Capital. 164

CHAPTER X.

Genoa and the Birthplace of Christopher Columbus.—Turin and Lake Como.—Back in Austria.—Trieste and its Environs. 179

CHAPTER XI.

A tramp of three hundred miles in the Austrian mountains.—The Adelsberg Caves.—Gratz.—Over the Semmering Pass.—Vienna. 195

CHAPTER XII.

Vienna.—Its Churches and Museums.—Through Bohemia.
—Prague.—Down the Elbe to Dresden. . 212

CHAPTER XIII.

The Beauty and Art Treasures of Dresden.—Over the Plains of Saxony.—Leipzig.—Lutzen.—Wittenberg.—Berlin. 229

CHAPTER XIV.

From Germany to Sweden.–Across the Baltic.—Stockholm.
—A Trip to Upsala.—Swedish Liquor Laws. . 255

CHAPTER XV.

Along the Finland Coast.—The Sights of St. Petersburg.—The Great Churches.—The Fortress of Saints Peter and Paul.—Tyranny of the Czar. . . . 265

CHAPTER XVII.

Visit to Copenhagen.—"The Platform of the Castle of Elsinore."---Lubeck.---Hamburg.---Bremen.---Tramp in the Teutoburgian Hills. 275

CHAPTER XVIII.

Hanover.---Brunswick.—Tramp over the Brocken.---Lost in the Woods.---Goettingen.---Cassel. . . 288

CHAPTER XIX.

Weimar and its Famous Men.---Jena University.---Over the Thuringian Mountains.---Coburg, Bamberg and Nuremberg.---Back once more at Stuttgart. . . 302

CHAPTER XX.

Farewell to Stuttgart.---Weinsberg's Women.---Heidelberg and Frankfort.---Down the Rhine Again.---Aix-la-Chapelle.---Inauguration of the Great Cologne Cathedral. 318

CHAPTER XXI.

From Cologne up the Rhine.---Spires.---Sesenheim.---Strassburg.---Basel.---Constance.---Spending the winter at Geneva. : 331

CHAPTER XXII.

I leave Geneva.---Embark at Marseilles for Egypt.---Land at Alexandria and go to Cairo.---Pyramids and the Desert. 350

CHAPTER XXIII.

Voyage from Egypt to Palestine.—The Suez Canal.—Landing at Joppa.—Jerusalem and Bethlehem.—The Holy Fire. 381

CHAPTER XXIV.

Moonlight ride from Jerusalem to the Sea.—Along the Coast of Asia.—Site of Ancient Troy.—Constantinople.—Athens.—Back in France. 395

CHAPTER XXV.

In France Again.—Paris.—Across the Channel.—London.—Stratford.—Ayr.—Glasgow.—Edinburgh.—Abbotsford.—Liverpool.—Ireland.—Voyage Home. . 410

A Student's Views Abroad.

CHAPTER I.

THE VOYAGE.—LANDING AT ROTTERDAM.—TRIP ON A DUTCH CANAL.—HISTORICAL SCENES AT DELFT AND RYSWICK.

A trip to Europe is the dream of every American student. If he has an especial fondness for history, biography and poetry the longing to visit the Old World is intensified. He can imagine no greater pleasure than to spend a quiet afternoon in dreamy reverie in the Poet's Corner in Westminister Abbey, or a week of study among the art treasures of the Louvre or the Vatican, or to wander among the colossal ruins on the banks of the Nile, or to stand on the Acropolis at Athens and gaze on the scenes which were once familiar to the philosophers and statesmen whose power over mankind has not yet waned.

In 1879, when not yet nineteen years of age I graduated from an Ohio college. In my school days I had dipped into general literature with a keener relish than I did into my text books and like many others I dreamed more of foreign travel than I did of choosing a profession and settling down to make my fortune. I could not reconcile myself to adopt any of the courses prescribed for law, theology or medicine. I preferred journalism but longed for greater opportunities for study and travel before entering on that profession.

In the summer after leaving college for the last time I began reading law with my father, in my native city, but was unable to settle down fairly to the work. I devoted more time to the perusal of the books in the city library than I did to the study of law. I continued to think of a trip to Europe for the purpose of a study of the German language but my plans remained as mazy as a dream.

In the course of the summer I reread Bayard Taylor's "Views Afoot" and my admiration for the pluck and enthusiasm of that famous traveler led me first to mature a definite plan of a trip to the Old World. After some elaborate figuring and considerable correspondence with various parties I came to the conclusion that I could go to Europe, spend eight or nine months studying German and see something of the Old World for three or four hundred dollars From various sources I got together sufficient funds, and accordingly set to work to prepare for the trip. I had made up my mind to choose journalism as a profession and expected that the knowledge of the German language and an acquaintance with the habits and ideas of the Old World would be a valuable preparatory to such a career.

I secured a passport from Washington to use in case of emergency and also a circular letter of introduction from the Secretary of State to the United States ministers and consuls. My subsequent travels largely exceeded my plans. I saw many more countries and spent more time abroad than I had ventured to think possible. Yet my experience has been that the very best thing any traveler can have is enthusiasm for literature and art. The wealthiest of tourists are generally the most complaining because their pleasure consists only in the luxuries of life and every little detail is therefore a source of annoyance to them. A man, who has an enthusiasm for the heroes of history, feels so much delight in viewing the classic scenes which they once made famous, that he does not brood over the petty annoyances incident to eating and drinking.

A man with enthusiasm for an idea in his breast will cheerfully brave the terrors of the frozen north and the horrors of the fever stricken south to attain his aim. He will hold as nothing the hardships by the way and will rather rejoice in overcoming them and feel renewed pleasure in every victory over unpropitious circumstances. The student who wishes to rough it in Europe should have in some degree a touch of the same enthusiasm. This delight in viewing the historic haunts of the "great of old" must be sufficient to make him forget the roughness of his fare and the hardness of his bed He must have sufficient interest in literature and art to make him indifferent to the unpleasant companions which are often thrust upon him.

> "Press on! for it is godlike to unloose
> The spirit and forget yourself in thought;
> Bending a pinion for the deeper sky,
> And, in the very fetters of your flesh,
> Mating with the pure essences of heaven."
>
> — *Willis.*

After a preliminary ride through the beautiful country along the Pennsylvania railroad, I embarked at New York on the "Schiedam," of the Netherlands-American Steamship line, shortly after the interesting hour of noon, on Saturday August 30th, 1879. About three o'clock the engine whistled several warning shrieks, which sent the visitors hurriedly ashore; the officer on the bridge growled a command, the cables were loosened and we were off.

The piers, the ships, the forts hurried past us. We dipped our flag in honor of the guardians of the Nation's peace, and then we were out in the open sea. I felt very little of the Byronic enthusiasm as I watched "my native shore fade o'er the waters blue." I could not forget the humble adage, "never shout until you are out of the woods," and I had too many misgivings about sea sickness on the morrow to indulge in premature sentimentality.

I climbed into my berth that night with the firm conviction that I would spend the next day leaning over the rail gazing steadfastly into the fathomless deep. I opened my eyes in the morning with considerable trepidation but was surprised to find the vessel moving on with a soothing motion which continued several days. As the time went by I gained confidence in my digesting apparatus, and when the waves did run high, I felt none of that "strong emotion" which many of my fellow travelers experienced.

Of course the first thing the ocean passenger does is to get acquainted with his vessel. Ours proved rather a slow one. It never made more than eleven miles an hour, and usually nine was the rate. It was baptised "Schiedam" in honor of the town near Rotterdam which is known far and wide on account of its 300 distilleries. One would think that it had rather a tipsy godfather.

Next after the vessel, one's fellow passengers claim his

attention. We had a pretty fair representation of nationalities, but the German element predominated. Of course there were some queer characters on board, which afforded us plenty of amusement. I mention but one. He was a German and a humpback with a roguish face. He had been one year in America in the milk business but his English was limited. He seemed to have been successful for he had a well-filled purse, on which he freely drew for the purchase of schnapps and red wine. He said he was going to the Rhine to get himself a wife. "American gal all false—all hoombug ; Doitch gal—rede cheeks—big—ah ! fine. Doitch gall all work."

For the first week out from New York we had no difficulty in amusing ourselves, but, after that, time seemed to drag along. We had cold and cloudy weather for ten days, which compelled us to remain below deck. At last on the afternoon of our thirteenth day from New York the sun shown out brightly from among the clouds and we were gladdened by seeing the Scilly Islands and the southwest coast of England. From that time on we had land constantly in sight. On Sunday, September 14th, we anchored on the Holland coast. As soon as the tide came in we proceeded up the Maas, past quaint villages and innumerable windmills, and at three in the afternoon, just fifteen days after leaving New York, we reached Rotterdam.

It was with the most agreeable feeling that I first set foot on the continent, which has been the home of the great of the ages. The scenes which had inspired the pencil of the artists and the pen of the authors whose names are household words were now before me.

In every direction strange sights met my glance. Here was a quaint looking house ; there a peasant in the oddest of costumes. I spent the evening in the streets watching the movements of the people, and the appearance of the canals, the boats and the houses. It was Sunday evening and the streets were filled with people in their holiday dress. The windows of most of the stores were brilliantly lighted and every one seemed in the best of spirits. At nearly every block I met squads of young men walking arm in arm singing popular songs at the top of their voices. Men in soldiers' uniforms were very numerous, and with the gayly dressed girls made a pleasing spectacle.

The next morning all signs of this jollity had disappeared Every one now seemed busy. But in their work they presented a still stranger appearance. Horses are very scarce in Rotterdam. What in America is considered sufficient load for a horse is there drawn by a man. Under most of the hugh handcarts are one or two dogs, hitched to the axle tugging away to help the man. Then there are carts pulled exclusively by dogs. Indeed it is no fun to be a dog in Holland. There they earn their tax.

I had always thought that the wearing of earrings was a relic of barbarism, but after being in Holland one thinks our ladies are very mild offenders on that score. In Rotterdam many wear immense metal ornaments projecting from the sides of the head like horns. But they have a more common and more pleasing custom than this. Every one from the humblest kitchen girl wears the neatest and whitest little caps ever seen. This combined with the splendid complexions which are almost equally universal, make the feminine element a valuable addition to the city in an aesthetic view.

At the hotel in which I lodged everything was strange. The kitchen had a floor and walls of tile and the brightly polished brass utensils which hung about the room were proof of Dutch cleanliness and thrift. The little room which was assigned to me contained a bed concealed in the drapery of snow white curtains.

In Holland there is a custom, which I think is exclusively Dutch, of having small mirrors just outside the windows, inclined at such an angle as to reflect the image of those on the pavement so that it can be seen by the inmates of the room without being seen themselves. This practice is almost universal but seems very strange to an American.

Rotterdam has about 150,000 inhabitants and boasts of a cathedral, two fine bridges over the river Maas and an extensive shipping. It was the birthplace of the famous Erasmus, to whom the city has erected a statue in the market place. The house in which he was born is occupied now by a produce and fruit store.

After having spent three days in the narrow streets of Rotterdam, I thought that it was about time to move. Accordingly I embarked on a little steamer on the canal for Delft, which is ten miles from Rotterdam. There were but two other passengers in the tiny cabin. One was a smooth faced conservative gentleman dressed in broadcloth. His coat was buttoned to his chin, and he still wore the old fashioned knee pantaloons which terminated in black stockings and these in still blacker shoes. A black silk hat crowned this midnight costume. "Well, my friend," thought I,

"You were born about two hundred years too late." The other passenger was a young man in a stylish suit. After we had gone a short distance the latter addressed me in Dutch. I turned loose my stock of words in that horrible language and told him I did not understand.

" Sprechen Sie Deutsch ?"

I shook my head sadly.

" Parlez-vous Francais ?"

I shook my head again.

" Do you speak English ?"

I quickly told him that I did, and "the polyglot" talked to me in my mother tongue. He was a specimen of the many that I found in Holland who could speak three or four languages. A student of the Leyden university afterwards told me that the Hollander never found anyone else who could speak his language, and so was compelled to learn other languages if he wished to have any communication with the rest of the world.

But as I soon found my newly made acquaintance had nothing to say in particular, I left him and went on deck. The canal was thickly dotted with boats of all sizes and descriptions. But here also was the same scarcity of horses that I noticed in Rotterdam. Most of the boats were pulled by men. Let me place it to the credit of the nation however that I saw none pulled by women. Here and there we passed one with a couple of dogs tugging at the rope. Then we would meet two large boats both pulled by one unfortunate horse.

The surface of the canal on which we were riding, like that of the majority of Holland's canals, lay above the surrounding country, so that our view was unobstructed. The land was in pasture and was covered with the greenest of grass. Not a fence was to be seen, but small canals or trenches filled with water formed an admirable substitute. Windmills were plentifully distributed over the country and their revolving arms gave a look of animation to the landscape. Lines of tall and slender trees relieved the monotony of the level plain and formed a background for the living picture.

As we drew near to Delft the houses along the canal became more numerous, and through the open doors I could see the women working at the eternal scrubbing and washing for which the Dutch are so noted. A sagacious old Holland gentleman whom I met on the steamer assured me that as gold is the god of the Americans, so water is the god of the Dutch. All that I saw made me willing to believe the latter half of his statement. I am not certain but that one may be uncomfortable clean as well as uncomfortably dirty.

However this may be, my meditations were cut short by our arrival at Delft. I gathered up my traps and walked up a street with the inevitable canal in the middle until I reached the Prinsenhof or Palace. By a move of the hand I made one of the soldiers, whom I found at the gateway, understand that I wished to enter. Accordingly he led me across an open court and through a door on the opposite side to the foot of the stairway. In the wall to the right are three small holes in the stone and immediately above them is an inscription recording the fact that here on the 10th of July, 1584, William the Silent, Prince of

Orange, and defender of Dutch liberty, was assassinated by a wretch animated by the hope of being rewarded with the gold of the blood thirsty Philip of Spain. To see these bullet marks and this staircase was the principal object of my visit to Delft. I paid that tribute to the interest Motley's narrative awakened in the character of the Dutch Washington.

After having spent sufficient time in imagining the details of the tragedy, I crossed the street to the "Old Church," and visited the monuments of the Admirals Van Tromp and and Piet Hein. Then I went to the "New Church," which is however no newer than the middle of the fifteenth century and saw the magnificent monument to William the Silent which was erected in 1621. The effigy of the prince in marble lies on a black marble sarcophagus beneath a canopy, supported by four clustered pillars and six isolated columns, all likewise of marble. In the niches of the pillars stand four allegorical figures, Liberty, Justice, Prudence and Religion. I confess I had been so enwrapt in the present that I had not realized that they were able to conceive of so beautiful a thing as early as 1621. But then I suppose that can be pardoned in an American.

I looked at the simple tablet to the memory of the scholar Hugh Grotius, who was born at Delft, and then went across the market place to the Town House, and was conducted to a neatly furnished hall, in which the honest burghers have met for over two centuries and a half. In the middle of the room is a large table which is surrounded by chairs, while before each is placed writing materials. The chairs are as angular as any Dutchman could wish. On the walls are hung the paintings I wished to see. They are principally portraits of the Orange family. Their history can be plainly traced in their physiognomies. The faces of the powerful princes, William the Silent, Maurice and William the Third are singularly strong and form a marked contrast to those of the two last princes.

I next turned my steps northward along the road to Ryswick and soon left the city of Delft behind. The road runs along the bank of a canal and is paved all the way. On both sides trees are planted at regular intervals, and between the road and the canal is a neat gravel walk lined with grass. The sod is so well kept that I was almost afraid to step on it, though it was in the open country.

I walked along slowly, watching the quaint craft on the canal, the little dog carts on the road and the dusky windmills in the fields beyond. But at last, the road led over a bridge across the canal and I soon reached the village of Ryswick, four miles from Delft.

It was here that the peace of 1697 was concluded between France and the allied powers headed by William III. of England. The house is not now standing but its site is occupied by an obelisk erected at the close of the last century. This peace has a place in American history, for the results of a few paltry scratches of a pen here were felt in the wilderness thousands of miles away. Then King William's war was ended and the Indian allies of the French ceased butchering the English colonists of New York and New England.

I had some difficulty in finding the obelisk. I walked in every direction but could see nothing of it. I asked a mail carrier whom I met but he did not understand, as I unfortunately did not know the Dutch word for obelisk. I was about to give up in despair, when I found it in a park almost concealed by the trees. It is very tall but very plain looking.

I then retraced my steps through the village to the church yard where I visited the tomb of Holland's favorite poet Tollens. He sleeps in a quiet nook behind the church among the less famous dead.

Dutch villages are models of neatness. In America the little towns are the most forlorn and unpicturesque places imaginable and generally combine all the bad qualities of both town and country. But in the Holland villages, the streets, the pavements, the houses and shops are as neat and bright looking and much cleaner than in the cities.

From Ryswick, I returned to the main road and walked a mile farther between two rows of majestic trees, reaching the Hague with its broad streets and handsome buildings long before the evening shadows appeared on the green fields of Holland.

CHAPTER II.

THE HAGUE.—FAMOUS SCENES IN HOLLAND'S HISTORY.—LEYDEN AND ITS UNIVERSITY.—AMSTERDAM.—ZAANDAM.—PETER THE GREAT AS SHIP CARPENTER.

I had been foot-sore from my rambles in Rotterdam and by the time I reached the Hague I barely had energy enough to move. But as the traveler must disregard weariness, I mustered up all my enthusiasm for the historical sights before me. Having found a hotel with a French as well as a Dutch sign, I went in and waylaid the first official I met. I recited to him the only sentence of any considerable length that I knew in his language, and expected an answer in the affirmative or negative. But as it is not in the nature of things for a public official to be so brief, he launched out in a long harangue in which I was swamped at the first word. I explained the difficulty and he called in the servant who did the English for the establishment. How impatient the traveler is of these English grinders when he first comes in contact with them! But let him be forced to do his talking in gestures and monosyllables for a week and he is quite glad to meet even these few worded gentlemen. They are not in the least embarrassed, however by the limitedness of their language. When they find you are an American they excuse their ignorance by serenely and contemptiously remarking that they do not understand American English.

I would very willingly have rested after the day's adventures but I had a call to make. Among the passengers on the "Schiedam," was an elderly gentleman from New York who was going to visit his brother at the Hague. Hearing of my plans he gave me his address and requested me to call on him and said he would show me some of the sights of the metropolis. All the time during the voyage he indulged in eulogies of Holland, notwithstanding my repeated assurance that my opinion of the Dutch people was very high.

Well, I had some desire to see the interior of a Holland home, and so I gathered together the remnants of my bodily strength the same evening I arrived at the Hague and started out to hunt up the address. I found the name and number attached to a magnificent house which faced on an open square with rows of tall trees and with the National Monument in the center. I rang the bell and was ushered into a marble-floored hall adorned with two statues where I waited while the white-capped servant carried my card to Mynheer H. He quickly appeared and drew me into an elegantly furnished room which was filled with those beautiful trifles which luxury only can conceive and which wealth only can buy. After some brief inquiries about my experience since we had parted in Rotterdam he concluded to begin the sightseeing at once by showing me the house and grounds. So taking his hat and pipe he led me through half a dozen different rooms which rivaled the first one in elegance, out into the garden. We walked slowly along the curved paths under green trees and shrubbery and past the flowers, and the statues, the fountain and the well-kept grass. He showed me the fancy fowls and then we went into the stables, where everything was scrupulously clean. Here I saw the fine looking horse which he assured me cost a thousand guilders. Then he showed me the carriages and the driver's livery. But at every turn he asked me:

"Is that fine or not?"

I drew pretty largely on the list of synonyms for the beautiful and then passed again through the elegant rooms out into the street. We went along the finely paved avenues and looked at the magnificent houses with their lawns adorned with fountains, statues and flowers.

"Is that fine or not?"

He triumphantly asked in his broken English. I assured him it was gorgeous. But on he went through streets, parks and squares, into public buildings, and over bridges, now stumbling in dark passages and then emerging into brilliantly lighted and thickly crowded thoroughfares. Every few minutes he would stop and out came that inevitable:

"Is that fine, or not?"

I ransacked the out-of-the-way corners of my brain for words expressive of incomparable excellence. Yet they were but fuel for the flames,

"Is that fine, or not?"

That was the greeting for every strange sight. He had heard some Americans, in America, ridiculing Holland, and I was to be sacrificed to satiate his wrath.

"Is that fine, or not?"

I verily thought I could go no farther, but on and on he

dragged me. Trees and houses and street lamps went by in a confused stream.

"Is that fine, or not?"

The query came out as strong as ever, but my answers were reduced to faint monosyllables. At last we were out of the city. We passed through the dark shadows of a large grove and halted in a dense crowd. Within a broad enclosure before us hundreds of people were sitting at small tables drinking and joyously conversing. Upon an elevated platform amid brightly gleaming lamps there were several dozen musicians. We had been there but a short time when they began to play, and even my unmusical soul might have shared the raptures of the multitude, but at that time I would have been indifferent to old Orpheus himself. I stood there in misery while several pieces were performed with interludes of the old query :

" Is that fine, or not?"

At last the worthy Mynheer was satisfied and we turned our faces toward the city. I wanted to rest a few minutes on one of the seats by the way-side, but he was afraid I would take cold.

" Is that fine, or not?"

The interrogatory still came every few paces, but as even misery has an end we finally reached my hotel and I bade my persecuter a feeble good-night. The next day he was suddenly called away to Utrecht and I was left to finish my sight seeing alone.

Although the Hague is chiefly a modern built city, it has several places of great historical interest. By the side of the fish pond in the center of the city rises a number of buildings, called the Binnenhof, surrounding an open court which is entered by several gates. Many of these buildings are very old, and the square which they inclose has been the scene of some great events in Holland history. It was here on the 24th of May, 1619, that the aged Grand Pensionary, John Van Oldenbarneveld, was executed through the influence of Prince Maurice, of Orange. The former was a distinguished representative of the Democratic element, while the latter was one of the greatest generals of the past. But the philosopher tells us that "every excess causes a defect ; every defect, an excess. Every sweet hath its sour ; every evil its good." The Prince was a great general, but the curse came with the blessing of power. He was impatient of opposition and perpetrated this judicial murder which will cast a cloud on his name forever. Instances, like this, of the clashing of two heroes are always painful, especially to the young. It produces the same uncomfortable feeling as hearing one friend express unlimited contempt for the opinion which we know to be defended by another who is equally dear to us. We like to think of characters as having decided shades either of good or of evil and any opposition of one admired hero to another seems unnatural.

East of the Binnenhof is the Maurice House Musuem of Paintings, which contains some very celebrated pictures. The most famous are the "Young Bull," by Paul Potter, and the "School of Anatomy," by Rembrandt. The former was carried to Paris by Napoleon in spite of an offer of thirty-six thousand dollars for it, by the Dutch Government. Having a guide book which told me what to admire, I could not help being enraptured by the right pictures.

At the Navy Office I saw hundreds of models of ships, guns and light-houses, all constructed with wonderful skill. But the saddest of all was the collection of relics of a party, sent in 1595, in search of the northwest passage to China, who fell victims to the rigors of the climate. The things were found and brought back only a few years ago. They are cooking utensils, instruments, guns and spears, books and fragments of paper with writing on them now no longer legible. These relics of their daily activity but more painfully remind us of their fate.

The Royal Library contains 160,000 volumes; among them the Librarian pointed out a great many which had been presented by the American government. They show also in the visitors' book a good autograph of the historian Motley.

One of the most interesting places in the Hague for me was the old Gevangenpoort prison, which is situated a short distance west of the Binnenhof. It was built over a gateway through which the busy throng of to-day passes unceasingly, each pursuing his pet hobby, unmindful of the gloomy memories which cluster around that ancient pile. Having been admitted through a heavy wooden door, I was left to ramble about the place at my leisure. The building is three stories high and contains about twenty cells, so I had enough to occupy me. On each massive door is an inscription in Dutch, French and English recording the fact for which the adjoining appartment is especially famous. The windows are small and have double sets of bars. I climbed up the winding stairs, which seemed to have as many branches as a tree, went through all the rooms and peered into the closets. Although I was not acquainted with many of the names of those who had been imprisoned there, still as I stood in the cheerless cells in solitude I could well appreciate that I was in the presence of another age. While wandering around I came upon one apartment that was singularly gloomy. It was a cell built within a cell. The rays of light that struggled through the bars of the outer window were almost entirely intercepted by the inner bars ; and beside the ordinary terrors of the place, the prisoner here suffered those of semi-darkness. The inscription on the door was :

CELL OF PISTORIUS.

While I was standing musing over the strange scene, the custodian entered with two soldiers. In a hoarse voice he explained to them the history of the place, and then lighted a match and pointed out some red figures on the wall all the time continuing his account, of which I could only understand the words Pistorius and blood. Every few moments the soldiers interrupted the speaker with dismal groans of horror. The blood marks on the wall, the red glare of the light, the sepulchral tone of the keeper, and the sighs of the sympathetic soldiers combined to work on the imagination and call to mind visions of that time when men thought to stop the rising of the sun by shutting their eyes and butchering those who saw.

But the custodian and the soldiers soon departed and I

was again left to pursue my wanderings. There is a cell on the ground floor which is labeled:

> **PLACE WHERE WOMEN WERE STRANGLED.**

In this there is a collection of instruments of torture. Here is to be seen every means of producing pain without death that diabolical fancy could invent. I gazed long and curiously at this collection. Before I went out I happened to open a closet door and there I found—not a heap of skulls or some objects in like harmony with the surroundings—no, not such, but a child's rocking-horse and a doll's wagon. "Ah! it is well;" thought I, "here are the sixteenth and the nineteenth centuries in contact. Here is love and hate, joy and pain. The love of child puts to shame the hate of man!"

But the "cellar of torture" was left yet to be visited. There I found among other things a bench and axe used in beheading. On the former were a great number of nicks, and perhaps every mark could tell a tale of death!

I have spoken of the tragedy of the Binnenhof. The Gevangenpoort was the scene of a somewhat similar event. In 1671 the DeWitt brothers, John and Cornelius, who had been opponents of the house of Orange, were taken from the Gevangenpoort prison by a mob and literally torn to pieces. The custodian pointed out a hole in the window-sash made by a bullet fired at the ill-fated men.

It was not without a feeling of relief that I left this place of torture and death and mingled again with the gay-faced multitude. In the evening I went by rail to the famous old city of Leyden.

Leyden was founded by the Romans. In 1574, during the war for independence, she resisted a terrible siege of the Spaniards, until relieved by William the Silent, Prince of Orange, who opened the dykes and flooded the country. As a reward for the faithfulness of the city early the following year the Prince founded the University, whose fame afterwards gained for Leyden the proud title of the "Athens of the West." There are at present about thirty-five professors and eight hundred students. Leyden means suffering and the name is appropriate for her greatness arose from her sorrow.

Soon after I arrived I met one of the students, who introduced me at their club and afterwards took me to a meeting to witness the initiation of some new men. Among the other things these candidates for fame were made to do, was talking to me in English. The poor fellows found it hard work to get their ideas into that garb and were rewarded with many uncomplimentary comments from the older ones. I will add, however, that the majority of those whom I met could speak English as well as several other languages.

On a mound of earth in the center of the city stands a low, broad tower, which is supposed to have been built by the Roman Drusus. During the days of the siege of 1574, the people crowded its summit to watch with heavy hearts for the appearance of the Prince's vessels in the flooded fields. I suppose it is the oldest structure in Holland.

Motley's history had inflamed me with the desire to see it above all other things. But I was disappointed. I expected to see a picturesque ruin but found a neatly built pile of modern bricks and mortar. They say it is "restored," but for my part I have no admiration for "restored" buildings. There is some reason in repairing old churches, where beauty and not age is the attraction, but I can see no sense in moderns rebuilding structures which are only interesting from a historical view. They tell us it is to preserve them, but we don't want them preserved. Let the arches fall, let the moss creep over the crumbling stones; these are the signs of age, these are the things that impress us. But in the name of the ages that are past, let no one defile their work with any prosy modern mud.

If you look at the map of Holland, you will scarcely notice the crooked, slender line which passes by Utrecht and Leyden and finally ends at the North Sea. Insignificant though you may consider it, that is the Rhine. The greater portion of the water of the famous river enters the sea through channels called the Maas and the Lek, but this feeble branch bears the name which is familiar to every ear.

Over a thousand years ago the mouth of the stream was filled up during a hurricane, and the water formed a vast swamp near the sea from that time until the beginning of this century. Under the reign of King Louis Napoleon a canal was dug and an immense dyke with locks constructed, and thus assisted the waters are enabled to reach the sea.

Near the mouth of the river lies the town of Katwijk aan Zee, six miles from Leyden. During the summer steamers afford a convenient means of communication.

Thinking that it would be neglecting the most prominent feature of Holland not to take a look at one of her sea dykes, I concluded to spend the remainder of the day in the trip to Katwijk. Accordingly, I was soon gliding down the smooth Rhine in a neat little screw steamer. There was nothing grand in the scenery, nothing there to make the Rhine synonymous with beauty. Imagine a stream not broader than our own Scioto, with not the faintest ripple on the surface to indicate a current. Picture to yourself this peaceful stream with low banks thickly fringed with willows, and you then see all that the Rhine is at Leyden.

The ride was only interrupted by the occasional slacking of the speed of the steamer to allow some heavily laden sailboat to pass without dashing the water over her side. I had formed my general idea of a dyke principally from the appearance of the Scioto levees, and was considerably surprised at the mountain of sand at the mouth of the Rhine. The Dutch proverb, "God made the sea, we made the shore," seems not out of place when one sees such gigantic bulwarks against the inroads of the ocean. The tides being out, I took a walk along the beach and then looked at the ponderous locks, which are opened at low water to let out the sluggish Rhine. All the strength of wood, iron and stone is here used in resisting the waves, and the massiveness of the gates seems entirely in keeping with the solidity of the dyke.

After my return to Leyden, an hour's ride by rail brought me to Haarlem, famous also for a fearful siege by the Spaniards in the war for independence. But she was less fortunate than her sister city, and was finally obliged to yield to the enemy. The perfidious Alva immediately violated the terms of the surrender and murdered about two thousand of the heroic defenders of their fatherland.

Haarlem has a large cathedral which was completed in 1516. It contains one of the largest organs in the world, which has four key-boards, sixty-four stops and five thousand pipes, the largest of which is fifteen inches in diameter and thirty-two feet long. It almost fills one end of the church. From one of the arches are suspended several small models of ships, commemorating the fifteenth crusade. The red-white-and-blue flags hanging at the diminutive mast heads are like those which are floating to-day in Holland.

According to the Dutch accounts Lawrence Coster, a sacristan of the Haarlem cathedral, invented the art of printing in 1423, seventeen years before the period assigned by the Germans to its invention by Gutenberg of Mayence.

Not knowing which one had the honor of bestowing that great blessing on mankind, I determined to reach the right one by paying my veneration to both. Accordingly I looked at Coster's statue in the market place and examined the specimens of his printing in the town hall, feeling very thankful that he made it possible for me to have "rolled" for a hand-press in my career as "devil" in a country office.

Having visited all the places I wished, I took the train to Amsterdam. The railroad is almost perfectly straight and passes along the northern edge of what formerly was the Haarlem Lake. It was so large that during the war for independence Motley tells us many naval battles took place on its surface. It was drained between 1840 and 1853, and seventy-two square miles of land recovered, which holds a population of 10,000, and is said to be worth 800 florins or 320 dollars an acre.

Amsterdam has been frequently compared with Venice, and there seems to be much that is similar in the situation of the two places. Venice is built on seventy-two islands; Amsterdam on ninety. Venice has three hundred and six bridges; Amsterdam about three hundred. Through Venice the Grand Canal winds its way; through Amsterdam flows the broad current of the river Amstel. But the Dutch metropolis has more than the Italian; it has broad streets as well as canals, and so the poetic fancy is robbed of the pleasing pictures of the gondolas. Without seeing the canals one can not realize the number there is in that small space on the maps of Europe allotted to Amsterdam. One meets with the tall masts of the vessels in every direction, and he can walk but a short distance without crossing a bridge. But Amsterdam has still another strange characteristic; all its houses are built on piling. The ground is so soft that without this precaution the walls would sink into the mud. The general appearance of the city is much like Rotterdam. The buildings in the business portion are narrow and high and built of the small brick peculiar to Holland. In the streets one frequently meets with the costumes of different provinces. I saw a great many women who were wearing skull caps of gold or silver under their bonnets and reaching the top of the ears. These ornaments are very valuable and are usually heirlooms in the families. On the canal boats I saw men in violet colored suits with full Turkish knee trousers. The other costumes resemble those in Rotterdam already described.

Amsterdam has immense harbors for ships, and one can find flags of nearly every civilized commercial nation flying from the masts of the vessels at anchor. On the quay there is a small round tower, built in the fifteenth century, which is called the criers' tower. It is said to have received its name from the fact that vessels sailed from here for all parts of the world and the weeping of friends at parting was constantly recurring at that place.

On the Sunday I was in Amsterdam, I was walking along one of the streets when I heard numerous loud voices which seemed to come from a street on the opposite side of the canal. I crossed over at the next bridge and was soon in a crowd of people of the lower classes. Along the sides of the narrow street were piled old clothes, old shoes, old utensils and many other things of like description. Then there were fruit stands and places where cheap articles of dress were kept. But before each of these classes of wares were men screaming at the top of their voices, some trying to induce the people to buy of them, while others were conducting auctions. The confusion of noises was awful. I never heard any like it, even in an American political meeting. It was the Jewish Quarter, where the worst specimens of that noble race were carrying on their trade. I extricated myself from the crowd as quickly as possible and sought something more pleasing than those filthy shops.

South of the city lies a large park of seventy-five acres, called Vondel's, in honor of the poet, who has received the distinguished title of "the Dutch Shakespeare." The park is far inferior to the Central Park, New York, and to the park at Haarlem, as far as beauty is concerned. In Disraeli's "Curiosities of Literature" he says that Vondel lived in great poverty, notwithstanding the popularity of his tragedies. One cannot help thinking as he looks at these broad acres, that if they would give the Vondels of the world a little more while they are alive, they would be satisfied to have less after their death.

It was Sunday afternoon that I visited the park, and returning to the city, I met hundreds of young people taking their holiday. The number of plug hats was truly alarming. Indeed he seemed to have attained the summit of human happiness, who had the tallest cylinder on his head, the longest and most crooked cigar-holder in his mouth, and the reddest cheeked girl on his arm.

The flood which made the Zuider Zee, left a narrow arm of land between Amsterdam and the North sea which cut off all convenient communication. But recently a large canal has been constructed extending from Amsterdam westward to the North sea. It is of sufficient depth to allow the largest and heaviest laden vessel to pass through and cost $14,000,000. I went about one third of the distance through this canal by steamer to Zaandam whose chief attraction to the tourist is the hut in which Peter the Great lived while working on the ship yards. The house is very small and seems to be on the point of falling to pieces. It is now protected by a large shed. The hut consists of two small rooms and a bed closet. The walls are literally covered with names; the desire to gain immortality by defacing a public building not being peculiar to Americans. I contented myself with inscribing my name and place of residence in the visitors' book.

However small the hut may be, monarchs have not considered it beneath them to do it honor. Alexander of Russia visited it in 1814 and left the following inscription :

> NOTHING TOO SMALL
>
> FOR A GREAT MAN.

The present Emperor of Russia visited it in 1839 and also left a tablet to commemorate the fact. The rigid scrutiny, which everything undergoes now, has spoiled the tradition in regard to the Tsar's residence in Zaandam, for it is now said that he only remained there a week in 1697, when the crowds which came to see him work obliged him to go to the dock yards at Amsterdam. Thus our golden legends are stolen from us ! They have destroyed William Tell ; Beatrice Cenci is going ; will they now take Washington's little hatchet ?

But Zaandam has one other wonder besides the hut of Peter the Great. There are about four hundred windmills in the vicinity of the town. Having an hour's spare time before the departure of the steamer, I took a walk into the country. The road served also as a dyke and wound around as though the builder was trying to increase the distance to the greatest possible extent. The windmills in some places are as numerous as houses in a city, and the revolving arms which meet the eye in every direction present a strange appearance. My walk extended as far as one of the farm houses, which seemed to be of the better class. It was square in shape with a tall roof which sloped on each side and was out of proportion with the lower part of the building. The dwelling house and the stable were under the same roof. Back of the house some men were engaged in threshing grain, but I could not distinguish the nature of the machinery. I only saw that they used an engine and that the separator was very small.

After returning to Amsterdam I went by rail to Utrecht. Although this city was founded by the Romans and rivals Leyden in age, although it occupies a prominent place in Holland history, still there is not much remaining at present to interest the tourist who can so easily reach more important relics of the past.

In traveling on Dutch railways I was suprised at the great care taken to avoid accidents. The railroads are enclosed within hedges and no one but employees are allowed to walk on the track. At every crossing of a wagon road are placed gates with a watchman to attend to them. There is usually but one approach to the stations, all other sides being securely fenced. At Utrecht I happened to go past the street leading to the station and then was compelled to walk completely around it before I could find the way. As the distance was over a mile, I felt it was a luxury to be free to get killed, which is unquestionably a part of American liberty.

CHAPTER III.

BATTLE-FIELD OF WATERLOO.—BRUSSELS.—UP THE RHINE.

THE CASTLED CRAGS.—ARRIVAL AT STUTTGART.

I went from Amsterdam direct by rail to Brussels via Rotterdam and Antwerp. The country between Rotterdam and Antwerp is a level plain, and the monotony of the journey was only interrupted by a glimpse of the ancient city of Dortrecht and by the passage over the bridge at the Hollandsch Diep. The breadth of that arm of the sea is over a mile and a half, and the length of the bridge exclusive of the approaches, is seven-eights of a mile.

Not far from Brussels we passed the village of Vilvorde, which has great interest for Protestants from the fact that it was the scene of the martyrdom of William Tyndale, one of the early translators of the English Bible.

At 2 P. M., we arrived at the depot at the northern end of the city of Brussels. As I wished to go on to Waterloo that afternoon, I walked directly through the city, taking but a brief look at the grand old market place. I bought a ticket for Braine l' Allend, the station nearest the battle-field and soon found a place in a car. As I approached the end of my journey I kept my eyes fixed in the direction of the battle-field, and in my eagerness made the rather amusing mistake of thinking for a few minutes that a boy on a haystack in the distance was the mound of the lion. But I was soon afterwards gratified with the sight of the genuine hill and on leaving the train at Braine l'Allend I took the road leading towards it. The way however proved longer than I had anticipated, and as I was passing a peasant's house I thought I would like to see the interior of one of them and quench my thirst at the same time. So I asked a woman who was standing at her door way, in Dutch, for a glass of milk. I thought that of course she spoke Flemish, but I soon found that she was French by her speaking "wee" like an orphaned pig. As I had not expected to go to Belgium I was totally ignorant of French. But I was determined not to retreat, and took out my phrase book and hunted up the French word. Not wishing to venture into the mazes of pronunciation, I pointed out the word on the page. She then led me into the house while she went to bring me the milk. I looked around me. The floor was evenly paved with large square brick and was sprinkled with sand. A crucifix stood on a table near by and made known the religion of the house. The furniture was bleached from numberless scourings, and its whiteness would not have disgraced a Dutch housewife. After I had drunk the delicious beverage I let the good woman pick out her pay from a handful of Belgian silver and copper. I then continued my walk and soon reached the battle-field.

The great drama of the 18th of June, 1815, was played upon a place worthy of its greatness. Even after visiting the great battle-fields of ancient history, Byron could not restrain his admiration for that of Waterloo. Military critics as well as civilians unite in declaring the field pre-eminently suitable for a great action. Although the battle receives its name from the little town of Waterloo, it took place three miles south of that village, immediately below a place called Mount St. Jean. The hills gradually decrease in size southward from Brussels, until at the battle field they appear as gentle undulations of the ground. Each of the two opposing armies occupied one of these slightly elevated ridges with a valley between them. The slopes was so gradual that a horse need not slacken his pace in ascending them. The Allies were posted at the northern part of the field and had the inwalled farm house of La Haye Sainte as a minature fortress a little in advance of their center. The French army had the inn of Belle Alliance in the middle of their line opposite to La Haye Sainte.

To the west midway between the hostile armies was the country seat of Hougomont, which was enclosed by a hedge and brick wall. This place was successfully held by the Allies in spite of the continued efforts of the French to take it. The principal fighting was done at Hougomont and at the center of the Allied line.

The appearance of the field is much the same as at the time of the battle. The principal additions to the scene are the monuments to Col. Gordon and to the Hanoverian officers, and the mound of the Belgian lion. This last is a cone-shaped heap of earth two hundred feet high, surmounted by a large bronze lion. The summit of the mound affords an excellent view of the country, which is entirely unobstructed by fences. On this elevated place I sat and watched the September sun sink in the western sky, and as its last beams gilded the landscape, I thought of the glory and the horror and the "rapture of the strife." Near the base of the mound the Duke of Wellington stood when he gave the order for the last charge. Far to the south I could see the hills over which the French retreated in wildest confusion after their defeat. To the east the heights were visible on which the Prussians under the brave Bluecher appeared in the afternoon of the battle and forced Napoleon to divide his strength, and thus contributed to his defeat. All around me lay the gentle slopes, every foot of which have been the scene of fierce conflict and cruel pain. Not until the darkness had deepened, did I descend from that mound which offered so many subjects for contemplation.

Among the thousands who fought at Waterloo, who are unknown to fame, was the gallant Sergeant-Major Cotton, of the 7th Hussars. After the battle, when the field became an object of interest to pilgrims of every nation, he settled there as a guide. Unlike the majority of that profession he followed his specialty as a labor of love. Not a book of merit on the subject of the battle appeared but he secured it for his private study. Not a general revisited the field of his scars and his glory, but the sergeant from his casual remarks and reminiscences gleaned some new fact for his wide store of knowledge. This constant contact with eye witnesses of the battle made the old guide familiar with every movement on that eventful day. To him the charge and the repulse were not as vague abstractions, they were real, real as everyday life. Until his death in 1849, the veteran sergeant continued at his post, and bequeathed to posterity a large and valuable collection of relics and a little book on the subject of the battle, "A Voice from Waterloo."

The sergeant's niece, now an elderly lady, possesses his library and museum, and has built a hotel at the foot of the mound of the lion. It was to this refuge for the weary pilgrim that I retreated as the night came on. I found it fully in keeping with the martial memories of the place. In the museum there are guns, pistols, swords, bayonets, daggers, shot, shell, armor, coats, caps, skulls, shattered bones, and in short nearly everything found on a battle-field. On the walls there are portraits of officers of both armies and engravings of scenes in the battle. There seems to be no end to the number of these warlike pictures. They are on every wall in the breakfast room and dining room and reception room. And even in the bedrooms as one falls sleep some picture of a gallant charge weaves itself into his dreams.

From Waterloo I sent some flowers to a friend in America, who in return sent me the following poem :

> "The roar of the battle is over,
> And only the song of the bird
> And the gentle lowing of cattle,
> On that field of blood is heard.
>
> Peaceful and calm is that meadow,
> With the sunlight shining o'er ;
> Peaceful and calm are the heroes,
> That sleep to wake no more.
>
> And over their silent faces
> This tender blossom grew,
> On the tomb of Napoleon's glory,
> On the field of Waterloo."
>
> —*A. F. Broomhall.*

Nearly every visitor to Waterloo wishes to procure some relic of the great conflict. Though occasionally the peasants find bullets, buckles and other articles, the majority of the things offered for sale are manufactured for that purpose. I noticed in Barnum's "Struggles and Triumphs," that in his account of his visit to Waterloo he expressed his satisfaction that some one was working that branch of the profession of profiting by the weakness of human nature. For my part I take more pleasure in the flowers I brought from the field than in the bullets I had the frailty to buy.

A walk of three miles brought me to Waterloo station where I took the train back to Brussels, which is a beautiful city. On entering the capital for the second time, I took a long walk, almost completely encircling the city. A large part of my way was along the boulevards which have been constructed on the site of the ancient fortifications.

Among others I passed the Palace of the Duc d'Arenberg, which was once the residence of Count Egmont, who was unjustly executed by the Duke of Alva. A short distance higher up is the site of the house, where the protest was signed which began the struggle for liberty. At the same spot the banquet took place at which the subscribers of the protest adopted the name of "beggars," which had been previously bestowed on them in contempt by a courtier, as they were presenting their petition.

A short distance farther I passed the palace of his majesty Leopold II. and then entered a beautiful park ornamented with numerous statues. Next I visited the cathedral, a fine specimen of ecclesiatical architecture.

After passing a column commemorating the congress of 1831, which completed the separation of Belgium from Holland, I entered the Rue Royale, at the northern end of which stands the house where the famous ball of the Duchess of Richmond took place on the eve of the battle of Waterloo. I looked with great interest at the building, as those lines from Byron, being a paternal favorite, have rung in my ears from earliest childhood :

"There was a sound of revelry by night,
And Belgium's capital had gathered then
Her beauty and her chivalry, and bright
The lamps shone o'er fair women and brave men;
A thousand hearts beat happily ; and when
Music arose with its voluptuous swell,
Soft eyes looked love to eyes which spake again,
And all went merry as a marriage bell ;
But hush ! hark ! a deep sound strikes likes a rising knell !

"Did ye not hear it ?—No ; 'twas but the wind
Or the car rattling o'er the stony street ;
On with the dance ! Let joy be unconfined;
No sleep till morn when youth and pleasure meet
To chase the glowing hours with flying feet—
But hark !—that heavy sound breaks in once more,
As if the clouds its echo would repeat ;
And nearer, clearer, deadlier than before !
Arm ! arm ! it is—it is—the cannon's opening roar !"

After wending my way through several attractive streets and passing a few monuments and statues I arrived at the market place. On one side I saw the grand town hall, of the fifteenth century. Upon the other side was the Maison du Roi, where Counts Egmont and Hoorne passed the last night of their lives, and in that square where I stood, those two nobles were beheaded. Our Prescott and Motley have made the characters of the counts familiar to the English readers, but their investigations have tended to lessen our admiration for them, although they are regarded as national heroes by the Netherlanders. The only claim of these restless nobles to the title of patriots, seems to be the fact that they suffered a patriot's death, and their fate confirms that sententious epigram attributed to Monckton Milnes,"as men die, so they walk among posterity." But, whatever one may think of the characters of the two counts, he cannot help being greatly impressed with the famous square. He stands on ground that has been the scene of many tragedies, and is surrounded by the same mediaeval buildings which looked down on the execution of the twenty-five nobles who were beheaded there by order of the Duke of Alva. The memory of this bloody act combined with the sight of those ancient buildings, is surely sufficient to touch even the most indifferent.

Not far to the south of the market place stands a not very modest fountain of a little boy, called the manikin. The water is squirted out in the natural way. Although this diminutive figure may not excite much admiration in the spectator, still it is a great favorite among the common people. In 1817 it was carried off by a thief and its loss was mourned as a public calamity. It was, however, recovered, and seems now in great prosperity. It possesses eight suits, in one of which it is dressed on each holiday, and has also a salaried valet. Some years ago an old lady bequeathed it a thousand florins. When I first saw the manikin, it was in the primitive garb of nature, but on returning from Waterloo, I found it dressed in a black velvet suit and three cornered hat, and sheltered by a small umbrella.

When darkness put an end to my sight-seeing in Brussels I took the train to Antwerp, and was soon walking through the well-lighted streets of that city.

The most prominent feature of Antwerp is the cathedral tower which is 402 feet high and is visible from a great distance. In front of the cathedral is a well with a canopy of iron, which was made by Quentin Massys, who was once a blacksmith but afterwards became one of Antwerp's most famous artists. According to legend, he fell in love with a painter's daughter, but was refused by her father who would give her to no one but a painter. The blacksmith did not despair, but exchanged his anvil for the palette, and not only won his bride, but also became a successful painter. It is a pleasing legend but we are assured that it is not true by our iconoclastic friends.

The famous painter Rubens died at Antwerp and his house is still to be seen. The cathedral contains his masterpiece, "the descent from the cross." In addition to this there are a great many of his best works in the museum. The array of masterpieces was to me perfectly bewildering.

From Antwerp I returned to Rotterdam and the next morning I started for Mannheim by steamer on the Rhine. Although the distance to the German line looks very insignificant on the map, it was quite dark before we came to Emmerich, which is the first place in Germany reached by the river. It was a dreary ride. High levees on each side hid the surrounding country from our view, and the towns which we passed were very small, so that there was almost nothing to see. The Rhine boats are built somewhat like sea going vessels with high hulls. The passengers have very little room to move about, and after having traveled in those large floating palaces of the Mississippi, where one has as much variety of amusement as on land, one finds nothing to admire in the small, inconvenient craft which navigate the Rhine.

We did however pass one famous old city before we left

the Dutch territory, and that was the ancient Nymegen, the site of one of Cæsar's camps and one of the residences of Charlemagne. The city is also famous for the treaty which was signed there in 1678.

The second day on the Rhine was not much more interesting than the first. It was too cold to be on deck with any comfort, and there was nothing but a flat country to be seen. We passed Dusseldorf during the day, and this afforded me a temporary diversion. I saw the new building for the Academy of Art, which is making Dusseldorf so famous, and farther to the south the blackened ruins of the old building were visible. But the bridge of boats soon opened, we passed through and left the city behind. As night came on I fell asleep and when I awoke we were lying at the wharf at Cologne, the city of churches. Just below us the line of lights on the railway bridge extended across the river, and above us lay the bridge of boats. I left the steamer and entered the gloomy-looking walls for a short walk in the famous city.

Cologne has one of the most famous cathedrals of Germany. It was begun in 1248 and the work continued until the close of the fifteenth century, but from that time until 1823 the cathedral remained in an unfinished state. Since this latter date four millions of dollars have been expended in finishing it.

In order to account for the stopping in the building of the cathedral, the people had the following legend : The architect had tried in vain to conceive of a plan grand enough for his purpose, when his sulphureous majesty offered him a sketch in every way suitable for the intended structure.

The shrewd builder knew that according to the time honored custom his soul would be demanded as the price of the gift. So he carefully committed the details of the plan to memory, and then told the dealer in brimstone that it did not suit him. As might be supposed, the lord of the lower world was quite enraged to find himself thus imposed upon. So he told the architect that he might build his cathedral but he should never finish it.

After threading the narrow streets I came to the vast cathedral looming up in the darkness. The scaffolding was still standing by the walls, and but little could be seen in the night. So I soon left the famous structure and after walking sometime, I returned to the steamer.

It was still dark when I went on deck the next morning, but I could see in the distance the lights of the university town of Bonn, the birth-place of the great Beethoven. It was bitterly cold, but my enthusiasm was not to be frozen, for we were at the entrance of that part of Rhine, which has made the river so famous for its scenery. The hills, which below Bonn are widely separated, come together there and press so closely upon the Rhine, that the stream has barely room to pass between the rocky walls.

About half an hour after leaving Bonn the summit of Drachenfels loomed suddenly up in the darkness just at the river's side. As I looked up at the lofty cliff, indistinctly outlined in the mists of the morning, that description of Bryon's seemed peculiarly expressive :

> " The castled crag of Drachenfels
> Frowns o'er the wide and winding Rhine,
> Whose breast of waters broadly swells
> Between the banks which bear the vine,
> And hills all rich with blossom'd trees,
> And fields which promise corn and wine."

Farther up the river we passed the convent on the island of Rolandswerth in which the legend says the fair Hildegunde, the bride of Charlemagne's paladin Roland, sought refuge in her grief, when she heard the false rumor of the death of the brave knight. On the hill to the right are the ruins of the castle where the returned Roland lived to feast his eyes on the dwelling of his lost bride.

As we proceeded up the stream, it gradually grew lighter, but still thick clouds obscured the sun. Yet I could not wish the weather otherwise, as the darkness of the day seemed to be in keeping with the dusky ruins that were visible at every turn.

The hills on the Rhine do not form a continuous chain of the same height, but rather a series of distinct elevations, so that the eye rests on a succession of gentle curves of unsurpassable beauty. The vines which form a prominent feature of the scenery, are planted in rows and trained upon short stakes. They do not differ much in appearance from Indian corn, when it is tall and green. Every available spot on the Rhine has been appropriated for the cultivation of the grapes and the hills present a surface on which the bright color of the vines mingles with the deep brown of the rocks.

Every traveler on this noble stream must despair of justly describing his sensations, or of awakening like feelings in the minds of his readers. The grandly flowing river, the green clad hills and the moss-covered ruins, all crowd upon the observer and produce thoughts of whose wonder and rapture words have no power to tell. The journey was to me one long poem of beauty. At one moment I was occupied in contemplating the ruin of some old castle, whose gray walls seemed a part of the eternal rock which formed their base. At another time a little village with its ancient church and crumbling walls engaged my mind. The deep toned bells were ringing at many of the places as we passed, and the merry winds seemed to be playing with the sound. Now they would take it away and one could hear it moaning in a distant hill. Then suddenly they would bring it back until it pealed joyously in our very ears. Boat-loads of peasants in their Sunday frocks were continually hurrying across the path of the steamer on their way to the churches, whose invitations were rung by the bells so clearly in the valley.

In contemplating such sights I passed the morning. But I cannot give any detailed description of what I saw. The views upon the river were so uniformly beautiful that it is impossible to select one spot and say it was the best. I thought each place the loveliest while it was before me, and immediately forgot it in the grandeur of the next.

Early in the afternoon we passed the mouth of the Moselle, under the frowning walls of the fortress of Ehrenbreitstein, Rhine's Gibraltar. In a short time we reached the Koenigsstuhl, a tower-shaped structure, eighteen feet in height, which stands upon the west bank of the river. The four Rhenish electors formerly met there, and it has been the scene of the election of many of the emperors. It resembles in appearance those pictures of the tower of the Northmen in New England, which are given in many of our school histories.

A few hours later we passed the famous cliff of Lorelei.

The rock rises almost perpendicularly from the river to a height of over four hundred feet. Here in the good old days that are gone the sirens of the Rhine appeared and with their irresistible beauty, enticed the fishermen to their destruction in the rapids which guarded their rocky home. This has been a favorite subject with German poets and nothing has done more to make the spot famous than the following poem by the sweet singer Heinrich Heine:

THE LORELEI.

I cannot divine what it meaneth,
  This haunting nameless pain:
A tale of the bygone ages
  Keeps brooding through my brain:

The faint air cools in the gloaming,
  And peaceful flows the Rhine,
The thirsty summits are drinking
  The sunset's flooding wine;

The lóveliest maiden is sitting
  High-throned in yon blue air,
Her golden jewels are shining,
  She combs her golden hair;

She combs with a comb that is golden,
  And sings a weird refrain
That steeps in a deadly enchantment
  The list'ner's ravished brain:

The doomed in his drifting shallop,
  Is tranced with the sad sweet tone,
He sees not the yawning breakers,
  He sees but the maid alone:

The pitiless billows engulf him!—
  So perish sailor and bark;
And this, with her baleful singing,
  Is the Lorelei's grewsome work.

A railway tunnel pierces the cliff and the trains of this commercial age rather rudely jar the dwelling of the sirens every hour. And, I may add here, through all this region which has been such a favorite of the muses, a railroad runs along each bank of the river. When one is dreamily contemplating some picturesque ruin upon a neighboring height, it is not unfrequently the case that a locomotive will dash across the foreground of the scene and suddenly recall the lover of legends to the unpoetical moiling of to-day.

We reached Bingen just before night came, passing the island on which the little square " mouse tower" stands. According to the legend which Southey has versified, the people of the adjoining district, "once upon a time," after a failure of the harvest, begged the wicked Bishop Hatto for a share of his hoarded grain. At last wearied by their entreaties, he summoned them to his barn, as though about to grant their petition ; but when they were within, he barred the doors and burned the building with all the people.

> " 'I' faith, 'tis an excellent bonfire !' quoth he,
> 'And the country is greatly obliged to me
> For ridding it, in these times forlorn,
> Of rats that only consume the corn.' "

But his jest was turned against him and ten thousand rats were sent for his destruction. He fled to his island tower, but the avengers swam the river and climbed the banks.

> " And in at the windows, and in at the door,
> And through the walls by thousands they pour,
> And down through the ceiling, and up through the floor,
> From the right and the left, from behind and before,
> From within and without, from above and below—
> And all at once to the Bishop they go.
> They have whetted their teeth against the stones,
> And now they pick the Bishop's bones;
> They gnaw'd the flesh from every limb,
> For they were sent to do judgment on him."

The vineyards near " Bingen on the Rhine " are said to be the best and most profitable in the country. The hill opposite the town presents a wonderful appearance. It is so steep that it has been formed into terraces and these are so numerous, that, if it were not for the green vines, the side would seem like a continuous stone wall from the base to the summit. We can readily account for this extreme care for every available spot, when we remember that the best vineyard in the neighborhood affords the owner a thousand dollars an acre annually.

As the boat lay at the wharf at Bingen I had abundant occupation in watching the gray-colored mills that are anchored in the middle of the river. They have side-wheels like a steamer which are turned by the current. Not a human being was to be seen on them, and their queer forms and constant motion gave them a strange appearance of weirdness.

Besides these, I looked with great interest at a little rock near the opposite shore which was marked with a black cross. In it reposes the heart of the Rhenish historian, Nicholas Vogt, tutor of Prince Metternich, of Austria.

Above Bingen the hills recede somewhat from the river. But as it was growing quite dark, I took a parting look at a distant castle, and then went down into the cabin and was soon fast asleep. I had been fifteen hours on deck, shivering with cold it is true, but still there were such hours as leave a lifetime impression. To me now that journey seems like a dream. In the morning the " castled crags " rose up, and with the day they disappeared. But never shall I forget

"That blending of all beauties; streams and dells,
Fruit, foliage, crag, wood, corn-field, mountain, vine,
And chiefless castles breathing stern farewells
From gray but leafy walls, where ruin greenly dwells."

It was about ten o'clock in the evening when I awoke

from a few hours sleep after the day's fatiguing experience of watching the vine-clad hills of the Rhine. The steamer was lying at the wharf, and the men were busily engaged in unloading a portion of the cargo. I did not have any doubt but that we were at the ancient city of Mayence, and accordingly set out to see as much as possible in the darkness. I soon found a street running perpendicular to the river, and bordered upon one side by what seemed to be an enclosed park. I walked a mile or two but could not find much town or many people. As there seemed to be indications of soon getting out into the open country, I retraced my steps and returned to the landing place. I was considerably astonished to find nothing but the most discouraging looking darkness in the spot where I had left the steamer.

The situation was not quite so bad as it would be, if one were suddenly set down in the night in some obscure corner of China, but still my knowledge of German was not sufficient to unraval so complicated a mystery and the condition of things began to look rather uncomfortable. However, before I had time to become very much alarmed, the ringing of a bell at an adjacent wharf announced the approach of another steamer. I hastened over to the office and asked the agent a series of questions in a language that must have startled him. The proverb tells us that "necessity knows no law," and truly my necessity paid very little attention to the laws of grammar. I may have violated every rule of syntax, but that did not grieve me, as I succeeded in discovering that the town was Biebrich and that the approaching steamer was going to Mayence.

Chuckling over my easy escape from the dilemma, I soon

regained the Netherlands boat at Mayence and then went through the city wall and stumbled about in the narrow streets, until I found the statues of Gutenberg and Schiller. After getting a glimpse of the cathedral I returned to the steamer.

After being delayed the next morning for some time by a fog, we finally reached the wharf of the town of Worms. There is scarcely a city in Germany around which the legends cluster more fondly than here. On the broad plain by the Rhine dwelt the heroes and heroines of the Heldenbuch and the Nibelungen Lied. Here in those glorious days lay the rose garden of Chriemhild, the fairest of the fair. Only a silken thread enclosed the ground, but the haughty beauty held her twelve strong champions as invincible and challenged the great Dietrich of Bern to a trial of strength with her knights. The hero thus defied rose in a rage and with eleven trusty followers went to battle with the proud lady's defenders. The reward of each of the victors was to be a rose-wreath and a kiss from the lips of the fair Chriemhild. As in all legends, the end is in accordance with our sympathies, and the champions of the boastful beauty were utterly defeated. Then the conquerors claimed their prize and to add to the mortificatian of the humbled lady her "cheek, a just punishment as it seemed, was scratched to the drawing of blood by the rough beard" of one of the victors.

This is but one of the many legends of the fairy beings which were created by the overflowing fancy of the nation in its youth. But these tales have left at least one memoral of their existence to this age of industry and the landing place opposite Worms is called Rosengarten or the garden of roses, Chriemhild's bower.

If there are any who are impatient of these childish stories, let them turn to that grand convocation of the 17th of April, 1521, at which the great emperor, Charles the Fifth, presided, while around were ranged imperial electors and ecclesiastics in all the pomp of state. But mark ye that pale and emaciated form that enters the august assembly unbefriended and alone. The proud monarch turns to the ruler at his side and expresses his contempt for the stranger. Yet every eye is turned toward him, for it is Luther, and this is the grandest, the sublimest moment of his life. The vicar of the archbishop of Treves questions him in the name of the church. On the following day he stood in the same place, and firmly maintained the diginity of reason and the right of private judgment. "It is neither safe nor prudent,' said he finally, " to do aught against conscience. Here I stand, I cannot do otherwise, God help me, Amen." You may search the annals of all time, but you cannot find a nobler example of moral sublimity than this, and when the memory of those kings and priests shall have passed away, the admiration of that act will make the Diet of Worms a familiar name in the minds of men.

With such thoughts it was not strange that I looked with great interest at the plain and town, although all has passed away but the ground where the famous deeds were done. In the time of Frederick Barbarossa 70,000 people dwelt in the city, but the thirty years' war and the successive French invasions completely annihilated the buildings which were so famous, and Worms to-day is entirely a modern town, with but 15,000 inhabitants.

The journey from this point to Mannheim was very much like that below Cologne. The banks of the river are low and the view is limited.

But I must not take leave of the steamer on which I spent three days and a half without saying something of the Captain. I had seen those brutal officers of the Mississippi boats, who never address their inferiors in rank unless to curse them, and I found a great deal to admire in this partriarchal commander on the Rhine. He was of true German proportions and consequently was quite a perceptible object as he passed to and fro on the bridge. At times he came down upon the deck with his large, long stemmed porcelain pipe, and talked with the crew and passengers in a really paternal way. Mirth twinkled in his eyes and smiled on his lips, and oh! how he laughed when he found that I could understand neither German nor Dutch! Dyspeptics might have complained that our gallant officer was too fond of the blessings of the table; else why did he stop his boat to pick up a duck which one of the crew had shot? But I was willing to pardon such healthy thoughts, and gave my hearty well wishes to the jolly captain of the Rhine.

At about eight o'clock in the evening I reached Stuttgart, the end of my journey, having come from Mannheim by rail, via Heidelberg. I was just a month and one day in coming from Circleville, and traveled almost five thousand miles.

CHAPTER IV.

WINTER AT STUTTGART.—STUDY OF THE GERMAN LANGUAGE.—FATHERLAND CUSTOMS.—CHRISTMAS IN A COUNTRY VILLAGE.

STUTTGART, February 7th, 1880.

On my arrival in this city last fall I found a comfortable room with Dr. Niethammer, a retired attorney. He lives in a flat on a beautiful square called the Feuerseeplatz which contains an artificial lake and an imposing new stone church in the most elegant Gothic style. Sunday mornings I am always awakened by the beautiful music from the church tower.

Dr. Niethammer is a fiery Republican and full of political spirit. He is intelligent and companionable, though advanced in years, and has done much to make my stay in Stuttgart pleasant. His flat is on the fifth story, which strikes an American as being a trifle high, especially in a country which has no elevators, but in Europe the number of flights of stairs seems to cut no figure. A nobleman, with whom I am acquainted, lives in a third story flat. The fifth story is therefore none too high for a simple citizen.

I pay twelve marks or about three dollars a month for my furnished room and give the servant girl fifty cents a month in addition. The girl carries my coke, builds my fires, blacks my shoes every evening, cleans my clothes and runs my errands. Americans will agree that she earns her fifty cents, although it is twice as much as she expected to receive.

My breakfast is furnished by my landlord at five cents a day. It consists of a cup of coffee and a roll, which is short rations for an American stomach. My dinners and suppers I get at a restaurant, nearly a mile from the Feuerseeplatz. These cost me from ten to twenty-five cents. It is evident, therefore, that my expenses are moderate.

I have been studying the German language with great diligence all winter, under the tutorship of Prof. Christian Schwartz, who lived over twenty years in the southern States and served a short time in the Confederate army. Prof. Schwartz was recommended to me by a gentleman employed in the royal library, and I was much astonished to find that he had also been the tutor of Mr. George Martin, of Lancaster, Ohio, an acquaintance and former student at the same college with me. Prof. Schwartz charges twenty-five cents for each lesson of one hour.

Dr. Niethammer's daughter, Fraeulein Marie, speaks some English and helped to give me such information as I needed to get started at my studies.

Among my later acquaintances is Count N., with whom I walk every day to Degerloch, a village on top of the mountain, south of the city. The count is studying English and our arrangement is to talk German going up the hill and English coming down. Occasionally other friends join us in our daily promenade.

Of the four kingdoms that are comprehended in the present German Empire, Wurtemberg stands third in size and last in population. In the times of Duke Ulrich, while Luther was yet alive, the country became Protestant, but she has never occupied a prominent position in the national history nor possessed rulers who have had a lasting influence on the culture of the empire. It is true, she has her Eberhards and Ulrichs and Wilhelms, but their fame has scarcely penetrated beyond her own hills and forests. As the birthplace of men of mental power, however, this little kingdom ranks among the most famous ; and from many of the villages which nestle on the hill sides around a church spire, like birds about their maternal protector, men have gone out whose praises have echoed in lands where these dukes and kings are never named.

Not quite three-quarters of a century ago in the last days of the year 1805, Napoleon, by the treaty of Presburg after the battle of Austerlitz, obtained additions of territory for his South-German allies and royal crowns for Bavaria and Wurtemberg. By a timely desertion of their benefactor in 1813, the latter succeeded in retaining their gains after the one who had won them had been driven from the field of Waterloo.

Thus Wurtemberg is forced to acknowledge that she has no grand historical character among her princes whose immortal deeds can give fire to the sluggish veins and lead the coming youth up the rugged, thorny path of fame. But she presents one claim which can not be disputed. She has more breweries to the square mile than any other land on the face of the earth. According to the latest statistics, 7,777 of these beer manufacturers are at work within this kingdom, and produce annually 85,300,000 gallons, which is equivalent to 46 gallons for every man, woman and child in the State.

Since 1321 Stuttgart has been the capital of the country and the residence of the sovereign. The greater part of the city is the growth of the present century, and consequently she gains in beauty and cleanliness while she loses in historical interest. The hills, which almost surround the town, have left a valley which is now completely filled with houses. The buildings at the edges of the city rise gradually up the slope for a short distance, while beyond them lie the beautiful vineyards, and still higher up, the forest trees cap the summits. The Neckar—the scholars' Neckar —whose rippling waters have just passed the university town of Tuebingen, flows by Stuttgart's suburbs, Berg and Cannstatt, and hastens on toward the famous hills of Heidelberg. A walk of fifteen or twenty minutes up a well-kept roadway brings one to summits which overlook the city. I have sat for hours and enjoyed the views. No clouds of smoke as at Cincinnati, hang over the town; but one can look through a clear atmosphere at the dwellings, churches and palaces that lie far beneath him.

The vineyards are laid out in terraces by walls and gutters of masonry, which contrast strangely with even the most particular farming in America. And then, too, the amount of work done by women is noticeable. They come trudging over the hills every day, dragging heavy wagons with milk or market vegetables. One meets them of all ages, from those who are in the prime of womanhood, to those whose furrowed brows and drooping forms tell of long years of toil, which have not sufficed to make old age a period of rest. Here one sees women working in the streets at the most menial labor. As I walk along and mark how a young girl on the threshold of life is tottering under a heavy burden, I look into her face expecting to see her upbraid the fate which grinds her under the wheel of toil ; but I notice the eyes brighten and a smile flit over the care-worn face when she meets the boy of her heart. There is poetry and sunshine, which come welling up not only in the lives of the rich, but even among the slaves at the tread mill. And oft where we look for curses we meet blessings and smiles.

This low condition of the working classes should form an item in the calculations of those who think that the degradation of the laborer advances in proportion to the progress in the use of machinery. He should well remember that the rewards and comforts of the workingmen in the great factory towns are not less than those of these peasants, whose implements are of the simplest kind. The question involves so many and such complex principles that the decision is by no means as easy as many imagine. I had far less difficulty in making up my mind that a German woman of the lower classes works as long and as hard as a Rotterdam dog.

I have said that Stuttgart is principally a modern city, but I may add that she has, nevertheless, three churches, which were built before Columbus sailed for America, and one old castle which was erected while Queen Elizabeth was ruling in England. There are many narrow streets to be seen bordered by houses constructed three centuries ago. They are mostly of that mediæval style, having each story project slightly over the one under it.

In the Neckar Strasse, near the royal palace, there is a gloomy looking building which is used now partly as the headquarters of the palace guard, but which was once the seat of a school established by Duke Karl Eugen, in the last century. From 1773 to 1780 Schiller spent the bitter days of his youth in this half prison, and wrote a portion of his first drama in moments stolen from the rigorous duties that were imposed upon him. Some persons affect to treat this dreary period of the poet's life as one whose trials were magnified by an aversion to discipline common to all school boys. But for my part I think the agonies he endured were as intense as those of deep affliction in the the prime of manhood. I know of no tragedy more mournful than the forcing of genius into a sphere contrary to its nature and in defiance of its aspirations. I know of no thought more blighting to the heart of man than to feel immortal melodies pressing to the lips and yet be compelled to ape the discordant notes set by fools, until the harp strings are shiveled with uncouth sounds that might have given forth Orphean strains of beauty divine. "Will a courser of the sun," says Carlyle, "work softly in the harness of a dray-horse ? His hoofs are of fire, and his path is through the heavens, bringing light to all lands ; will he lumber on mud highways, dragging ale for earthly appetites from door to door ?"

In a square next to the old castle is the famous Thorwaldsen's statue of Schiller, which was erected in 1839. The poet is clad in a long gown whose folds are partly gathered up by the right arm, with which he holds a pen. The left hand clasps a book, while the laurel-crowned head bends slightly forward. From the attitude one would imagine that he had left his desk and had been pacing the floor until a new thought had enrapt his mind and stopped him in his walk. The artist has succeeded in throwing in the back ground the hard features, the large acquiline nose and protruding under lip, which are so prominent in the statues at Mannheim and Mayence. I doubt if bronze ever represented more vividly that dreamy look which glows in the poet's face in the hour of inspiration.

From the new royal residence a beautiful park stretches toward the north for several miles and ends finally on the banks of the Neckar. Four rows of magnificent forest trees line the walk and the carriage ways, affording a refreshing shelter from the summer heat.

The old castle is an irregular building which has received many additions since its construction in the middle of the sixteenth century. It is nearly square and has large round towers at three of the corners. The broad moat has been entirely filled up, but one can still see the grooves at the two gateways where the draw-bridges once rested. As the castle is situated in the midst of the city, it, of course, loses much of the romantic interest which it would otherwise have.

On passing through the gateway one enters a court in which stands an equestrian statue of the first Duke of Wurtemberg, Eberhard im Bart. Several galleries or porches encircle the square, rising one above another and being supported by numerous Corinthian columns. On one side before a grated window on the third story a sentinel is pacing to and fro. It is the chamber where the crown jewels are deposited. Upon the other side are the entrances to the royal chapel, which is used at the present day. At one end there is an elevated platform, where the king and the members of the family sit. The queen, who is a sister of Emperor Alexander II. of Russia, belongs to the Greek church and has a chapel of her own. The king is nearly fifty-seven years of age, and his hair and whiskers are quite gray. He is rather fine-looking and appears at the chapel in a plain officer's uniform with sword and epaulets. Immediately in front of this platform for the royal family, which is protected by a railing, are the seats for the nobility. The rest of the space upon the ground floor is assigned to the ladies, while the gentlemen have places in the gallery. The Germans seem to be convinced that where men and women are gathered together the devil is in the midst of them, and they make it a religious duty to separate the sexes in the churches.

Nothing is more noticeable to the American than the number of friendly salutations that are used by the Germans. When one walks in the country he is met everywhere with a cordial " Gruess Gott, " which is as untranslatable as the English " good-bye." As one passes along the streets at noon he hears in every direction parting friends saluting each other with a " Prosit," or a " Guten Appetit." German etiquette, too, requires one to doff his hat to gentlemen as well as to ladies. Nor is this a half hearted movement as in America, but one vigorous and decided. Many of these actions are ungraceful and some are really laughable, but still I think that the warm salutations, which are so universal, are indicative of a national feeling of that good nature which prefers kindness to malice.

Sometimes I took walks on Sunday afternoons. I would ramble among the forests on the hill-tops, stopping occasionally to watch a party of young folks in a vineyard, who would fire off a pistol and then send up a merry peal of laughter as it was answered by another from a distant slope. Sometimes I would thread my way through a village whose narrow streets were filled with little wagons and wine-tuns. Then I would return to the city, passing the unending stream of people that was pouring out to the numerous public resorts. Master and servant, maid and mistress, officer and soldier, in short, all grades of society make these excursions on pleasant holidays. No other place affords the same advantages for seeing German character in its various phases. Readers of Goethe's Faust can obtain some idea of the strange contrast in the people on these walks from that scene before the city gate, where soldiers and students, servant girls and fine ladies, laborers and profound burghes successively pass before the eye :

> "From the dark, low rooms, scarce habitable;
> From the bonds of work, from trade's restriction;
> From the pressing weight of roof and gable;
> From the narrow, crushing streets and alleys;
> From the churches' solomn and reverend night,
> All come forth to the cheerful light."

Among the innumerable other things which attract the attention of an American, when he arrives in Europe, are the soldiers whom he sees here on every hand. It seems that every knife is sharpened, every gun is primed, and all is in readiness for a common destruction. The energies of the nations are strained to their utmost to raise the means for the gigantic preparations. Each State watches eagerly the movements of the armies of its neighbors, and upon the least provocation loudly accuses them of aiming at conquest. War is the subject of reminiscence in America; but in Europe it is treated as one of the possibilities of the present. Each nation grinds its sabers, loads its guns and claims to be an apostle of peace. Some of the papers suggest, as a much more rational way of maintaining public tranquillity, that a congress of the jealous powers adopt a fixed and reasonable proportion of their standing armies to their population. Thus they would gain by common concession that peace which otherwise is maintained by common terror.

The kingdom of Wurtemberg, with but 7,658 square miles of territory, has as many soldiers as the United States, with their area of over three millions. According to a statement published a few weeks ago, there are 3,700 men in garrison in this city. One meets them in all parts of the town, either singly or in troops. Handsome officers throng the promenades and places of amusement. I never saw a set of men so uniformly fine looking as those who carry the swords of the German army.

The life in the barracks is shared by so many that it leaves a lasting impression on the national character. College life in America has a similar, but not such an extended influence. The awkwarkness of the raw recruits, the incidents on the watch and all the petty adventures of lively spirits subjected to rigorous discipline combine to form a series of memories that are never forgotten. I doubt not that every one of these soldiers will tell long and interesting lies in after years of what he did at the barracks, even as Justice Shallow and all our college students spin their endless tales of what was done at school.

Americans think the Germans are heathen for presuming to enjoy themselves on Sunday. But they would be astonished to know that the feeling is reciprocated. The Protestants celebrate a great many festival days here which I never heard of before I came to Stuttgart. The other morning as the servant brought me my coffee she announced that it was a sacred day. I assured her that I knew nothing about it and then her contempt for the Protestants of the New World was unbounded. "Humph!" said she in disgust, "the Americans are of no account if they don't celebrate to-day."

Nature seems to resemble those tender hearted mothers, who, after severely whipping their children, give them sugar candy as a compensation for their pains. While the people of the northern zone shiver in the wintry blast, they gain that greatest of all blessings, a home. When we are weary of parks and palaces, when the cold immensity of the heavens does but chill us, we turn with never ending pleasure to the memories of the cheery fireside, which was the delight of our childhood.

Of all the nations of the earth perhaps none has loved the joys of the home better than the German. Surely no land has a richer store of those legends which bloom like flowers around the family hearth. The facilities for rapid transportation have indeed made city life almost alike the world over, but in the numerous villages of Germany it is still possible to find those customs, which the authors have so delighted in describing. Several years ago I read with intense interest the details which Richter gives in his autobiography, of life in a country parsonage. Since then

A STUDENT'S VIEWS ABROAD. 73

I have not been more eager to see the Rhine, than to pass a week in a German village. At last an opportunity to have my curiosity gratified was presented in the invitation to spend Christmas with a steamship acquaintance living in the country West of the Rhine, between the rivers Nahe and Moselle. So in spite of the extremely cold weather I left my temporary home at Stuttgart about the middle of December, and on the evening of the second day reached Kirn on the Nahe, thirty-three miles from Bingen. The whole distance was not more than two hundred miles, but I had been in five states and ridden on six different trains. The traveler can hardly fail to wish that the Imperial Chancellor would expend some of his unifying force in making some reasonably long railways out of the innumerable short ones.

From Kirn I went by the diligence up the Hahnenbach valley to Buechenbeurn. There was but one other passenger, a burly farmer, who immediately began to inquire about my past history and future prospects. When he found that I had some difficulty in understanding him, he concluded that I was deaf, and then shouted his questions close to my ear in a tone that would not have disgraced a workman in a boiler factory. But this unusual exercise soon exhausted him and he dropped back into his corner and was soon fast asleep. After leaving the diligence a walk of three-quarters of an hour brought me to Hirschfeld, which was my journey's end.

As is perhaps generally known, the German farmers live in little villages instead of being scattered over the country in the independent style of America. Every one of these little communities has an inn, whose proprietor is usually also a grocer on a small scale. This abundance of places for entertainment of the traveler has made Germany the pleasantest of all countries for tourists afoot.

The first sight of a village is hardly in accordance with one's expectations. The houses are built to face whatever point of the compass was agreeable to the owner, without any regard to the bearings chosen by his neighbors. The streets are so crooked that one could easily believe that they had once been cow-paths. The buildings have walls of plaster which are strengthened by cross pieces of wood. The barns are frequently built from clay mixed with straw. As there is an abundance of slate in the neighborhood of Hirschfeld, these humble structures are covered with substantial roofs. Although the snow covered the ground during the entire course of my visit, still I could see enough to convince me that the people were by no means fastidious in their tastes. Heaps of stable refuse lay before each dwelling as though it was considered an ornament.

The farmers have one principal room in their houses in which the eating and ordinary occupations of the family take place. Immediately behind this is the kitchen. The people universally use an ingenious stove, which is built in the wall, so that while standing almost entirely in the main room, it opens out into the cooking apartment.

As carpets are a rarity even in German cities, of course there are none to be seen in the villages. For the covering of the beds one has a mountain of feathers. When the national customs are summed up, I think that along with the pretzels, beer and tobacco, one should place the feather beds.

Not long after my arrival a man who was holding a dog by a chain, blew a flourish on a horn in the street in front of the house. The sheep which came running towards him from all directions told me plainly that this was the shepherd. I was further informed by my friend that he took the sheep every day from the village out into the open country, and that the office of shepherd is a regular profession. Later in the day another man passed along the street and blew a whistle, which the hogs obeyed as promptly as the sheep did the shepherd. I was told that the business of swineherd was similar to the other.

Before the close of the first day we went to the house of the district overseer to report my arrival. We did not have much difficulty in convincing the honest officer that the tranquillity of the community was not endangered by any machinations of mine. As it was not in his power to pronounce the name of Circleville and as his ideas of the land beyond the sea were rather vague, the investigation was not pursued very far.

On our return to my friend's house, we passed the common bake-oven which is used by the entire village. Every day I could see the house-wives going along the street balancing on the head or shoulder a long board upon which were placed four or five loaves of dark-colored rye-bread. In this region bread of wheat flour is regarded as a luxury and when a father returns from a journey he brings some rolls or buns for his children, who receive them as gladly as little folks would confectionery in Ohio.

In spite of the labor-saving machinery of the world, the spinning-wheel still maintains its place in the German villages. In the evening at my friend's house the table was pushed back into a corner, the lamp was suspended from the ceiling and the girls from the neighborhood came in with flax and spinning wheels to spend the long winter evening. Soon after these came troops of young men, who ranged themselves along the wall upon the chairs and benches, and gossiped or smoked or slept, according to their pleasure. But all this time the girls in the center of the circle never ceased their skillful spinning, but constantly fed the insatiable wheels, while continuing the conversation with easy readiness at the same time. As I watched the groups before me, I could not help entertaining the fear that it was emblematical of the relation of the two sexes. The girls were working as industriously as bees, while the boys were maintaining the dignity of their lordship by grumbling and befouling the air with vile tobacco smoke.

I thought I could discern in most of the faces about me a great deal of latent ability, which would find a better field for its exercise in the land beyond the Mississippi. The majority of the boys had that massiveness of feature, which indicates solidity of each faculty and the power of doing a vast amount of work. But in the little village their mental shrewdness is expended on such contracted themes, that even the sharpest and brightest minds are apt to be corroded for want of use. My friend had been some years in Philadelphia and New York City, and had very little patience with the trivial subjects of conversation which engaged the attention of the evening circles. "They are talking about dogs now," said he in contempt once after we had left the room, "pretty soon they will begin to talk about cats, and rats, and mice." A simple-hearted old lady was one day amusing herself by asking me such odd questions as how old my mother was when she was married, but her investigations were cut very short by an icy interruption from my friend, "you don't need to know that."

After having seen the spinning of flax we went to see it woven into cloth. The loom was very much like those used by the rag carpet weavers who still linger in our land in spite of the great factories. I was told that a man could make fifteen ells in a day. The flaxen cloth is used by the people for bedding and clothing in the place of muslin. We also saw at another house some men weaving wool. One was making a piece which had two colors, and had to count the threads of the wool in order to know when to change the tints. Twenty-five cents a day with board are the wages of a farm-laborer, so it is possible to earn as much at this slow work of weaving as at the severer drudgery of the field

I had hoped to find the morals of the village in that simple condition which seems in keeping with the pariarchal habits of such communities. But I found the people discussing their little scandal case like their brothers across the sea, and if the report is true, these peasants are as eagerly chasing the almighty dollar as the most accomplished leader in "high life." When a young man applies for the hand of a young lady, I was told the parents of the latter note the area of his piece of land and examine the store of rye he has in the loft, and his fate rests upon the impression produced by these worldly goods. And even if the suitor passes through this test, his trials are not over. For when a couple exchange vows, they are compelled to notify the "higher powers" at Buechenbeurn immediately. A notice of the engagement is then posted in a conspicuous place at the village, and for three consecutive Sundays the preacher reads the announcement in the church. Upon the fourth Sabbath, if the couple has continued faithful to the end they can be married.

"They could do that much quicker in America," said my friend.

"How long would it take?" asked a curious rustic.

"Half an hour," was the laconic answer.

Although the village is about two-thirds of the Protestant faith, the Catholics have a separate school. Both are much alike in their arrangements and their scholars are between the ages of six and fourteen. As I wished to visit the schools, we called on the Protestant teacher one evening. He proved to be not only are presentative of higher knowledge, but also of more advanced civilization. So he soon conducted us from the common room into the parlor. The furniture was like that one sees in the German cities. In one corner stood a piano on which the gracious school-master played and sang during the course of the evening.

On the following afternoon we went to the house again through a crowd of children who stared at "the American" as though he was a strange animal. The teacher led us upstairs into the school room, and the scholars soon came trooping in after us. The work of the day began with the youngest ones on the front seats. The little foreheads became wrinkled, and the chubby, dimpled hands twitched nervously in the intense effort to answer the questions.

During one of the studies of animals, the teacher thundered out, "where is the lion found?" "In America!" eagerly answered a bright-eyed boy, who no doubt thought all kinds of wonders were to be found there. Thus the work went on until it came to serious tasks in arithmetic for the larger boys and girls on the back seats. I enjoyed the afternoon very much and was quite pleased to find the scholars had almost as much trouble in getting their thoughts into grammatical German, as I had mine.

To many this plain village life will hardly seem to deserve the love which Jean Paul and many others have so warmly expressed for it. But all men become poets when they think of their childhood, and that idealizing spirit transforms the vilest clods into richest gems. As Emerson says, "the loathsome worm takes wings and flies away a beautiful, rainbow tinted butterfly."

The approach of Christmas was the signal for a new activity in the little village. As I have related before, a course kind of rye-bread is the ordinary article of diet. But during the holidays every one considers himself entitled to something better than what he has had all the year round. And so for several days before Christmas the housewives were busy kneading dough and hurrying to and from the village oven carrying the delicacies that were to delight the children as well as the old folks. If there had indeed been a dearth of sweetmeats at other times, there was an abundance then. Monstrous cakes several feet square were baked as substantial additions to the fantastically shaped small ones for the children. Some of the fond fathers waded through the deep snow to the forest and brought back evergreen boughs for Christmas trees.

The Germans have two festal days at Christmas (Weihnachten) on the 25th and 26th of the month. The churches have services at both times as well as on New Year's day, so that however it may be with other people, the preachers have no vacation at that season.

On Christmas eve we went to a neighbor's house to see the brilliantly lighted tree. The children were rejoicing over the simple presents and indulging themselves in an immoderate quantity of cake. The men set to work to celebrate the evening by playing cards for walnuts, while the women amused themselves by asking me questions about America. One old lady wished to know whether I would have to cross the sea when I returned home. Notwithstanding the immense emigration to America, and in spite of Germany's splendid school system, there is considerable ignorance among the people in regard to the New World.

The peaceful village of Hirschfeld is jarred by no religious discords. Protestants and Catholics live quietly together and even worship in the same church. As I wished to attend the Christmas service I was put under the care of the school-master, who conducted me to his elevated seat near the pulpit, from which I could see both preacher and audience. The church was a dismal place. There was no fire to warm the feet of the faithful, and no elegant pews in which to slumber. The rough benches were almost as thick as they were broad and one cross-piece was the only support for the back. Along the front of the gallery were painted several dozen hideous pictures of saints, who were labeled in order to assist in their identification. The cold stone pavement and bleak looking walls added to the general discomfort, while the snow that was blown against the window panes looked coldly in on the shivering people. The only relief which the eye could find in all this dreariness was the two Catholic altars, whose tastefully arranged ornaments and flowers formed a strong contrast to the barrenness that surrounded them. After the service had begun the schoolmaster stood up with his gloves, furs and overcoat and started a hymn. The people clutched their books with hands that were blue with cold, and let their voices follow his, but at such a distance behind it that they might have been mistaken for its echo. In answer to my anxious questions in regard to the comfort of the preacher, my friend had told me before I went to the church, that he was better off than the rest of the people as "he could knock his feet together and in that way keep warm." And as I watched how vigorous the speaker was in making his gestures, I could not help entertaining the suspicion that physical as well as spiritual warmth was the object of his movements.

After the service I went at the invitation of the schoolmaster to his house to lunch. The little folks there were in high glee over the dolls and toys which the children's saint had sent them, and little Karl, a bright-eyed, three year old boy, seemed quite warlike with a helmet and sword. I soon began to feel at home at the hospitable fireside in spite of the difficulties of the language, and forgot the many miles that lay between me and my native land. The children called me "der Onkel" and confidently brought me their playthings to be admired. As we were at the table Karl's mother asked him where "der Onkel" came from. "Aus

Amerika," answered the little fellow promptly. Of all the memories of my visit to Hirschfeld none will cause me more pleasure than that of this family circle at the village school-master's.

I did not venture to the church on the second festival day but obtained a glimpse of something new that evening. On each of the great holidays of the year, the proprietor of the inn at the neighboring village of Holbrueck provides music at his dance-hall, to which the lads and lassies come from miles around. In spite of the bitterly cold wind my friend and I went down across the plain to see the sport. After climbing one flight of steps, we entered the large dancing-hall which had several smaller rooms adjoining it with tables and chairs, where the merrymakers rested and drank. The ceilings were not more than eight or nine feet high and the upper four feet of the atmosphere was principally smoke. I first thought of a conflagration or the dislocation of a stove pipe, but I soon found that the smoke came from the vilest kind of tobacco. I had been on a German steamboat, in German railway cars, depots and restaurants, and thought I had seen some of the smokiest places in the world, but they were all mild compared to this. The wildest tales of student life never tell of the verdant freshman encountering such befouled atmosphere as this, even at a "smoking out." The musicians stood on a store-box in one corner, and although their feet were visible, they disappeared like mountains in the clouds.

We groped our way across the main hall and into the side room, and at last found some seats. After my eyes had become somewhat accustomed to the smoke, I saw that the room was filled with the stout boys and girls of the country. Before each couple stood a bottle of wine and a glass. The boys were smoking and talking to their partners. Occasionally one would take up the glass and drink the smallest amount possible and then refilling it, he would give it to the girl at his side who drank a similar quantity. But soon a few introductory flourishes upon a horn called the dancers to the hall. The boys seized one of the hands of their partners, and they climbed over the benches together with an ease that would astonish the frail daughters of America. As soon as they reached the floor they clasped each other in a manner, of which the American waltz will give a remote idea. Thus locked in one another's arms the couples pranced around the room in a circle, varying the style of their movements according to the music. The boys looked blandly over the shoulders of their partners and continued their smoking as though they were sitting quietly in a chair. But the buxom maidens seemed to hold out the longest, and I noticed more than one fellow resign his place in the arms of a stout country girl to some fresh friend who had been standing outside of the circle. When the music ceased there was another scramble for the seats, and feats of agility were executed that would seem marvelous to the fair daughters of the west. After we had seen the different varieties of dancing we made our escape to the fresh air and returned to Hirschfeld.

The 27th of December is the moving day, (Wandertag). It is the time when the servant girls change their places, and is ranked among the village holidays. I could not see anything unusual until late in the afternoon when numerous bands of girls passed through the streets singing and seeming to feel quite happy. When they met a woman or girl, a general handshaking would take place and sometimes the jug of whiskey which one of the party carried, was brought into use. Long after dark one could hear these singing groups of girls passing by the house. But it must not be thought that all were going to new places to work for one of each band was moving and the others were her companions, who were accompanying her to her new home.

I have spoken of pigs and sheep, men, women and children, but have neglected to speak of the horses. Although every man in Hirschfeld is a farmer, there is not more than half a dozen horses in the whole village. The people use cows or oxen in their place. The reason as I was told, is that while a horse always decreases in value and at last is worth nothing, the farmers can fatten the oxen every year or two and sell them, and thus never lose the money they invest. Of course this kind of reasoning indicates a limited amount of work with no necessity of speed.

After I had spent nine days in the village I felt that I had taken vacation enough, and so set out one evening to walk to Buechenbeurn in order to take the post to Kirn on the Nahe. As my friend was sick I found that two stout country damsels had volunteered to accompany me. Accordingly one seized my traveling shawl and the other my small valise, and after the farewells were said, we passed the crowd of villagers who had assembled to see "the American" depart, and were soon on the open plain. My friend had enjoined me to let the girls carry my traveling equipments and although I claim a little of the American chivalrous spirit, my feeling of awe for the manly muscles of those daughters of the plain, and a sense of my Lilliputian strength induced me to hold my peace. Soon after we had left the village it began to rain and blow violently. Yet the two stormproof maidens went on undisturbed through the darkness, wind, snow and rain. After nearly an hour of rather severe walking we reached the office at Buechenbeurn and my bodyguard left me with many repeated invitations to visit Hirschfeld again.

At three o'clock the next morning I began the ride of four hours by diligence through sleeping villages down the Hahnenbach valley. Then I bade farewell to the Hundsrueck country and returned to Stuttgart.

I have been devoting the latter part of my stay in Stuttgart to preparation for my travels in the coming summer. I have been reading whatever I can find relating to the history of the places I intend to visit.

I have also made various little excursions afoot into the surrounding country. One pleasant day I walked to Marbach, the birth-place of Schiller. Another day I visited Solitude palace. Every time the sun shines brightly it makes me eager to begin my summer's trip.

CHAPTER V.

BEGINNING OF THE SUMMER'S TOUR.—HOHENSTAUFEN CASTLE.—ULM AND AUGSBURG.—THE ART TREASURES OF MUNICH.—INNSPRUCK.—OVER THE BRENNER PASS INTO ITALY.

I took leave of my Stuttgart friends and started from the city, March 24th, for my summer's tour. I left the most of my baggage with a friend and carried nothing but a knapsack and rubber coat as my outfit for a five months trip.

The traveller from Stuttgart by the Rems Valley Railway on approaching the Swabian Alps obtains occasional glimpses of two lofty peaks which tower far above their fellows. One seems conical in shape, the other like a prism. The former is Hohenstaufen, the seat of the famous Swabian emperors. The latter is Rechberg, upon whose summit stand a ruined castle and little chapel.

The train winds around among the hills, passes the village of Waldhausen, according to tradition the birth-place of Emperor Frederick Barbarossa, and skirts the hill near Lorch, where a Benedictine monastery stands which contains the graves of a dozen of the Hohenstaufen family. Finally the cars reach Gmuend, an ancient city with a fine location on the banks of the Rems. The Romans called it "the joy of the world." Here I left the train and after spending some time in looking at the quaint buildings, I took my knapsack on my shoulders and set out for Rechberg.

The road led gradually up the hill, but I turned off upon a foot-path which promised to be nearer. I soon came to a place where it was so steep that the earth was cut into rude steps, which looked romantic enoungh but made it fatiguing work to ascend. As I paused to rest, I was startled by shouts of childish laughter above me, and soon saw a number of little girls with baskets coming down pell-mell through the forest at a rate that would have put Putnam and his horse to shame.

After they passed on into the valley I picked up my knapsack and started off again. The path became steeper and steeper and above the forest became as near to a perpendicular as was possible. A misstep would have sent me rolling down the rocks but in the animation of the moment I thought nothing of such possibility. I at last reached the summit all breathless and threw myself on the grass to recover.

Near me on the highest point was the chapel from which sounded the subdued tones of the holiday service. The preacher's dwelling was the only other building upon the mountain. This spot, so far from the noise of the workman, has heen set apart for the worship of the Unknowable and perhaps the peasants who leave their labors in the plains and ascend this mount, feel a higher and purer reverence for the Deity.

Old Dr. Johnson never allowed anyone to talk of the weather in his presence, and stoutly maintained that its variations had no effect upon the human mind. If he had traveled more he would undoubtedly have moderated his views and pardoned the tourist for attaching so much importance to the nature of the weather.

I was particularly fortunate in this respect, for not a cloud could be seen in the sky. It was one of those days which the Germans designate as Italian weather. If there was a slight haze perceptible, it was to be ascribed to the effect of the great extent of the view. Upon one side I could see the long chain of the Swabian Alps. The terraces and various colors upon their sides made it seem but a few weeks since the waters had dashed against their summits. Upon the other side my view was over a hundred villages, whose roofs and spires shone in the bright sunshine amid the forests and fields.

I remained so long looking at the landscape that the people came from the church before I had departed. Taking my knapsack once more upon my back I hurried through the crowd of worshippers and went gradually down the hill. Before going very far I passed the ruins of the castle Hohenrechberg, whose towers and battlements can be seen for miles. From there I walked about four miles and a half to the village of Hohenstaufen which lies upon the side of the mountain from which its takes it name. I opened the churchyard gate and entered the little chapel, into which Frederick Barbarossa once walked. Under the eaves are the arms of many famous cities in Germany and Italy which were subject to the lord of this lofty mountain. The chapel was partly restored in 1860 and the work is yet in progress.

Leaving the churchyard I followed a good path which led up the side of the peak. The summit I found also much better arranged for the convenience of the traveler than Rechberg. Numerous benches are placed so as to command the best views. A beautiful rustic building about the size of an American summer house has been erected for the protection of the visitor in unpleasant weather. There is an inscription over the entrance which ought to touch the heart of every vandal :

> "From wind and rain I screen thee
> Be kind enough to spare me."

The ancient castle of Hohenstaufen was one of the many which were destroyed in the Peasants' War, and the material was afterwards used in building the castle at Goeppingen. All that now remains upon the peak are a few remnants of walls, but the sight of these and the magnificent view made me feel abundantly rewarded. The prospect is even better than that at Rechberg, for one can see in all directions from the same spot.

Hohenstaufen affords an excellent opportunity to muse upon the mutability of human affairs. On this mountain once dwelt proud Emperors whose power was felt from the Mediterranean to the North Sea. To-day a few scattered stones alone are left to tell of what has been. The peasants who plow the fields under the shadow of the hill, have almost forgotten the nobles who ruled their fathers. Only the red bearded Frederick lives yet in the legends like England's king of the table round and the people have long expected that in times of trouble that the beloved emperor will again appear and overcome all the nation's enemies.

Taking a loose piece of the wall of the castle and a few leaves from the hillside as a memento I descended into the plain and walked about five miles to Eislingen, a station on the railway.

Early the next morning I left with the train for Ulm. As we proceeded we penetrated farther into the mountain range, and the grade became steeper and the valley narrower. The peculiarities of German fields soon disappeared and the thickly wooded peaks that lay around us differed but little in appearance from the summits of the Alleghanies. After reaching the elevated table-land the train ran for miles along its level surface and then descended toward Ulm. The immense fortifications loomed up in the distance, and as we drew near to the city we passed the citadel Wilhelmsburg, where General Mack surrendered his army of 30,000 men to the French in 1805, without trying to defend his flag.

At noon the train arrived at the fine new depot at Augsburg, and I set out with high expectations to view the magnificent relic of the greatness which the rich free cities attained in the middle ages. The buildings on the broad avenues in the neighborhood of the station are entirely modern, but they are constructed in a style which shows that wealth has not yet deserted the place which once boasted of a Fugger. After wending my way through a number of crooked streets I reached a broad one called Maximilian's-Strasse, which is the main artery of the city. At its northern extremity stands the fountain of Augustus which was erected to the memory of the emperor who founded Augsburg and gave it his name.

Passing down the street one sees a large, old looking house, which belonged to Fugger, the merchant prince of Augsburg. The walls are covered with frescoes, representing events in the history of the family.

The few collections of artistic and historical value in Augsburg would scarcely suffice to detain the tourist who is going to Munich, but the entire city is a relic of the past such as is seldom seen. The houses are mostly of the sixteenth and seventeenth centuries and are finished in a way that shows the riches which flowed into the merchants' coffers from the trade in the Levant. The streets are nearly all narrow and crooked, and the aspect of the city is as antiquated as the Dutch towns and much finer than they in regard to the style of the building.

Modern Munich has little more than its name and coat of arms to remind one of the austerities of the monks, after whom it is called. Though lying on a plain that is swept by the cold winds of the Alps, art and wealth have raised the capital of the Kingdom of Bavaria to one of the finest cities of Europe, whose influence is felt in all parts of the world and whose praises are on the lips of every traveler. Here are fine palaces and churches, magnificent avenues and gates in endless variety and unsurpassable taste. One might well wonder what astonishment this scene would give to the great Roman Tacitus who looked upon Germany much as we regard the island of Iceland. And rightly might he marvel at the change that has come over the bleak, inhospitable country.

The treasures of painting here are contained principally in the old and new Pinakothek. The former is a gallery of works of the old masters of the Dutch, Italian, Spanish and German schools. Though perhaps none of the first three can be as fully studied here as in their native countries, still it is a collection that may well deserve the attention of the artist. Rubens' best works are to be seen in Antwerp, but even here are twenty or thirty of his paintings that should not be neglected by his admirers. Murillo's pictures are to be studied in Spain, but his "beggar boys" are the admiration of the visitors to the old Pinakothek. Finally many of the famous works of Raphael, Titian, and the other Italian masters can only be found transplanted upon this northern land.

On the south side of the building is a long gallery, called the Loggien, which is finely decorated with frescoes representing incidents in the lives of the great artists and allegorical paintings in honor of the patrons of the wielders of brush and chisel. The minute details of the work are so well done that one feels repaid for the pains he gets in straining his neck to contemplate the ceiling.

The new Pinakothek is a collection of modern paintings. The outer walls are adorned with frescoes, but those on the south and west sides are almost completely destroyed by the heat of the sun. The contents of the gallery are of course not so interesting as those of the masters in the old Pinakothek, yet they have an especial interest from the fact that many of them represent incidents in modern history. The last Franco-German War has already formed the subject for a large number of paintings, so that one can now turn from the rusty old pictures of the combats of knights to the more prosy battles where cannon and musket play the leading part.

The Glyptothek is the treasury where Munich's possessions in sculpture are stored. It is a building in chaste Ionic style with statues of the masters in niches in the walls.

The first hall that one enters contains several strange looking Assyrian bas-reliefs. The second has a number of specimens of Egyptian sculpture of different periods, from the rude, unnatural statues of the age before the Ptolemies down to the finer finished ones which show the influence of the Greeks and Romans. In the center of the hall stands one of those obelisks of syenite which have been the chief object of plunder among the Europeans who have visited the land of the pyramids. The remaining rooms are filled with statues and busts of the different periods of Roman and Greek art. It is pleasant to look at the long series of busts which are nearly two thousand years old and which represent those great men whom we hate most bitterly in our early school days and afterwards learn to love. The entire collection was to me exceedingly interesting and I would willingly have devoted a longer time to its study.

South-west of the city in the midst of a broad common stands a tall figure which seems of moderate dimensions when contemplated from a distance, but which is one of the largest statues in the world. It is 62 feet high, has seventy-eight tons of metal and cost $97,000 exclusive of the pedestal. After having obtained a candle of the custodian I ascended the stairs upon the inside. After winding round and round until I had climbed a hundred and twenty-six steps I reached the top and entered the monstrous head. In front of me I could see the shape of the eyes and nose, which are between one and two feet in length. Upon each side is a seat of metal which is cast to resemble a cushion. While I was looking through the little openings toward the city, a great, burly German came puffing up the steps and squeezed himself through the narrow entrance. Pretty soon two more came up and the head seemed nearly full. The figure represents Bavaria standing by a crouching lion with an uplifted wreath in one hand and a sheathed sword in the other. It was begun Oct. 15th, 1843, and finished Oct. 15th, 1853. "This colossus," says the inscription, "erected by Ludwig I., King of Bavaria, is planned and modeled by Ludwig von Schwanthaler, and was cast in bronze in the years 1844–1850 and set up by Ferd. Miller."

Just behind the statue is the Hall of Fame, an open structure with Doric columns. It contains a large number of busts of distinguished Bavarians from the early times down to the present. The student finds many faces among them that he has long since learned to honor, but the artist is still more gratified as the majority of them have been of his profession.

In this city of statues nothing would be more suitable than a visit to the place where many of them were cast, and an inspection of Miller's foundry is especially interesting to Americans, as some of the best monuments in our land are from his workshop. So I walked to the northern end of the city, and spent several very agreeable hours in the royal establishment. The men were engaged upon two large subjects. One was an equestrian statue of the prince of Servia, which is almost finished and is destined to be erected in Belgrade. The other is an immense statue of Germania, which is to be placed on the summit of the hill opposite Bingen on the Rhine, as a monument to commemorate national unity.

The guide who conducted me through the building was a

good natured fellow, and became particularly gracious when he found that I was an American. After he had delivered himself of his usual speech for each subject he was glad to gain any information in regard to our country. Many of the models have been preserved and some of them looked quite familiar. Only a few fragments of the Cincinnati fountain remain, but there are still a large number of others to be seen which are well known. Among them are the capital doors at Washington, Lincoln and the slave, the Washington statue at Richmond and the soldiers' monument at the Cincinnati cemetery.

When I awoke on the morning I had fixed for my departure from Munich I heard the unwelcome sound of falling rain. Hoping I might be mistaken, I went to the window and found my impression was only too true. The chilling wind from the Alps seemed all the colder for the bright spring sunshine of the previous weeks. As I had no time to wait for pleasant weather, I was forced to abandon the long cherished plan of a journey afoot across the country to Innspruck by way of the Bavarian Lakes, and be contented with the sights of a trip by rail. After shivering through the rain to take a farewell look at the old Frauenkirche, I accordingly left Munich by the train for Rosenheim.

After going several hours along the elevated plain upon which Munich stands, we entered a more uneven country. The clouds which still lingered in the southern sky seemed almost transparent. Presently they began to drift away, revealing the snow-capped summits of the Alps. Peak rose over peak, until it was impossible to distinguish mountains from clouds.

Changing cars at Rosenheim we started up the valley of the Inn. The way became constantly narrower, until the snowy summits towered far above us on each side. Towards evening we passed a chapel by the road side, which was built to commemorate the parting of the Queen of Bavaria in 1833, with her son, Otto, who was on his way to accept the crown of Greece. Immediately afterwards we crossed the frontier and entered the empire of Austria. A few minutes later the train rolled into the depot of Kufstein, where we alighted for the custom house inspection. I threw my knapsack down before an officer, who was evidently convinced that there could be nothing contraband in such a receptacle. He merely asked me if I had any tobacco. Upon my answering with an emphatic negative, he said with a flourish of the hand, "ganz recht, all right."

As it was already late and I wished to travel in this interesting land by daylight, I concluded to spend the night in Kufstein. The town has a fine location in the valley upon the right bank of the river. In the center a lofty and solitary rock rises abruptly from the plain and is crowned by an impregnable fortress. Only one steep path leads to this Gibralter of Tyrol, and all provisions and supplies are drawn up by means of an inclined place. Modern cannon might produce some effect upon the battlements, but to the unskilled eyes of a civilian starvation seems the only enemy that could conquer its defenders.

I found the style of the peasants' cottages in Kufstein already different from those of Southern Germany. The high roofs and plaster walls with painted wooden supports, which one sees everywhere in Swabia had disappeared entirely. In their place were low houses with flat, wide-spreading eaves, which are characteristic of Alpine scenery. Along the fronts upon a level with the attics are balconies with railings of carved wood. The roofs are covered with immense stones as a precaution against storms. The hats which the peasants wear, partake of the same tendency as the houses, for they are broad brimmed and flat.

I could detect in the faces of the people the influence of the mountains. The eyes were brighter and indicated a quicker working of the mind than among the sluggish Swabians. The maidens, too, were blessed with more beauty than their cousins of the north.

The temperature at Kufstein was rather cool and the sight of the snow on the mountains did not tend to lessen the sense of coldness. When I left the next morning the ground was white with the heavy frost. The cars were without fire and I shivered so on the way that I was perfectly indifferent to the scenery. As I alighted at Innspruck, I was almost numb with the cold, but there was no fire at the station. I suppose the natives are used to it, but I felt like taking the next train south.

The chief curiosity of the city is the church of the Franciscans which was built in the middle of the sixteenth century. At the left of the entrance is the monument which covers the ashes of Andreas Hofer, whose very name sends a thrill to the heart of every lover of liberty. His remains were in Mantua from the time he was shot by order of Napoleon, until 1823, when a battalion of Tyrolese brought them to Innspruck, where they now rest in honor. It is needless for me to praise the mountaineer. His name is venerated by his countrymen as much and as deservedly as the Revolutionary heroes are among us.

But the chief object of attraction in the church is the magnificent monument of Emperor Maximilian I., according to whose will the church was erected. He also wished his bones to rest here, but this was not complied with by his successor and they lie at his birthplace, Wiener-Neustadt, a city about thirty miles south of Vienna. The monument consists of a large sarcophagus, upon which the emperor is represented kneeling, while around it are ranged the colossal statues of twenty-eight heroes, which the observer is to consider as pall-bearers and attendants, although they in reality stand entirely apart. The figure, which is universally considered as the best executed, is that of Arthur, King of England. It has a certain grace of posture which the majority of the others lack. The sarcophagus itself is covered with twenty-four bas-reliefs in marble representing historical scenes. The work is extremely delicately wrought and commands general admiration. The famous sculptor Thorwaldsen pronounced them masterpieces of their kind.

There is also another event which makes the church historically interesting. Christina of Sweden, daughter of Gustavus Adolphus, the champion of Protestantism, made a public confession of the Catholic faith here on the 3d of November, 1654.

In the Nation's Museum are a great many relics of the struggle for freedom in 1809. Portions of Andreas Hofer's dress, his amulet, sword and gun, and specimens of money coined under his administration are exhibited together with similar articles that were made sacred by having been used by his fellow-leaders.

I left Innspruck in a snow storm not at all sorry that I was again going toward the south. Soon after leaving the station we passed through a tunnel and then the character of the scenery became changed. At Innspruck the railroad parts with the broad and fertile valley of the Inn and follows the course of its tributary, the Sill, which plunges down a narrow gorge that is wild and picturesque. The snow at first was but a thin coat that lay lightly on the boughs of the evergreens, and only made them brighter and fresher. The grass too was visible and the entire landscape had that pleasing appearance which we like so much in the first snow of a season. Around the peaks overhead rolled the thick clonds, while far below it the water dashed foaming down the rocky channel.

Tunnel followed tunnel as we went on up the mountain range, and the character of the landscape was again changed. The snow became deeper and deeper until all the vegetation was hidden and it seemed we had returned again to the time of mid-winter. Meanwhile the valley became broader, cultivated land appeared and towns were occasionally passed. When we stopped at a station, we could see the people wading slowly about in the snow in a way that seemed dreary enough to those who had but a few hours previous seen the sun shining brightly on the budding fields of Southern Germany.

At several places along the line we saw traces of avalanches and land-slides and this naturally gave rise to some comment among the passengers. As children tell ghost stories at night and sailors during a storm relate harrowing tales of shipwreck, so it was equally appropriate that the snowy peaks of the Alps should lead my companions to speak of the disasters of the past. Wild and weird seemed the tales that were told of the dread avalanche's destructive falls, and as we whirled round a curve a young man pointed to an immense mass of rock that had come from the summit and destroyed the road and railway track.

Before reaching the top of the mountain range we passed the Lake of Brenner, which is the source of the river Sill, which we had followed from Innspruck. It was completely covered with ice. About noon we arrived at Brenner station, the highest point on the road. It is 4,485 feet above the ocean level and forms the watershed between the Black and Adriatic seas.

The train stopped five minutes to give us an opportunity to get a farewell German lunch of bread and sausage before descending into Italy. The snow lay five or six inches deep on the ground and there was nothing to tempt us to tarry. Just south of the station the Eisak comes plunging down the mountain side in beautiful, though diminutive waterfalls. Down the valley worn by this stream the railroad picks its way, making at times great bends to avoid an obstruction, and at others dashing boldly through the heart of a peak. The descent was very rapid.

The horse-shoe curve on the Pennsylvania railway is the object of considerable admiration, but it is far surpassed by the bends in the Brenner road. The most remarkable of these is south of the summit, where one can see the track hundreds of feet almost perpendicularly below him. In summer great numbers of people leave the cars at the station on the hill and descend by a foot-path to another station below, where they arrive ten minutes before the train. Nor is this all, for the lady opposite me said one could enjoy in the interval a glass of beer at the excellent brewery near the depot. But as the snow was on the ground when we passed, not even this could induce anyone to leave their seats and go down a-foot.

The traces of a warmer climate soon began to be visible. The pines gave place to chestnut trees and vineyards. Even the manner of cultivation of the grapes betokened the nearness to Italy. Instead of being closely trimmed and fastened to short stakes as in the unfavorable climate of Germany, the vines are allowed to grow long and are trained upon trellises. The character of the people became different. The sun-browned Tyrolese disappeared with his big blue umbrella and in his stead came the still darker skinned Italian. All my German companions left me before reaching Botzen and their hearty good wishes were the farewell sounds of the northern tongue. I then amused myself with listening to the musical accents of the new passengers. The language seemed as melodious as the murmur of a brook, and our northern words in comparison were as harsh as the clash and clatter of a factory loom.

Toward evening we arrived at Trent, where I had determined to spend the night. Starting out in search of the "albergo," which I had chosen, I made my first inquiries in German, but was answered in the other language. The next time I stopped a soldier and let off at him a portion of my stock of Italian. The fellow looked at me despairingly and said quickly: "Ich versteh' Italienisch nicht." Well, I thought, this is rather mixed. Again as I was entering the inn a couple of German soldiers across the street called over to me : "Hey ; you're a German, are you not ?"

After getting my baggage safely in my room I went for a look at the place. Trent is supposed to have been founded by the Etruscans and has the appearance of a genuine Italian town. The flat roofs of the houses are covered with queer tiles, whose variations of black and white make them seem like the crumbling stones of a ruin. As in many other places the city wall is completely preserved except on the side where the nineteenth century has demanded space for a railroad. The numerous high fences of stone, the fantastic shapes of the houses and the occasional beggars lounging in the streets were among the many indications of the Italian nature of the town.

I visited several of the churches and among the others was the one in which the celebrated Council of Trent was held. Across from my room stood an old structure with battlements and towers which was used as the barracks for the troops. In the courtyard in the rear of the inn a fountain noisily poured forth a constant stream. In the midst of such surroundings I could dream of the sunny clime of the south, although the sky was black with clouds and the snow-capped mountains were visible upon every side of the city.

CHAPTER VI.

VERONA.—VENICE.—FIRST GONDOLA RIDE.—ST. MARK'S AND THE PALACE OF THE DOGES.—RAVENNA.—ARRIVAL AT NAPLES.

From Trent I went by rail to Verona, where I saw the arena, an amphitheater which is supposed to have been erected in the reign of Diocletian about the year 284 of our era. As the first specimen of a Roman circus which I had seen, it was of course very interesting. The outer wall is composed of a series of arches rising one above the other. It is of the same class of structures as the coliseum at Rome. As I had not yet seen that monster, I could not look upon the arena as a thing of no consequence.

It would be needless to describe the churches which I visited, even if I could. A few days in Italy are sufficient to show one the hopelessness of any such attempt. A splendid prospect of lofty arches and a confusing array of paintings along the walls are what the traveler sees on every hand, and he is unable to recall the impression produced by the different churches as a whole, much less of the thousand details of their interiors.

But I must not neglect to tell of another excursion which I made, that will probably be of interest. The name of Verona has been published more in the distant world by

Shakespeare's plays than by any other means, and even the least sentimental traveler has a desire to see the tomb of Juliet. Having gone through a great many narrow and crooked alleys and passed the old city wall, I was suddenly accosted by several children, who danced about me crying, "Tomba di Giulietta." Following them I was admitted by a porter into the garden of a suppressed monastery. He conducted me along a narrow path which terminated in an ugly apartment of a house. The walls are rough and upon one side stands a sarcophagus that is still rougher. It is of red Verona marble without anything resembling a lid. A slight depression at one end marks the place where the head was supposed to rest. The scene was barren of everything to excite a poet's imagination, especially as the skeptical loudly maintain that there is no authority whatever for calling it the tomb of Juliet. Upon a table in one corner of the room I saw some copies of the drama in English, German and Italian. Above the sarcophagus a number of withered wreaths and bouquets are suspended to commemorate various visits to the shrine of unfortunate love. A card attached to one of these, bears the name of a descendant of the "thousand souled" bard who visited the place in 1874.

From Verona I went direct to Venice, "the city of a hundred isles," whose mouldering palaces and great canals would indeed be a favorite with the traveler apart from any other association, but genius has made them doubly sacred and the charm of history is mingled with that of romance.

"Ours is a trophy that will not decay
With the Rialto : Shylock and the Moor,
And Pierra, cannot be swept or worn away—
The keystones of the arch ; though all were o'er,
For us repeopled were the solitary shore."

Everybody has a foolish desire for auspicious beginnings and lays especial stress upon the character of first impressions. I longed to draw near to the romantic city in the favoring light of an unclouded sky and see her as Byron taught me to expect.

> "A sea-Cybele fresh from ocean,
> Rising with her tiara of proud towers
> At airy distance, with majestic motion,
> A ruler of the waters and their powers."

But in all this I was disappointed. I left Verona in the afternoon in the rain. A glimpse of the steeples of Vincenzia and Padua and the sight of the flooded country were the preparations for my entry into the city that we deem within the bounds of fairy land. It grew dark and the rain beat dismally against the windows. Here and there the car door was opened to admit a passenger dripping with water or to allow one to go out into the darkness and rain. The bells at the station sounded uncertain and mournful. The railroad agents shouted huskily. But above all we could hear the constant, depressing sound of the falling flood. The train lights emitted a funereal gleam upon the dark waters of the lagune as we dashed over the long bridge to reach the island city. I disembarked at the station and pushed my way through the dense crowds of passengers and noisy porters until I reached the quay. The grand canal was covered with boats of all kinds and each boatman was shouting at the top of his voice in a jargon that no stranger could understand. An officer in a great rubber coat accosted me:

"Una barca ?" inquired he.

"Nein, I want a gondola," said I, slightly mixed.

After considerable preliminary shouting a gondola came up to the steps, and the boatman assisted me to descend into the box that is fitted up for the traveler. After giving the name of my hotel to the gondolier, he went back to his post and I settled myself in my seat to enjoy the ride as well as possible under the circumstances. The form of the gondola is known to everyone. The low, narrow box in the middle has a place for one or two persons. There are windows in front and at the two sides and the passenger can stretch himself out at full length and enjoy an admirable view. Mark Twain's comparison of the whole thing to a hearse is good. The gondolier stands at the stern and works a single oar upon a pin which gives the boat a rocking motion from side to side.

I pushed back the blinds after my gondolier had shoved off from the wharf, and had considerable pleasure in the trip in spite of rain and clouds. The palaces loomed up darkly from the banks of the canal and we glided along past the occasional lamps, whose light gleamed on the face of the water, and all the unpleasant realities of stormy weather could not dispel the poetic effect of such a scene.

Just before reaching the Rialto my boatman left the grand canal and began picking his way through a series of narrow channels, where his progress seemed almost miraculous. Not even once in the entire voyage did the numerous projecting obstacles scrape the sides of the gondola, so great is the skill of the boatmen. I finally saw some masts at the end of the narrow canal in which we were going and recognized that I was approaching my destination. We soon passed under a bridge which I almost instinctively felt was the Bridge of Sighs, that mournfully interesting relic of a bigoted age. A thrill of joyful suprise came over me as we glided out into the broad channel and I saw the Doges' palace and the column with the winged lion of St. Mark upon the right. A few minutes later we reached the wharf. The gondolier opened the door and said, "ecco, here it is!" I was pleased so much with my first ride that I did not grumble when I was charged double the tariff.

The hotel in which I had chosen to rest is on the grand canal, and the view the next morning was quite entertaining. In the broad channel lay several steamships and a number of sailing vessels and flitting about among these were hundreds of small boats. To the south the spires of the churches on the opposite islands terminated the view, while toward the east the Adriatic could be seen as far as the eye could reach. On the quay in front of the hotel the gondoliers and fruit-sellers were keeping up a constant confusion by their discordant cries.

After visiting St. Mark's, the palace of the Doges, and some other places I spent a great deal of time in threading the narrow lanes that form a net work of communication throughout all Venice. Strangers are apt to think that the island city has no streets whatever and even the shortest trip must be made by water. But this is a mistake. Venice has as many land passages for pedestrians as any other city in Europe, although some of them are scarcely a yard wide. For ordinary purposes these lanes are used by the people exactly as pavements are in other places. The gondolas represent the carriages and the larger boats the wagons of heavier traffic. A workman no more expects to go to his business in a gondola in Venice than one does to use a cab in America.

The narrow lanes have a great many bends and often seem to end abruptly in a brick wall. I walked about regardless of the points of the compass, trusting the paths would lead me somewhere. Occasionally I would fail to find an outlet and would be compelled to retrace my steps, which was by no means facilitated by the hooting urchins who delight in tormenting foreigners. In spite of the discouraging stares of the natives, I followed the narrow lanes into all quarters and saw the various shades of Venetian life. At one part I met the dainty mustached, gold ringed, nice young gentleman with little feet and smaller brains; at another I passed the squalid mother chasing strange animals among the tattered locks of her child.

In walking in the extreme eastern end of the city I came unexpectedly upon the park. It is rather limited in extent and conveys but a feeble idea of the bright green earth on the mainland. Yet there undoubtedly are thousands in the city who have never seen a larger piece of vegetation than this. I was still more surprised to find within the enclosure a track marked as a "course for horses." Upon it a man was riding a little nag as fast as it could go, trying to get a taste of the joys of equestrianism. It was the only horse which I saw in Venice and it seemed rediculous to see him used in such a way. But of course it is quite natural that the natives of the city should place an extravagant value upon such a ride, however small it might be.

Altogether there is a great deal in Venice to remind the traveler of the cities of Holland. Of course this has much more romantic interest than the prosy, commercial towns of the Dutch, but the aspect of the canals is very similar. For a dreamy ride I prefer a gondola in Venice, but for the ordinary purposes of life the clean, honest, hard working natives of Holland are by far the best.

St. Mark's Square has long been the center of life in Venice. The famous church and the palace of the Doges border it upon one side, and formerly the chief offices of the government were located in this vicinity. By the water's edge stand two columns, upon one of which is the winged lion of St. Mark, the patron saint of the city. Upon the other is the emblem of St. Theodore, the protector of the old republic.

Between these two slender marble pillars, on the quay, which were themselves trophies of the conquering arms of the city, formerly took place the reception and parting of the great generals who maintained the dignity of Venice abroad.

Many a brave Venetian soldier has been nerved in the hour of battle by the ambition of a triumphal entry under the shadow of the winged lion. The proudest bearers of the triple crown and the bravest of the emperors of the North have landed at these columns, not disdaining to be the guests of the mistress of the sea. Indeed this place was woven into the affections of the Venetians as deeply as the forum was in those of the Romans. Here was to be seen all the glory of their native city. The masterpieces of art and the trophies of a hundred campaigns were visible on every hand. In the distance the blue Adriatic smiled upon her lord, and here the Venetian might stand and utter with truth those seemingly extravagant words of the younger Foscari :

> "My beautiful, my own,
> My only Venice—this is breath! Thy breeze,
> Thine Adrian sea-breeze, how it fans my face!
> Thy very winds feel native to my veins,
> And cool them into calmness."

The fantastic architecture of the church of St. Mark is the first thing that attracts the attention of the stranger. It was begun nine centuries ago, and is built in a combination of styles. It has a large dome in the center and a smaller one upon each side. The façade is in the form of five arches supported by an immense number of varied colored columns. Above these are historical scenes in rich mosaics. Immediately in front of the portals are three tall flag-staffs, from which once floated the colors of Cyprus, Candia and the Morea, in token of the sovereignty of Venice over those lands. Above the entrance are four bronze horses which have had a checkered history. Probably of Roman origin, they successively adorned several triumphal arches, were carried by Constantine to his new capital, and were brought to Venice by the Venetian conquerors. They were taken to Paris by Napoleon in 1797, but were restored in 1815 to their former place, where they have since remained.

The exterior of the church conveys an admirable idea of the wealth of the old Republic. The style is of Oriental magnificence, such as could only come from the lavish hands of princes.

The interior is fully as magnificent as the exterior. A beautiful mosaic pavement covers the floor, while the columns and vaulting are adorned with scenes on different subjects, also in rich mosaic. This magnificence, however, seems to attract more visitors than worshipers, and the crowds of priests pursue their service almost alone. The church was dedicated to St. Mark, whose remains are said to have been brought to Venice from Alexandria in the year 829, but it also contains some other relics which might well be considered interesting, if there were not so many similar ones in Europe. Among these wonders are "a piece of the true cross," "a portion of the skull of John the Baptist" and "a vase containing blood of the the Savior." I saw a picture in the Academy of Fine Arts which represents the miraculous discovery of the "true cross" in one of the canals. The adjacent bridges and windows are thronged with spectators, who piously contemplate the scene. Under the water can be noticed the long robed forms of several priests who are diligently searching after the treasure, while in the center is another who has just appeared above the surface, holding aloft the sacred relic in triumph.

On the north side of the church, upon the exterior, is the tomb of Daniel Manin, who was President of the short-lived Republic which was established when the Austrians were expelled from Venice in 1848. The monument was covered with fresh wreaths, which shows that he is still remembered kindly by the Venetians. One of the floral testimonials bore the familiar name of Garibaldi, and the date showed that it had been but recently deposited there.

South of the chuch stands the great palace of the Doges, which is as unique if not as magnificent as the cathedral itself. The wings of the building leave an irregular shaped court in the center, and around this runs a gallery, which is at present ornamented with statues of distinguished natives of Venetia from ancient times down to the present.

The principal apartment of the palace is the grand council chamber, where the highest nobility formerly held their assemblies. Its walls are covered with historical paintings, except the wall back of the President's chair, which bears a picture of paradise. Of course it represents a multitude engaged in those silly occupations which some people dream will be the business of the future world, but which would scarce suffice to amuse the simple fancy of a child for a moment, much less still the complicated wants of a rational man for eternity. The principal interest, however, attached to the picture is an account of its being the largest oil-painting in the world.

On the frieze of the hall are seventy-six portraits of different Doges who have ruled in Venice. I looked with a great deal of interest at the black tablet which covers the place appropriated to Marino Faliero, and which produced such an impression upon the mind of Byron. He said truly that the black space causes more interest than any of the monotonous row of faces. The inscription in Latin proclaims that "this is the place of Marino Faliero, beheaded for his crimes."

I next turned my steps toward the famous Bridge of Sighs, which connects the rear wall of the palace with the prison, which stands on the opposite side of the narrow canal. The bridge is a covered structure, with two grated windows upon each side. A partition separated it into two divisions, one of which was appropriated to the passage of criminals and the other to the prisoners of State. Of course I peered through the iron bars at the outer

A STUDENT'S VIEWS ABROAD. 113

world and repeated to myself Byron's well known lines:

> "I stood in Venice, on the Bridge of Sighs;
> A palace and a prison on each hand:
> I saw from out the wave her structures rise
> As from the stroke of the enchanter's wand:
> A thousand years their cloudy winds expand
> Around me, and a dying glory smiles
> O'er the far times, where many a subject land,
> Look'd at the winged lion's marble piles,
> Where Venice sate in state, throned on her hundred isles!"

The attendant led us then down into the dungeons where the prisoners were incarcerated. The narrow aperture in the wall does not deserve the name of a window and the light and air of heaven can scarcely penetrate into these dismal tombs for living men. The stones were dripping with water and even in my momentary pause I shivered with cold. Here the unfortunate victims were left without so much as straw for bedding and many a wretched man has sat within these walls while the grim monsters of disease were slowly destroying both mind and body. What tales of horror these dungeons could unfold, if they were endowed with the power of speech! What shrieks of despair would there be heard; and what wild prayers and hysteric laughter of phrensied brains! There could be no better commentary upon the thoughtful sentence of Burns that "Man's inhumanity to man makes countless thousands mourn."

Among the cells which we visited was one where Byron spent twenty-four hours in order to get a more vivid idea of the horrors of the place for the composition of his tragedies. An English lady, who was with my party, remarked that he chose one with a board lining, that was therefore not so damp. It looked cheerless enough, however, in spite of the trifling improvement over the others.

The guide next pointed out the dungeon where Marino Faliero was confined and showed us the place of execution. We saw the little window at which the priest received the last confession of the cendemned, the aperture in the stones where the light and crucifix stood, and finally the pins to which the ropes were fastened for strangulation, the trough for the blood of the beheaded, and the secret door by which the bodies were conveyed to the canal. Indeed there seems to be a great deal of truth in Ingersoll's pointed saying that it has only been about fifty years that this world has been fit for a gentleman to live in.

On the second evening of my stay in the city I had stood on a lofty tower, called the Campanile, in the square of St. Mark, and watched the sun sink beyond the plains of Lombardy and its crimson colors fade into darkness upon the spires of town and the broad surface of the misty sea. But the morrow was black and cloudy and the water seemed to pour instead of drop. I pulled on my great rubber coat and started for the grand piazza in company with an American student in similar attire. Before the church and palace were moody looking groops of travelers, trying to get a glimpse of the wonderful architecture in spite of the rain. The respectable Venetians looked from the snug cafes in pitying contempt at the crazy "Inglesi," who ventured out in such weather. But the street boys hooted and took a fiendish delight in perplexing the tourists. Occasionally a crowd would rush out from shelter to demand a soldo of the dripping sight-seers, and then dash screaming back when it was refused. It would be difficult to find a more discouraging prospect and I concluded to retreat. So taking a farewell look at the old square I tumbled my effects into a boat and was soon among the prosy scenes of the railroad station. After a cheerless ride across the Venetian plain we reached Padua where I rested for the night. The April storm continued however to pursue me and I fled the next morning toward the south. I looked across the fields in the direction of the village of Arqua where "repose the bones of Laura's lover." We crossed the rapid Adigo and the broad Po and stopped at the station at Ferrara.

The storm ceased for a time and I was enabled to visit the few places in the city that have been made sacred by past associations. Motives of economy as well as the dictates of choice lead me in my excursions to depend mainly upon my natural means of locomotion, and I have a particularly warm ill-will against the builders of Italian railways. They have the faintest possible sense of the eternal fitness of things when they choose a place for their stations. If they locate the station within a mile of the outskirts of a city, they think they have fully discharged their duty toward mankind.

It may be said, however, in palliation of their offense, that the present mediæval customs of the towns compel them to keep without the walls. Every large city in Italy has preserved her ancient ramparts, not indeed as a means of defense, but as a portion of her custom house machinery. A duty is levied on all comestibles which enter the corporate limits and the net-work of guards around the towns is as intricate and clumsy as that on the frontiers of a country with a protectionist regime.

I had a little adventure with the officers before I learned of the system. When walking from the station into the city of Verona, a villainous looking fellow in an indifferent uniform accosted me. I supposed that he was one of those impudent porters whom I meet everywhere, and attempted to pass on my way. He prevented it though, and I at length found that he wanted to inspect my baggage. From my silence and my efforts to get rid of him, he concluded that I had something contraband and I was accordingly compelled to open my luggage. A respectable looking knapsack was familiar enough to the eyes of the officers on the frontiers of Tyrol to let me go through without question and it seemed rather humiliating to be compelled to submit to inspection in order to enter an Italian town. But I consoled myself, as I always do, with the thought that I was getting experience at least. In ordinary cases a simple declaration by the traveler that he has no comestibles is sufficient to pass his baggage without examination.

As soon as the visitor enters Ferrara he preceives that its glory has departed. The long streets are deserted and the unbroken rows of houses seem as lifeless as a continuous wall. Here and there a petty vendor of eatables has established his stall in a broad doorway that once was the avenue of commerce in keeping with its proportions. The aspect of the city and the contrast with its former condition reminds one of those worn out ships that are dragged upon the beach and used for fishermen's huts. From a population of a hundred thousand Ferrara has now shrunk to twenty-eight thousand.

As the nearest place of interest I turned my steps toward the house which the great poet Ariosto built for himself, when he was living in the favor of the brilliant court of Alphonso the Second. It stands in the Via dell' Ariosto which is at present so quiet that I could scarcely find a person of whom to inquire my way. It is a plain, two storied building without anything remarkable either in size or style. The inscription on the house is said by the learned author of the "Curiosities of Literature" to have been written in answer to some friendly taunts at the smallness of the structure. It is little, said the poet, but suitable for me and offensive to no one. The house was bought by the town in 1811 and a statue has been erected to him in the Piazza Ariosto. Indeed it must be allowed that the Italian cities have universally exhibited a laudable care for the places made sacred by the masters, which has by no means been fully imitated by those northern lands which affect to look down on the degenerate sons of the south.

Upon ringing the bell I was admitted by a motherly faced old lady into an ample hall. She then conducted me by a stairway to the right into the upper rooms. One of these was used by the poet for a study and the table is still shown upon which he was accustomed to write. The apartments below were used for dining room and kitchen, and all are paved with tile as is usual in Italy. After inscribing my name in the visitor's book, the custodian lead the way to the garden in the rear of the house. Its size is scarcely larger than the building itself but it was filled even in those early days of April with sweetly smelling flowers, which looked all the brighter for the recent rain. At my request the kindhearted old lady made me a beautiful bouquet for a souvenir of the place.

I then turned to the center of the city and passed the queer looking diamond palace, which receives its name from the curious appearance of its outer wall, in which all the stones are hewn to a point and thus present a regular series of jutting ends. Not long afterwards I saw the lofty towers of the ancient palace of the house of Este and soon paused in the square to contemplate the interesting structure. It is a vast building of brick, surrounded by a moat which is crossed by several of the old fashioned draw-bridges. It has four towers at the corners and a broad court within the walls. Altogether it is one of the best preserved examples of a mediæval castle that are extant. It bears no signs of decay and despite the fact that it is used for town offices and the telegraph bureau, it exhibits no visible indication of the influence of modern hands. It stands there grand in its simple massiveness and sternly keeps its bridges and moat like a hoary veteran clinging to bygone styles.

Under one of the towers the dungeon is pointed out where the last act of that dreadful tragedy was played which Byron has given to the English public in his poem of "Parisina." The fact is horrible enough in itself and we are glad to dismiss it from our minds, but such subjects had a strange fascination for the moody nature of the passionate Byron. Carlyle beautifully defines poetry as the effort of man to be at harmony with his existence, when he rises above his own selfish aims and feelings and looks on life from that lofty standpoint, where evil dissolves into universal good. But Byron seemed to have none of this ecstasy. He searched the chronicles of the darker times for the unjust victims of inexorable law and tuned his harp to accord with groans from rocks and shrieks from dungeon vaults.

Proceeding farther in my walk, I visited the cathedral, crossed the square and reached the university. Pressing through the crowd of students who stared at me as critically as they do over the sea, I was conducted by the porter to the library, which contains some precious relics. Among these are manuscripts by Tasso and Ariosto of their respective masterpieces. I saw one of the finger bones of the last named poet, which is preserved in a glass case, but it seems a sacrilege to thus make a show of the remains of an honored man, in order to gratify a vulgar curiosity. It were far better, I think, to let them moulder undisturbed within the sheltering veil of the tomb. Let Shakespeare's curse be extended to all and let no inquisitive hands presume to rudely handle the bones of the great. Ariosto's tomb was moved to the library from the church of St. Benedetto in 1801. His chair is also preserved at the same place.

I finally visited the hospital of St. Anna, in the basement of which is the dungeon where Tasso was confined for seven years by his former patron, Alphonso the Second. The proverb seems true that the vinegar of wine is sourest and the hatred that is begotten of love is the bitterest. The prison is small, and damp, and dark, such as would now be thought unfit for the vilest malefactor. The prophesy in Byron's grand "Lament of Tasso" seems to be literally fulfilled and the poet's cell is a place of pilgrimage. The walls are covered with names and Byron is among the rest. Although we may despise the practice, we of course must acknowledge that the presence of these inscriptions is indicative of great interest in the place. It is a melancholy duty which Ferrara now has to show the dungeon where her lord once confined the poet.

> "And Tasso is their glory and their shame.
> Hark to his strain; and then survey his cell;
> And see how dearly earn'd Torquato's fame,
> And where Alfonso bade his poet dwell:
> The miserable despot could not quell
> The insulted mind he sought to quench, and blend
> With the surrounding maniacs, in the hell
> Where he had plunged it. Glory without end
> Scattered the clouds away—and on that name attend
> The tears and praises of all time. * * *
> Peace to Torquato's injured shade! T'was his
> In life and death to be the mark where wrong
> Aim'd with her poison'd arrows, but to miss.
> Oh, victor unsurpass'd in modern song!
> Each year brings forth its millions; but how long
> The tide of generations shall roll on,
> And not the whole combined and countless throng
> Compose a mind like thine? Though all in one
> Condensed their scatter'd rays, they would not form a sun."

From Ferrara I went to Bologna, one of the oldest and most famous cities on the Adriatic coast, known principally in America on account of the sausage which is named after the town. Bologna university was founded in 1119 and is one of the oldest in the world. At one time it numbered 10,000 students. It has now only 400. Bologna took a prominent part in the wars of the Guelphs and Ghibellines and was one of the allies of the Pope against Emperor Frederick II., whose son Enzio was taken prisoner by the city and held a captive for twenty-two years until his death. King Enzio was a gifted poet and his love for Lucia Vendagoli throws a romantic halo over his captivity. The great church of San Petronio was the scene of the coronation of Emperor Charles V., Feburary 24th, 1530. Among the tombs it contains is that of Princess Elisa Bacciocchi, sister of Napoleon.

Bologna has two leaning towers but neither of them compare in beauty with the one at Pisa. One tower is 272 feet high and three feet and five inches out of the perdendicular. The other is 138 feet high and eight feet and a half out of the perpendicular.

From Bologna I went to Ravenna and spent the day. Ravenna was the principal harbor of the Roman empire but the sediment brought down by the rivers filled up the port and now even the sea is quite a distance from the city. Ravenna was the residence of several Roman emperors and Gothic Kings. Ravenna was preferred by Byron to all other Italian cities. It is indeed a most interesting place and contains many magnificent churches. The church of San Vitale was built during the reign of Justinian in imitation of St. Sophia at Constantinople. Near it is the church of San Nazario e Celso, which was founded A. D. 440 and contains the tombs of Emperors Honorius and Constantius III. and Empress Galla Placida. These are the only monuments of ancient Roman emperors which remain undisturbed. The mosaics on the walls and the curious tombs make this the most interesting church in Ravenna.

Dante's tomb has an interest which can not be rivaled. It is in a beautiful marble mausoleum, embellished with medallions of Virgil and Dante's patrons and friends. The visitor looks through the iron gates at the marble urn which contains the poet's ashes.

> "Ungrateful Florence! Dante sleeps afar,
> Like Scipio, buried by the upbraiding shore;
> Thy factions, in their worse than civil war,
> Proscribed the bard whose name for ever more
> Their children's children would in vain adore
> With the remorse of ages;   *   *
> Happier Ravenna! on thy hoary shore,
> Fortress of falling empire! Honor'd sleeps
> The immortal exile."

On my way from Ravenna to Naples, I passed Faenza, noted for its pottery (faience) ; Forli and Cesena, both ancient towns; and the river Rubicon famous for its passage by Cæsar. I spent some time at Rimini made famous by the Malatesta family whose fate is sung by Dante and Byron.

Not far from Rimini is the little republic of San Marino, the smallest in the world, perched on the mountain top. It was founded in the reign of Diocletian and has retained its independence through all the changes which have taken place around it.

I stopped a day at the beautiful seaport city of Ancona and paid a visit to the son of a German friend. The view of the mountains and the sea is charming. Later in the day I went to Loreto, situated on a hill and commanding grand views. The little town attracts half a million of pilgrims annually. In a handsome church is preserved the house of the Virgin Mary which was transported by angels to this spot from Nazareth in 1294. The house is encased in a marble screen adorned with sculptures of great merit. The house contains an image of the Virgin and Child executed by St. Luke the apostle.

After seeing Loreto I went direct by rail to Naples. The route is down the Adriatic coast and then over the Apennines.

CHAPTER VII.

NAPLES.—THE FILTHIEST CITY IN THE WORLD —THE CHARMING BAY OF NAPLES.—ASCENT OF MT. VESUVIUS.—POMPEII.

NAPLES, April 27, 1880.

This is the largest town in Italy, and I think, the dirtiest one in the world. All the filth of the cities of the eastern coast of Italy could not prevent me from being startled at the aspect of Naples. I am homesick for a breath of the clear, fresh air of Ohio, and a sight of the beautiful fields and smiling brooks that have not been polluted by the slime of these wretched people. Two weeks' residence amidst this filth has not sufficed to accustom me to its appearance nor reconcile me to the thought of the possibility of a civilized man living here without retrograding a little into barbarism. We think on general principles that the contemplation of beauty is suited to cultivate a refined taste and brighten every faculty of the mind. But it would be difficult to find a more impressive spot on earth than the Gulf of Naples, and, alas! It would be equally difficult to find a city where one encounters sights and sounds more jarring to the sensibility than those of Naples.

Over half a million of people live in these narrow streets, and will no doubt continue to dwell here the rest of their days ; but all the beauty of the bay, the tropical luxuriance of vegetation, and the cooling sea breezes that fan the city, would be powerless to tempt me to erect my tent poles in this region. I would certainly languish away at the sight of so much filth and wretchedness; and if I did not, I would curse myself for lacking sufficient fine feeling to do such a proper act.

The streets of the town are about wide enough, as a rule, for two vehicles to pass, but are innocent of any particular place for pedestrians. Men are expected to take their chances among the donkeys and horses, and it seems wonderful that so few are run over. The drivers keep their animals at a rapid trot and continue shouting and cracking their whips in order to warn the foot passengers, who avoid the vehicles as easily as if it was an instinct. The horses of Naples are very small, and it requires considerable practice for a stranger to learn to distinguish one in a crowd of people at night.

The sights and sounds of these narrow streets beggar description. Hawkers of all kinds of wares throng them constantly, and make one's ears ring with their discordant shouts. They keep this up all day long, and whenever I wake up at night I hear the same noise, and I suppose, therefore, it is a perpetual plague. Donkeys with immense loads on their backs are continually passing through the streets, and they have a very provoking disposition to bray in tones more fitting for the last agonies of dissolution than for the ordinary routine of every day life. At evening hundreds of goats are driven into the town, and their cries and the noise of their bells contribute another element to the general babel. What is lacking to complete the confusion is abundantly supplied by the children, who can scream louder, longer and more dismally than any others on the globe.

The houses which line these noisy streets and alleys are in entire accord with their surroundings. They tower up to the seventh and eighth story, and before each window is a balcony, which does service as a back yard. On this little hanging shelf they keep household utensils, flowers, chickens, and what not? Clothes lines cross the street in every direction holding articles of toilet continually, although no one ever sees the inmates with anything on that could possibly have been lately in the wash.

Provisions are drawn up to these lofty dwellings in baskets, and so the narrow alleys do not seem unlike a mine. Housewives stand on these balconies and gossip with their neighbors in tones that would be more suitable for the officers of two ships hailing each other during a storm. They scream at their children in the streets till it makes your hair stand on end. As for chasing vermin in youthful heads the mothers seem to have a mania for it, and the pedestrian can see them engaged in that entertaining sport on nearly every door step. The people have a regular Spartan indifference for the public in making their toilet, and are only rivaled by the Dutch in the infringement of our notions of modesty.

Pauperism has reached a terrible extent in Naples. Nearly every step one is accosted by some one, man, woman or child, and asked in most cringing tones for a donation. It would be impossible to meet the half of these petitions with even the smallest sum, as their number is legion. I would not willingly live within sight of so much real and feigned misery. It is very hard on the feelings of a sensitive person to be compelled to turn paupers away every minute, and a few cases of deception make one suspicious of the whole tribe. For instance, when one is followed by a wretch who cries, "signore," in the most whining, piteous tones imaginable, and just as you have concluded to give him something he has abandoned the chase and leaves you with some insulting words ; and then a revulsion of feeling comes over you and you think it were well that the whole race should be exterminated.

I try not to be too severe towards Italy, but I think she has a greater and more urgent need than meddling with the boundary lines of Austria. I think there is something more necessary to her future importance in European politics than the maintaining of a bloated army and navy. I think the regulation of her lower classes would be the surest step toward a prosperity that is solid and enduring. This stagnant scum must be cleared from the surface and then the pure springs can pour up from the fountain. How the evil should be encountered is a subject for wiser heads to determine. But let the grim monster be attacked that is sucking the life blood of the nation. There is no prosperity for society except in the healthy condition of all its members ; and for my part I think the proper way to remedy the disease that is blighting the vitals of Italy is to transport the paupers to the country and let the process of regeneration be exercised in nature's own manner. Like the fabled monster, a man receives new life when he touches ground, when he returns to the simple rules of nature.

The habits of the Neapolitans have produced a general

physiognomy peculiar to themselves. The matted, unkempt hair, the black eyes, the celestial nose, the irregularly cut mouth; who that has seen the picture can forget it? You cannot find its counterpart in Venice, or Bologna, or anywhere else ; it is a face that belongs only to the noisy, narrow, filthy streets of this metropolis.

The people have also a language of signs, which they use constantly. The gestures which they make seem arbitrary, but I am told that each one has a peculiar meaning. In the Northern States we know almost nothing of the significance of signs. But in the first European city we enter our introduction begins. In Rotterdam I learned that a shrug of the shoulders means I do not understand. From that time I found the meaning of some others, but the Germans use few in comparison with the Italians. It seems to afford them relief in expressing their thoughts, and they use them as a sort of emphasis.

As for the sights of Naples itself, there is not much to be said. There are very few buildings that have any interest either for the architect or the historical student. The greatest and almost sole wonder of the town is the museum, which contains the antiquities found at Pompeii and Herculaneum. This is one of the most interesting in the world, and no doubt affords the best opportunity one will ever have to study all the details of Roman life. The managers have shown a faithfulness in prosecuting their work that is commendable. The reverence for each fragment of the ruins is all that the most critical enthusiast could demand. Though nothing of a specialist in this department, I thoroughly enjoyed the rainy day I spent within the walls of the museum.

I visited the catacombs in the northern part of the city, but failed to appreciate them. I expected something dark and awful, but saw merely some holes cut in the rock, which were once covered with frescoes and mosaics but which look dingy enough now. I climbed all through the caves, peered into all the dark holes, and tried to look pleased at the places where the guides expected it, but it was all a failure. I resign to others the satisfaction of going into ecstasies over the catacombs of Naples. I thought they had neither beauty nor grandeur, nothing to delight or terrify me.

The only historical spot that I have been able to find is the Largo del Mercato, the square where King Conradin, the last of the Hohenstaufens, was beheaded when only sixteen years of age, by the usurper, Charles of Anjou. As I had recently been on the spot where the castle of that great house once had stood, I felt great interest in the place which had witnessed the tragic end of the last of the royal line which had produced a Barbarossa and a Frederick the Second. The square is now used for a market, and nothing but the memory of the past could attract the stranger to the spot. In the adjoining Church of Santa Maria del Carmine I visited the tomb of the ill-fated King. Over his ashes is a marble statue which was erected in 1847 by Maximilian the Second, of Bavaria. I like to stand at these places which we honor for their history, and muse over the days that are past, but I can not think, at least can not think pleasant thoughts, when a troop of beggars are whining their grievances in my ears. There is no land where one longs more than in Italy for a quiet hour among the ruins of the glory that is gone. But we long in vain. Beggars haunt every place. They drag their filth after you into churches; they lie in wait for you at the street corners. No square is so broad, no alley so narrow, but that you meet them driving their trade. I honor the master minds who have lived in this land, but I shall feel better when I am back among the Germans, where the people are generally honest and wash themselves sometimes.

I have been two weeks in this famous city, and have gone every day down by the seaside to look at the smoking peak of the Vesuvius. The most of the time the clouds hung over the landscape and made an excursion to the summit impossible, but finally the day came when everything was arranged and I was ready for the ascent. So I arose earlier than usual and hastening down to the harbor, was glad to find that the weather was clear enough for the attempt. The smoke of the volcano was curling lazily upward, and the view was only dimmed by a slight haziness of the atmosphere that would be thought but a trifle at any other place than the Bay of Naples.

Filling a little satchel with refreshments, and taking my large cane, I felt fully equipped for the undertaking and went by rail to Portici, the first station upon the road that runs along the side of the gulf. Declining the assistance of some four or five hackmen and guides of various degrees of uncleanliness, I walked in a few minutes to Resina, which is built on the lava stream that covers Herculaneum. Here four guides fastened themselves to me in spite of my protestations to the contrary. I disregarded all their directions, and procured the necessary information as to the road from some tolerably clean looking citizens who could not have much interest in deceiving me. It has been my practice all over Italy to ask the better class of merchants for any explanations I may need, for I find that as trade overcame the despotism of the knights, so it now is the best teacher that honesty is the best policy. I did not, however, succeed in ridding myself of my escort, for three of them pursued me constantly as far as the observatory. Whenever I stopped to rest upon a stone by the wayside they suddenly felt that they were also weary and halted too. They became rested in the same time that I did, and the moment I began to continue the ascent they followed as closely as my shadow.

For the lower part of the distance up the mountain there are two roads—a smooth, new one for carriages, and a rough, old one for pedestrains and peasants. The latter was of course the one which I chose. It became worse and worse as I ascended, and with such a villainous crowd around me I might be excused for feeling a little uncomfortable. This was but a momentary thought, however. I went constantly on, determined to go through with the part I had commeced. Some distance up the path I met a young stranger who was coming down the road with that confused precipitation which is peculiar to an excited German. He stopped when he reached me, and I found that I had guessed his nationality correctly. His agitation prevented him from giving a coherent account of himself, but I gathered from what he said that he suspected he had been deceived as to the way and was going back. Pretty soon a treacherous looking guide came rushing down the hill, and following him was a fat German. They both were disposed to return, and I went on. But they soon overtook me, having been induced by my nationality to think that I would get through all right. I found then that my stout companion was a citizen of Brooklyn and his friend was a native of Bohemia. They had but a faint idea of the way to ascend the Vesuvius, and had hired that brigand, who was more interested in extorting money from them than in safely piloting them to the crater. For the rest of the day we remained together, and though our conversation was principally in German, it was pleasant to be with even an adopted son of the American Eagle.

Soon after this incident we reached the lava stream of 1872. There are acres and acres of this black colored mass, which stretches from the cone far down into the plain. From a distance it resembles the dark soil of an American valley after it has been plowed into deep and irregular furrows by a spring flood. But a nearer view reveals the most intricate and fantastic convolutions imaginable. All the forms which molten liquids assume under powerful influence of gases are here preserved in a solid mass. It is like a great monster that has been writhing and plunging in pain, and has then been suddenly transfixed, leaving every fold indicative of the great struggle. Indeed a lava stream is the Laocoon of Nature, sculpturing the terrific lineaments of her countenance when wrought up by the fiercest forces that slumber in her bosom.

After passing the old hermitage and crossing the lava field, we reached the observatory, which was built in 1844 expressly for the observation of the phenomena presented by the Vesuvius. It is 2,216 feet above the sea, and stands upon a slight ridge of ground between two streams of lava. This long and narrow space contains the nearest vegetation to the crater. At this point my companions' villainous guide demanded his fee, and notwithstanding my protestations, they concluded to pay him, preferring his absence to his company. We now left the road and took a rugged foot-path across the lava field to the cone, only stopping occasionally to look at the complicated shapes assumed by the lava, which were as intricate as the folds of a woman's back hair, and in appearance very similar, though on a mammoth scale.

The fifty-eight recorded eruptions of the Vesuvius each caused a change in the height and aspect of the volcano. In the time of Augustus the surface of the mountain was flat and sterile. Now the appearance from Naples is that of two twin peaks, from the higher one of which the smoke pours. This is the Vesuvius proper and the adjoining summit is Mount Somma, the two being separated by a deep valley called the Atrio del Cavallo. In the center of a vast field of lava rises the cone of the volcano, which has the appearance of an immense sand hill seven or eight hundred feet in height. The sides have an inclination of about forty-five degrees, and present a pretty formidable task to the climber. Upon one slope a path has been constructed which facilitates the ascent somewhat, while upon another there is a straight road which is used in descending. Of course we had the misfortune to stumble upon the latter, and bitterly did we rue it. Many of my readers have climbed sand hills in their juvenile days, and can perhaps form at least a faint idea of the seriousness of undertaking an ascent of many hundred feet under such difficulties. At every step our shoes disappeared in the sand, and the fatigue was so great that we found it necessary to rest every twenty or thirty feet. The fiery Bohemian went up the slope pretty rapidly, leaving me with the fat German to struggle slowly along. Soon some other travelers came plunging down the path and told us we had missed the road, which did not tend to make the toil of ascent seem any pleasanter.

"Oh!" groaned the German, "Oh, for a drink of water!"

"Well," said I disconsolately, "it will have to be a fine show if it pays for this."

"Yes, yes," moaned the German, and then we floundered along a few steps farther. Finally, after spending two hours and a half in this miserable ascent, we reached the top, my fat friend having chartered a bronzed bandit to tow him for the last part of the distance.

On the other side of the cone we could see other tourists climbing up the path, and it did not seem so much easier than the precipice which we had so unfortunately chosen. The usual way for those who need assistance is for them to take hold of a strap and be pulled by one of the natives. Very feeble persons can be carried up in chairs by four stout men, but I would hesitate to trust my life to such a machine. A single misstep of one of the bearers would send the passenger rolling down the slope, and it would be a matter of little consequence where he would stop. Taken all together, the ascent of the volcano is a severe task, and only the grandeur of the scene at the summit can repay one for the exertion.

But all this toil and trouble will soon exist only in the note-books of past travelers, and within a few weeks the tourists will ascend the Vesuvius as easily as he can cross the Gotthard, where the tunnel is finished. A splendid carriage road has been built to the cone of the volcano, and from this point the traveler will be transported to the summit by an inclined plane railway, as quickly and as easily as at Price's Hill or Mt. Auburn, at Cincinnati. The track is already laid, the buildings are erected, and its completion is only a matter of a few weeks' labor. The engine is to stand at the foot of the cone, and the car will be carried up by a double set of wire cables, which work on two large wheels at the summit. A number of lava walls have been built at the top to protect the railway, but of course the first eruption will easily overcome these trifling obstructions and destroy in a few minutes the work of months. But notwithstanding this, the enterprise will no doubt pay, and the ascent of the Vesuvius will be robbed of all its romance.

The scene which awaits the traveler at the summit of the cone is one of surpassing grandeur. Before him lies a rough sea of cold lava that is circular in shape and rent in every direction by great fissures, whose sides are encrusted with sulphur and present all the varied hues of the rainbow. From these chasms pour smoke and deadly gases unceasingly. In the center of this sulphurous field rises another cone about thirty feet in height, which is at present the active crater. The smoke rises in a continuous stream, and every few minutes it makes great spurts that are accompanied by showers of red hot ashes and a loud sound like that when water is thrown on fire. At these times, too, the reflection of the molten mass within is visible on the smoke, and forms that appearance of flames that is seen from Naples. A number of tourists climbed to the top of this inner cone to look at the crater itself. We tried it, too, but when we were half way up, the wind veered and drove dense clouds of sulphurous gas and smoke upon us, and this, with a shower of ashes from the crater, made us glad to retreat. The guides said nothing could be seen by those who did not ascend the crater, but those who made the experiment said they saw merely a large round hole from which the smoke was pouring. The fumes of the sulphur were so overpowering that I had no desire to repeat the attempt.

A stout, gray-bearded Englishman, who had successfully accomplished the feat, was quietly knocking the ashes from his shoes, as I passed him. There are moments of enthusiasm which overcome even the proverbial stiffness of that nation and the old gentleman could not resist the temptation to ask me if I spoke English. I answered that I was an American, whereupon he suggested that I might be like the darkey who said, "if you bring the old Vesuvius over to our country the Niagara will mighty soon put out his pipe for him."

The view of the country from the summit of the volcano is such as one obtains but few times in his life. We were between four and five thousand feet above the sea and the most magnificent bay in the world lay before us, viewed as from a balloon. The blue waters glistened in the sun and innumerable small boats danced about on the waves. Far in front of us was Capri, the scene of Tiberius' revels after he retired from Rome. Then nearer, we could see the white houses of Sorrento, where Tasso was born. Closer to us yet, was Castellamare, where the elder Pliny perished, and to the left of this the dark columns and ruined walls of Pompeii formed a marked contrast with the village around it. Then we could see the coutinuous line of houses which borders the bay until far beyond Naples toward the north. And down the sides of the mountain the dark streams of lava extend among the fertile fields whose owners live on in forgetfulness of the demon that breathes fire and smoke from the Vesuvius. Over the summit by Virgil's tomb, we could see the Bay of Puzzuoli where St. Paul landed on his way to Rome. Beyond this, the Cape of Miseno and the islands of Ischia and Procida were visible—all scenes of the crimes and exploits that darken and illumine the history of the ancient nobles. Think of such a view, where these great memories are combined with the loveliest aspect that nature wears. Who could forget the day that revealed such a sight?

But even the best friends must part, the brightest visions must fade and at four o'clock we were compelled to bid adieu to the smoking crater and start downwards towards the landscape we had just been admiring. The descent of the cone was a matter of a few minutes, as those who have climbed around in gravel banks when boys, can easily imagine. Taking immense strides our feet would sink deep into the ashes and the absence of anything hard to jar us made the novel descent rather pleasant.

By the time we reached the vineyards it was growing dark and we had a view of a beautiful sunset beyond the hills of Naples. The hush of eventide came over nature and all the beggars in Resina could not prevent us from enjoying the return to the city.

The visit to the ruins of Pompeii is a companion trip to the ascent of Mt. Vesuvius. I made two visits to the ancient city, one during the week when an admittance fee is charged, and I was conducted about by a guide, and again on Sunday when admission was free and I was left to wander about as I pleased.

Preparatory to the trip I studied the contents of the Naples museum, which contains the articles found at Pompeii, and also read Bulwer's Last Days of Pompeii. The train runs in a little less than an hour from Naples to Pompeii, and stops near the ruins which lie on a slight elevation. The walls are preserved as high as the top of the first story. The pavements of the streets are perfect and show the deeply worn ruts caused by thousands of passing wheels. I wandered around among the temples, shops, dwellings, baths, villas and tombs. It was like being transported back two thousand years and visiting a city recently destroyed by fire. The street of the tombs is the most impressive part of Pompeii and its aspect is nearly the same as before the eruption which destroyed the town.

The discovery of the ruins of Pompeii in the last century was like a revelation of the past. Every kind of utensil used by the Romans was found. The artisan was surprised at his work, the theater was covered with ashes when crowded with spectators, the prisoner was engulfed in his prison. After seventeen centuries all was uncovered and the modern world was afforded opportunity of studying the habits and civilization of the ancient Romans.

CHAPTER VIII.

FROM NAPLES TO ROME.—FIRST IMPRESSIONS OF THE ETERNAL CITY.—THE FORUM.—COLISEUM AND ST. PETER'S.—THE RUINS IN AND ABOUT ROME.—EXCURSIONS IN THE VICINITY.

ROME, May 20, 1880.

I wasted no time in lamenting my departure from Naples. The constant recurrence of scenes of wretchedness and filth made me heartily glad to escape. The unique shades of life that can be found there afford abundant material for the artist and amuse the casual observer for a time, but for a longer stay the place is almost unendurable. when I was once in the cars I did not even care to look back at the city but turned my eyes toward the Vesuvius until its summit was hid from sight.

The journey to Rome was entertaining but presented few objects of extraordinary interest. At Caserta I had a glimpse of the old royal palace of the Bourbons. The country in this neighborhood is remarkable for its fertility and the vegetation is of tropical luxuriance. It was the ancient Campania and is now called the Terra di Lavoro. On the borders of this plain we passed the famous city of Capua where Hannibal's army succumbed to the allurements of an effeminate life. The view from the train constantly embraced the sight of the mountains and in some places we even saw peaks covered with snow. About the middle of the forenoon we passed the foot of Mount Casino, upon which a monastery is situated that was founded by St. Benedict, and which has ever been known for the learning and liberality of its monks. I wished much for time to stop and obtain a glimpse of such a life under its best form, but it could not be.

At midday we came within sight of the Alban mountains, and then crossed the ancient Appian Way and entered the Campania. The innumerable ruins on every side and the long line of the arches of the Marcian Acqueduct were the first hints of the majesty of the ancient city. Soon we entered the Aurelian wall, which is a monument of the greatness as well as the weakness of the old empire. In a few minutes we stopped at the station. After leaving my baggage, and without waiting even to look at the ruins of the baths of Diocletian, I hastened by the shortest side streets toward the forum. The houses near the station are as new and fresh looking as those of an American city. Everything betokens that wealth has not departed from its ancient seat. The contrast between Naples and Rome is wonderful, and the traveler is fully prepared to appreciate the Eternal City.

Descending the slope of Mount Viminal, I passed the ancient arch and the three beautiful Corinthian columns which are all that remain of the forum of Augustus, and then reached a railing surrounding an extensive excavation that was covered with ruins. This is the Roman Forum— one of the most famous spots on earth. This was the center of the life of that great city which led the world captive at her feet. Immediately before me lay the Sacra Via, along which kings have passed in chains, serving as a mere item in the long triumphal trains which bore countless treasures of everything that could excite avarice or lust. To my right was the arch of Septimus Severus, whose reliefs celebrate victories in the Parthian wars. Beyond this I could see the temples of Saturn, of Concord and Vespasian, each of which marks an epoch in the history of Rome. Above the scattered columns which are all that remain of these once grand structures, rises the hill of the Capitol, which bore the citadel of the ancient city. In front of me and to the left lay the broken stones which indicate the sites of the Basilica of Julia and the Temple of Castor and Pollux. Beyond this I saw the massive arches of the palaces of the Cæsars, on the Palatine hill, where Romulus first built his city. Within this small space before my eyes moved the great spirits of that ancient world. Here the sturdy Roman saved his daughter from the worst of the "wicked ten." Here Catiline laid his fell schemes. Here Cicero uttered his great speeches. Here Cæsar, and the long line of Emperors held their sway. Who could be too enthusiastic over such a scene? Who could fully realize the grand history that is attached to this place?

But I could not pause long here. I hastened on past the temple which the good Marcus Aurelius built, glanced at the Basilica of Constantine, and walked through the Arch of Titus which commemorates the fall of the Jewish nation. There I stood before the Coliseum, the grandest ruin in the world. Byron has taught us to expect much but no one is disappointed. The towering walls have resisted the powers of both nature and man and remain the most impressive monument of ancient Rome.

From the Coliseum I turned again toward the Capitol after taking a hasty look at the stolen beauties of Constantine's arch. Ascending the roadway to the summit of the hill, I crossed the terrace upon which stands the equestrian statue of the Philosopher-Emperor, Marcus Aurelius, and then descended the great staircase into the modern city.

There were still two other places which I wished to visit before evening and I went therefore directly onward until I reached the first of these—the Pantheon. This temple of Agrippa is the only structure of ancient Rome that has been preserved entire and every one must grant that it is worthy of the majesty of the Empire. The circular opening in the roof is the sole means of lighting the interior, yet nothing could be better illuminated. Crossing to the chief altar opposite the entrance, I stood before the tomb of Italy's late lamented king. Its ornaments are simple. A golden crown rests on a cushion of marble and before these stands a small bronze eagle with outstretched wings. Beneath it a plate bears the plain inscription :

Vittorio Emanuele, Re d'Italia.

From the floor to the beginning of the curve of the dome the wall is covered with wreaths of all sizes testifying the love of the people for the king, who united the governments of Italy. On the right of the altar a plain inscription on the stone records the fact that it is the resting place of the bones of Raphael, who has done so much to make Rome attractive. No flowers are near to proclaim his honor but the admiration for him is none the less deep and strong.

From this interesting relic of antiquity I walked to the bridge of St. Angelo, which Hadrian built. Here I first saw the Tiber, whose name is so familiar to the reader. I found it as muddy as fame had reported it, for there is nothing that would make it interesting but its history. It is about of the size of our own Scioto, but is never as clear. But still this stream, though it is dark and muddy, has been consecrated by contact with the great, and its ugliness is sacred.

Crossing the bridge, which is terminated on the opposite bank by the shapely castle of St. Angelo, which Hadrian built for his tomb, I took the street toward the west, and soon reached the elliptical Piazza of St. Peter's. Merely glancing at the grand colonnades and the Egyptian obelisk in the center, I hastened up the steps to the entrance of the church. The effect of the immense proportions of the interior is wonderful. Without appreciating the distances fully, one has still a feeling of awe as though before the immeasurable size of a mountain cavern. One stands at the foot of the columns and his head scarcely reaches to the top of the ornamental grooves which form their bases. Then he may well wonder that human hands should build so great a pile. The canopy which covers the altar under the dome seems but small in comparison to the arches of the roof, and yet it is ninety-eight feet in height. Without pausing then to examine the details, I walked around the walls enjoying the general view of the endless variety of artistic forms.

I felt now that I could sleep quietly, and returned across the Tiber to the modern quarters of the city. I was completely suprised to find how new and prosperous everything seemed. The glittering shops were all that one could expect in an American town. I had thought of Rome as a gloomy, half-ruined place, with narrow, crooked streets, but found comfortable buildings and magnificent avenues, all alive with business. Everything was like paradise, compared to the slimy alleys and hideous houses of Naples. Rome to-day is not what Rome once was, but she may yet regain her ancient prestige, and though the barbarians beyond the sea and Alps refuse to bow the knee, she may lead the redeemed Italy to a place honored among the nations. Not knowing of ill, let us hope for good.

One of the numerous excursions which I have made has been to that part of the city lying south of the Aventine Mount. In ancient times this would have been a walk through busy streets thickly bordered with houses, but that district now wears the aspect of the country. Following the road along the banks of the Tiber, I paused sometimes to look at the scene on the river. A half dozen small sail boats and two little steamers were all the shipping visible on this stream which in the Roman times was crowded with vessels from all the ports of the Mediterranean. The Tiber has left so much of its mud in the bed of the channel that it is navigable now only for the smaller craft.

A short distance farther down the stream, I left the road and made a visit to the site of the ancient quay. Pope Pius Ninth caused excavations to be made here which brought to light numerous remains of the old works. The most noticeable are two stone slabs which contain holes for the fastening of the vessels, and a portion of an inclined plane used in landing heavy goods. These fragments of the Roman wharf lie entirely outside of the modern city. The region is covered with wild vegetation, and the only indications of life are the few drowsy fishermen that are scattered along the bank.

The main road to which I returned, skirts the base of the Aventine Mount, affording one a view of the ivy-covered ruins and beautiful cypresses which stand on the summit. Before reaching the Aurelian wall which shows the extent of the ancient city, I turned off the main road and visited the old and new Protestant cemeteries. The latter is a small but tastefully arranged ground, shaded with cypress. Its chief interest for me, however, was the fact that it contains the grave of Shelley. I wandered sometime among the tombs searching for it and looking at the varied character of the epitaphs. The cemetery contains the graves of non-Catholics of all nations and as each one's monument is marked in his own language, there are, of course, some strange contrasts in the people that lie side by side. English and German are by far the most numerous, but I noticed also French, Russian, Greek and Chinese. After looking nearly everywhere in vain for Shelley's grave, I at last caught sight of the words "Cor cordium," on a stone, and then I knew my search was at an end. A simple horizontal slab of marble close to the city wall marks the grave, and bears the following inscription: "Percy Bysshe Shelley,

Cor Cordium, Natus IV Aug. MDCCXCII : Obiit VIII Jul. MDCCCXXII.

> 'Nothing of him that doth fade,
> But doth suffer a sea-change
> Into something rich and strange.'"

Here the sweet voiced poet sleeps under the waving cypresses and within the shadow of the wall of ancient Rome. What a great spirit he was! The world has not thought fit to build him a grand monument, but as long as beauty has admirers marble and brass will not be necessary to perpetuate his fame.

The old cemetery adjoins the new one and has also an imperishable claim upon the reader of English literature. Near the entrance is a tomb which bears evidence of recent attention, and under it reposes the body of Keats. Observers of the state of public opinion tell us that his popularity is steadily increasing, and the fresh testimonials at his resting place seem to indicate that it is true. The tasteful monument bears the original inscription : "This grave contains all that was mortal of a young English poet, who on his death-bed, in the bitterness of his heart at the malicious power of his enemies, desired these words to be engraven on his tombstone, 'Here lies one whose name was writ in water.' Feb. 24th, 1821." Some of his admirers have caused a large marble tablet to be inserted in an adjacent wall bearing a bas-relief of the poet and the following lines in verse :

> "Keats! if thy cherished name be 'writ in water,'
> Each drop has fallen from some mourner's cheek;
> Asserted tribute, such as heroes seek,
> Though oft in vain, for dazzling deeds of slaughter.
> Sleep on! not honored less for epitaph so meek."

Immediately in the rear of the old cemetery is the prominent tomb of Cestius which is built in by the wall of Aurelian. It is a pyramid one hundred and seventeen feet in height with smooth sides composed of marble blocks. It is one of the best preserved tombs that have come down to us from the Roman times. Cestius was a prominent man of the last century before our era but I believe all our knowledge of his character is gained from his epitaph.

The gate of St. Paul is in this neighborhood and as a fire was then raging in a building just without the walls, I had an opportunity to see a Roman department at work. In the morning when on the Palatine Mount I had seen the blaze and smoke and heard the buglers in a neighboring barrack blow the alarm for a half hour. It was late in the the afternoon when I reached the scene of the conflagration and I found a sight worthy of minute description. Several companies of the army were on the spot assisting the numerous firemen. Two small hand-engines were standing in front of the building and two others were at wells in adjoining yards. The hose attached to these instruments was about of the same size as that used for garden purposes in America. I went to the yard where one of the engines stood and found that they were using an ordinary pump and a bucket in order to raise the water from the well to the machine. They found it impossible to throw a stream to the top of the house from the yard and therefore placed the two engines near the wall and carried the water to them in buckets. When I arrived the extinguishing process had been dropped to give the workmen an opportunity to rest. The building that was burning seemed to have been a sort of warehouse and a few bales of straw had been dragged into the road. The interior was blazing with a zeal that mocked the puny efforts to stay it. A few of the firemen were on a ladder contemplating the conflagration ; some others were giving orders which no one heeded; but the majority were reclining on the rescued bales and complacently chewing the straw. One portion of the burning building was occupied by a restaurant which had been spared by the flames and its proprietor was doing an immense business in supplying the firemen and soldiers with wine and other refreshments. The calmness with which the extinguishing corps could sit and drink while another part of the building was burning was something beautiful to witness. Late the next day from a hill several miles distant I saw the smoke ascending as strong as ever, and there can be no doubt that the house burned until everything combustible was exhausted A week after I first visited the scene, I passed the spot while on another excursion. The engines, ladders, hose and firemen were still there. Water was still in the buckets. But the fire was dead—it had died for want of food.

When we remember that to these firemen have been entrusted the relics of ancient Rome, let us rejoice that brick and stone are not combustible. We have no Coliseum in our noble country, but we have fire departments that would surprise the Italians. For these blessings let us be thankful.

The process of uncovering the remains of ancient Rome is progressing slowly but constantly, and many once nameless walls have been found to be a part of ruins grand in their proportions and interesting in their details. By far the most imposing and extensive of these are the imperial palaces which cover the Palatine Hill. It can scarcely now be said that:

> "Cæsar's chambers and the Augustan halls
> Grovel on earth in indistinct decay."

The excavations since Byron's time have brought to light a series of structures that, next to the Coliseum, are perhaps the most impressive in Rome. They give us a fair idea of the vastness, if not of the magnificence, of the ancient palaces. Time has shorn them of their ornaments and made the object of many parts uncertain, but time could not cause the gigantic walls to crumble entirely to dust, and enough remains to awe the beholder with the majesty that hath been.

The visitor to the Palatine Hill first rambles through a number of large, half-buried apartments, whose use cannot be indicated with certainty. The lofty arches and massive foundations tell of the vastness of the original structure and the fragments of mosaic and statues give a faint hint of its magnificence. These are the remains of the palace of Caligula. A few arches are still pointed out of the bridge which he built over the Forum to the Capitol in order to have a direct communication with the temple of the Capitoline Jupiter, "whose image on earth he pretended to be."

From these chambers the visitor ascends to the ground which lies above them. This is laid out into a pleasant garden, and the air is fragrant with the blooming roses, which border the paths. This hill has had a great part in the history of Rome. Here the real Romulus built his city, which became the fruitful germ which produced the empire. Here Cicero, Mark Antony, the Gracchi, and many others of

Plutarch's divine men have lived. Then, the hill was appropriated by the emperors for their palaces and now nature has claimed her own and ivy covers the walls where monarchs dwelt in their pride.

On the opposite side of the Palatine from the vaulted chambers, of which I have spoken, a small house has been excavated, which was the only private dwelling in the vicinity of the Imperial palaces. It is supposed that it was the residence of the father of the Emperor Tiberius. This was gathered from the inscriptions on the lead water pipes of the house. From what strange sources do we get our history! In the direction of the Coliseum the visitor comes upon the indistinct pile of brick and stone which once belonged to the temple of Jupiter Stator that Romulus is said to have founded. Back of this is the palace of the Flavii, which is the only portion of the ruins whose uses can be accurately determined. How it startles the fancy to walk through these apartments and think of the scenes that once were here! In a side chamber fragments of the imperial household gods greet the stranger. In the grand salon adjoining this, the emperors sat on their throne and gave audiences to their subjects. One still sees the semi-circular apsis in the wall where the monarch's seat once stood, but there is little else left to tell of the glory of the place, for palaces fall to ruin as surely as hovels. The next apartment is where the emperor pronounced his legal decisions. He sat on a tribune at one end of the room, and was separated from the people by a marble railing. The traveler can muse over the fragment that remains of this, but time has broken down the dividing line and, alas for the monarch! he is now no more than one of the common herd. In the rear of these apartments the visitor enters the spacious dining hall, and from that reaches the fountain room, which contains a large elliptical basin with a shelved elevation in the center, upon which were ranged the flowers that were sprinkled with the spray from the fountain. A few of the marble slabs remain, but the earth there bears a ranker growth of vegetation now than when the imperial star was in the ascendancy. Lizards creep about the spot that ministered to the monarch's pleasure, and perhaps a resurrected Cæsar would be disgusted to find that even his scepter has been powerless to stay the inroads of time.

A path along the hillside leads to another series of ruins on the opposite extremity of the Palatine Mount. These are the palaces of Commodus and Septimus Severus. The details of the building are less distinct than those of the other structures, but the immense walls form a much more impressive spectacle. Another path runs down the slope to some ruins which were once a school for the imperial slaves. The plaster bears to this day scrawls which afforded a momentary occupation for the idle hands of mischief makers. Some scratched their names on the walls, while the more artistic drew unsightly caricatures. It seems to have been as severe a task seventeen centuries ago to " teach the young idea how to shoot," in the right way, as it is at present. We are undoubtedly entitled to conclude that the bad boy is not an invention of modern times.

Continuing along this path near the base of the hill, one passes an ancient altar dedicated to the unknown God. The simple shrine has long been deserted, but, if I read aright, this mute stone rebukes the creed of modern Rome which adorns her churches with portraits of the Almighty.

Not far from this emblem of a forgotten faith, a portion of the first wall of Rome is exposed to view. By the side of this fragment of the ancient fortifications is a small cave which tradition identifies with the Lupercal Grotto, in which the wolf took refuge, when driven by the shepherds from the babes, Romulus and Remus. I have in this trip touched a great many of those places with which our first Latin books make us unpleasantly familiar. But if the history of all the ruins of the Palatine could be known with certainty, the hill would be of unequaled interest. Even as it is, a ramble through the nooks and corners is as entertaining and impressive as any similar excursion in Rome.

> "Cypress and ivy, weed and wall-flower grown
> Matted and mass'd together, hillocks heap'd
> On what were chambers, arch crush'd, column strown
> In fragments, choked-up vaults, and frescoes steep'd
> In subterranean damps, where the owl peep'd,
> Deeming it midnight:—temples, baths, or halls?
> Pronounce who can ; for all that learning reap'd
> From her research hath been, that these are walls—
> Behold the Imperial Mount! 'Tis thus the mighty falls."

Across the valley in which the Coliseum stands, on the slope of the Esquiline Hill, are a number of ruins which are less extensive than those I have described, but are hardly less interesting. This was the scene of the conflagration during Nero's reign, and is the site of his famous golden palace. But the tryant's mansion soon fell into decay, and Titus built above it the vast baths which bear his name. Thus there are three different structures here—the remains of the original houses and the two buildings of Nero and Titus. The character of the ruins is much the same as those on the

Palatine, being vast arched chambers and halls. With the aid of torches one can trace the lines of many of the beautiful frescoes which adorned the golden palace of Nero. Some of these were models for Raphael in decorating the Vatican. The visitor is conducted to the dining and bath rooms of the palace and is shown the niche in which the famous Laocoon group stood. At one place a portion of the mosaic pavement of the house of Mæcenas has been uncovered, for that patron of letters had a residence here before the great fire, and its remains were afterward hidden by the buildings of Nero.

Thus on the Esquiline and Palatine the palaces of the mighty are crumbling to dust. Scarcely a fragment of their ancient glory remains, and a longer existence of the ruined walls will not be owing to the imperial power, but to the protection of scholars.

One of the latest lines of railway communication which have been opened in the vicinity of Rome is the route which leads to the mouth of the Tiber. This makes the trip a convenient excursion for a single day and I accordingly set out by the early train, hoping for pleasant weather, although I have ceased to have any confidence in the Italian sky after six weeks' experience of frequent rains. Yet the country looks so fresh and green that I can almost forget my disagreeable encounters with the storms when I get out among its beauties.

The railroad passes along near the Tiber affording occasional glimpses of the muddy stream which is rarely disturbed by the boats. As we drew near to the sea the train stopped a few minutes at the station at Porto, which takes its name from the harbor constructed here by Emperors Claudius and Trajan. The Tiber at present has two outlets. The deposits of the river have caused the coast line to advance about twelve feet annually and the sand had so accumulated at the mouth in the first century of our era that it was found necessary to excavate a new channel toward the north of the old one. Although the canal is much narrower than the main stream, it is used exclusively by the vessels. At the point where the Tiber entered the sea, Trajan constructed the harbor of Porto, but the deposits of the river have constantly increased and the ancient haven is now a shallow lake two miles from the coast. I obtained a glimpse of its waters as the train passed on its way.

A few minutes later we reached Fiumicino, a small village which has taken Porto's place at the mouth of the Tiber. The river deposits continue, however, to advance into the sea and after a century or two this town will no doubt be far inland. I walked out to the extremity of the mole which has been constructed at the mouth to facilitate the passage of the vessels. The water in the neighborhood of the outlet is polluted by the sediment of the Tiber and looks as muddy as the yellow stream itself. Here an unpleasant looking fellow in a shabby suit of fashionably cut clothes, came up to me and wanted to shave me. To prove that he meant business he drew his tools from his pocket and showed that he was ready to begin operations at once. His face indicated that he had very recently tried the process on himself and his cheeks were hacked in every direction as though he had been fighting a German student's duel. I have submitted with a tolerable degree of patience to be worried from morning to night by guides, beggars, hawkers, street boys, hack drivers, hotel runners, and other plagues, but to be accosted by an itinerate barber upon the sea-beach, a half mile from a human habitation, that is a great deal too much. I gave that fellow distinctly and emphatically to understand that I did not propose to be skinned just then and there. He withdrew to the background but continued to eye me, as though he longed to have my scalp.

I returned to the village and crossed the floating bridge to the Sacred Island, which is formed by the two arms of the Tiber. It is a large, low tract of land, covered with pasture where herds of fierce-looking cattle are feeding. A new gravel road afforded me a rough but dry walk of three miles to the ferry on the opposite side. Two men upon pack-horses far before me formed a characteristic feature of the scene. When I reached the other arm of the Tiber I found the riders had hitched their animals and were within a straw shanty drinking wine with the boatmen. I sat on the bank until they were ready to cross. When they finally came out, I found the ferryman one of those big whiskered, loud-voiced, jovial sort of persons, who seem peculiar to the fisherman class. He gave the orders in preparing the boat with a sunny egotism, and exhibited a supreme contempt for those who know nothing of his art. We lazily crossed the stream which is two or three times as large as the other branch.

From the point where we landed the ruins of the ancient town of Ostia extend for a mile up the stream. I entered a field where numerous mounds in all directions mark the spots where great houses once have stood. The ground is thickly strewn with fragments of stone and brick and the present cultivators of the place no doubt curse the old Romans for spoiling the soil. After passing many nameless ruins I reached the large, quadrangular temple of the Magna Mater, which towers far above the rest of the ancient city. I climbed up the steps and then descended to the basement, but a few pieces of the rich marble are all that remain of the glory of the ancient shrine.

I next visited the buildings that have been excavated near the temple. A part of the old pavement still preserves the ruts worn by the toil of other days. Some of the houses bear remnants of frescoes but desolation rules over all. How sadly one's foot-steps echo within the deserted walls as he walks along the streets where gayety once reigned. It is a mournful task to contemplate the fate of man and mark how the hero who has ruled the world dwindles to a paltry heap of dust, but it is scarcely less sad to view a city in ruins and note the broken arches, fallen columns and sunken pavements, where beauty once held its sway.

I resumed my walk and passed another long series of indistinguishable ruins and at length entered the street of the tombs. A number of marble sarcophagi are to be seen and pieces of the cinery urns are still imbedded in the walls of some of the tombs, but the fate which destroyed the homes of the living, has not spared the resting places of the dead. Man builds great structures to keep his dear dust from mixing with vulgar clay but nature rends his frail heaps of stone and claims her due.

A few minutes more brought me to the modern village

of Ostia. It has a picturesque castle and is surrounded with walls, but it does not contain a hundred inhabitants and it looks more like the courtyard of a stronghold than a place aspiring to the dignity of the name of a town. The meanness of the present village is a great contrast to the prosperity of the port under the early Romans when mariners of every nation thronged its streets. But we are creatures of time.

I returned to the ferry by a path along the river, passing the ruins of the baths where some beautiful marble columns are still standing. The ferryman was jolly as ever and I bought a couple of papal coins which he found in one corner of his pocket. One would not be much suprised to find old Roman money in use among such antiquated fisherman who are scarcely influenced by the present civilization. After walking across the island I found the train ready to start from Fiumicino and an hour later I was in Rome.

One of the most prominent and pleasing objects comprised in the grand view which one has from the hills of Rome, is the Albanian range of mountains, whose wooded heights form the background of the scene, toward the south west. They deserve a visit not only for their natural beauty, but also on account of their historical associations. The ruins to be seen are not extensive, but it is interesting to trace the places that have played so great a part.

I left Rome by the early train, one morning, and, after an hour's ride reached Frascati, a town situated on the lower part of the slope of the mountains. It seems to be nothing better nor worse than an ordinary country place with a tolerable degree of prosperity, and I only paused a few minutes to look at the two churches. The newer one contains the monument of Charles Edward, the young pretender, who died at Frascati, January 31st, 1788. The inscription records, of course, the fiction that his father was James III., King of Great Britain, Ireland and France.

The principal attractions of Frascati are the villas which are admirably situated on the hillside above the town. These are places of refuge for numbers of Romans during the heated term, and their grounds afford all the advantages of a public park. My course up the mountain led me past the villa Ruffinella, which is the most famous of all. It is a large and rather plain building, but its location is very fine. It was once the property of Lucian Buonaparte; afterwards it was owned by Maria Christina, Queen of Sardinia; and at present it belongs to the crown. It is the scene of one of Washington Irving's sketches, "The Adventure of the Artist." The sky was unusually clear, and I enjoyed the view of the Campania, from a terrace in front of the house. The spire of St. Peter's stands boldly out above the rest of Rome, when seen from a distance, and then we can appreciate its immense height.

From the Villa Ruffinella, I ascended the mountain for a half hour by a beautifully shaded road. At length I reached some scattered ruins and an ancient pavement, which indicated that I was approaching the site of Tusculum. This place is said to have been founded by Telemachus, son of Ulysses, and was the birthplace of Cato the Censor. Cicero had a famous villa in the neighborhood. It is supposed that it stood on the spot now occupied by the Ruffinella, but the guides of the country who are innocent of learning, have attached the orator's name to one of the ruined buildings which have been excavated at Tusculum. Only a few ancient structures can be seen which retain any definite shape. Among these is a theater, whose stone seats are nearly all preserved entire. A short distance beyond this is an elevation upon which the citadel stood. It was used as a castle during the middle ages by a race of lords who were allies of the Emperors and was therefore taken and destroyed by the Romans in 1191. A path, over fragments of stone, leads past some ancient cisterns to the summit, which is now almost level. On one of the loftiest points some of the old blocks have been piled up to the height of about ten feet, and a large wooden cross placed above these. From this artificial elevation one has a fine view in all directions. But the sky was already partially obscured by the clouds, which this treacherous spring weather seems never tired of sending, and I found that my rejoicing over the clear atmosphere was somewhat premature.

Four or five miles distant I could see Mount Cavo, the highest peak of the Alban range, rising far above the surrounding summits. The town of Rocca di Papa on its nearest slope was the next object of my movements, but between us lay the broad valley, covered with thick underbrush, through which the road passes. A complicated network of paths which are sometimes indistinguishable, is the only means of communication, and it is no ordinary task for a stranger to find the way. As long as I am within a half day's march of a railroad I have confidence in myself in spite of the fact that my knowledge of Italian is extremely meager, and so I set out boldly, hoping for a safe passage through the labyrinth. After descending the hill by Tusculum and crossing a small stream I entered a pasture field by a path which seemed to lead in the right direction. But it soon disappeared and I was left to flounder along through the wet grass as best I could. After surmounting this difficulty, I wandered about in some cornfields till I finally found a path leading through the matted underbrush. But like the other it constantly dwindled in size until I was compelled to struggle through the bushes with the faintest possible clue to the way. My perseverance was at length rewarded, and I emerged into a larger road, and, after an hour's walk, reached Rocca di Papa. The town is built on so steep an incline that the houses seemed piled up one upon another. There is nothing whatever to be seen in the place and the importunities of beggars and street boys effectually dispel any desire to stop. I ascended to the upper part of the town and was about to enter the open country again when it began to rain and I was forced to seek shelter under the eaves of one of the houses. It seemed but a passing shower and I soon set out for the summit.

On reaching the open space immediately above Rocca di Papa, I found an extensive circular valley spread out before me, which was surrounded by a ragged ridge, which plainly indicated that it had once been a volcano. The vast crater now bears the name of Camp of Hannibal, from a tradition that the Carthagenian General once encamped here during his campaign against Rome.

From this point a good road leads to the slope of Mount Cavo, coinciding at the upper part with the ancient Via Triumphalis, by which those Generals who had been denied a triumph at Rome ascended the peak and celebrated one on an independent basis. The road is paved with blocks of basalt and remarkably well preserved. I had not proceeded very far up the mountain until I was enveloped in clouds like a thick fog, and the rain began to descend in torrents. I crouched under the overhanging trunk of a tree and kept tolerably dry until a peasant woman came along and pointed out a place of shelter under a shelf of rock. I stood there for two hours, watching the flood pouring down over the stones and thinking of those eight miles I had to make to the railway station before seven o'clock.

The storm finally moderated a little, and I started to run for the summit. Above, below and around me the clouds hid everything from view except what was in the immediate neighborhood, but I dashed on up the Via Triumphalis in a very untriumphant manner, and reached the monastery at the top just as the storm began afresh.

After an hour of melancholy gazing at the rain, the clouds gradually parted below and disclosed the bright, green Campania, smiling in the sun. I shall never forget the thrill of pleasure it gave when that scene suddenly appeared far beneath my feet. The sight was so unexpected and the change of feeling was so great, that I was completely mastered by the agreeable surprise of the moment. Then the misty curtain rolled back farther and I saw the placid waters of Lake Albano, nestling in the depths of the forest and enclosed by a range of hills. By its side lay the long, green ridge, where Rome's early rival, Alba Longa, stood. But still the clouds rolled back, and the Lake of Nemi appeared, glistening in the sun, worthy of her ancient name "the mirror of Diana, the gem of the Alban Mounts." Far over the distant Campania I saw the blue line of the sea near the horizon. On this grand peak, Childe Harold ceases his song with that immortal address to the ocean, and if Byron saw this scene as I have seen it, he did well in choosing it for a worthy conclusion. I forgot the dreary waiting, forgot the long walk before me, forgot that I was cold and wet, forgot all in rapture of the view. I forgave the storm and felt fully repaid for anything I had undergone.

Finally, after three hours of constant rain, the clouds passed partly away and I was able to descend the mountain. At half-past four I reached Rocca di Papa, and then turned toward Albano, having two hours and a half in which to make the eight miles to the station. I had no such difficulty as in coming from Tusculum. I found paths, but the trouble was I found too many, and could not tell which one I wanted. I was compelled to turn back a great many times and try another road. The dense underbrush hid the mountain from view and I had forgotten my compass. Not a house was to be seen, and the thick black clouds that were gathering in the sky added to my distress. Time was passing surprisingly, and my chances for getting back to Rome that night seemed very poor. I ran this way and that along the slippery roads, until I had the satisfaction of emerging from the woods and seeing a town in the distance. I thought I saw a train and concluded I had missed my way and this was a railway station. I did not stop to debate the question, but left the road and started directly across the fields. I had not gone far, however, before I became entangled in an immense thicket of brush. I was a half hour in penetrating this and the rain had commenced to fall, but I rushed on to the town, and found that I had not seen a train but the side of a lofty viaduct, by which I recognized that the place was Ariccia, three-quarters of a mile from Albano. And so with all my difficulties I had come in the right direction, and made the distance quicker than is set down in the guide books.

As I descended the long stretch of two miles and a half from Albano to the railway I met, I think, nearly all of the laboring population. The peasants of this district are celebrated for their beauty, and I never seen the working class anywhere so good looking. One would suppose such handsome faces were the idols of the drawing-room instead of the slaves of the cornfield. I reached the station ten minutes before the train and was soon resting from my long and wearisome walk in the cars that were whirling towards Rome. Such was one day's pilgrimage.

I made a day's excursion to Tivoli, seventeen miles from Rome, to see the famous falls and the temples and villa of Hadrian. At other times I walked out the ancient roads to see the relics of antiquity which are scattered along their sides.

In my three weeks stay at Rome I was busy every day visiting the numberless churches, the Vatican and Capitoline museums, the ruins, the villas, and the countless other places of interest. I ascended the lofty dome of St. Peter's and studied every part of the gigantic structure. I spent hours and hours at the Vatican and Capitol. At the Spanish staircase I saw the most picturesque artists' models in the world. Peasant girls in rainbow tinted costumes and drovers from the Campania were there in their peculiar garb. I visited the burial chapel made of bones of monks. I went through the gloomy catacombs. To describe Rome properly would require a volume itself. I must be content with the notes I have already given.

CHAPTER IX.

FAREWELL TO ROME.—UP THE COAST TO LEGHORN.—ARRIVAL AT FLORENCE.—THE ART TREASURES, CHURCHES AND TOMBS OF THE TUSCAN CAPITAL.

Three weeks' residence in Rome made me so familiar with the streets, palaces and ruins of its seven hills that it seemed like parting with an old friend when I was compelled to take my leave and continue my pilgrimage. I went across the Tiber for a farewell look at the grand interior of St. Peter's and afterwards rambled for several hours among the scattered stones of the temples in the Roman Forum. In the evening I walked down to the Coliseum to watch the effect of the moonlight upon that monster ruin. The lines of Byron, which we used to declaim at school, made me eager to see the Coliseum under similar circumstances:

"Upon such a night I stood within the Coliseum's wall,
Midst the chief relics of Almighty Rome;
The trees which grew along the broken arches
Waved dark in the blue midnight, and the star
Shone through the rents of ruin; from afar
The watch-dog bay'd beyond the Tiber; and
More near from out the Cæsars' palace came
The owl's long cry, and, interruptedly,
Of distant sentinels the fitful song
Begun and died upon the gentle wind.
Some cypresses beyond the time-worn breach
Appear'd to skirt the horizon, yet they stood
Within a bowshot—Where the Cæsars dwelt,
And dwell the tuneless birds of night, amidst
A grove which springs through levell'd battlements,

> And twines its roots with the imperial hearths,
> Ivy usurps the laurel's place of growth ;—
> But the gladiators' bloody Circus stands,
> A noble wreck in ruinous perfection !
> While Cæsars' chambers, and the Augustan halls,
> Grovel on earth in indistinct decay.—
> And thou didst shine, thou rolling moon, upon
> All this, and cast a wide and tender light,
> Which soften'd down the hoar austerity
> Of rugg'd desolation, and fill'd up,
> As 'twere anew, the gaps of centuries,
> Leaving that beautiful which still was so,
> And making that which was not, till the place
> Became religion, and the heart ran o'er
> With silent worship of the great of old !—
> The dead, but sceptered sovereigns, who still rule
> Our spirits from their urns."

But the final moment at length arrived and I took my place in the train for Leghorn. We ran around the walls to the north west, obtaining hurried glimpses of the city spires and the green cypresses which wave over Shelley's grave. Then we crossed the muddy Tiber and entered the broad plain. The hills to the right soon hid the Eternal City from view and I felt that the farewell might be forever.

The recent frequent rains have made even the bleak Campania wear an unusual look of freshness, but apart from the green landscape there was little to be seen until we reached Civita Vecchia, a distance of some sixty miles. This place has in modern times assumed the importance of the sea-port of Rome, as the harbor facilities at the mouth of the Tiber are not sufficient for vessels of larger draught. I could see but little of the town from the train but the part that was visible was much cleaner than I was taught to expect. The funnel of a steamship near the light-house was sending up dense clouds of smoke and it seemed impatient to get away from the dull town and float once more among the blue waves of the sea.

All of my fellow passengers left the train at Civita Vecchia and for the rest of the day I had an apartment to myself and for a portion of the way I was the only person in the entire car. The scenery for the next few hours was of the same general appearance. Upon the left I obtained frequent views of the sea. Upon the right the uncultivated plain stretched far away to the foot of the Apennines whose towering peaks formed the boundary of the scene. Houses and villages are very rare and fields of grain are seldom passed. Swamps are of frequent occurrence. This is the Maremme district which is famous for its malaria. The inhabitants are engaged in cattle grazing and charcoal burning. During the summer they move to the mountains and do not return until October. The lack of cultivation of the land is the cause of this fearful extent of the malaria and the condition of the country during the middle ages is said to have been even worse than the present. Many of those I saw at the stations exhibited the effects of the destructive ravages of the fever. The country is under a curse which only the toil of centuries can mitigate.

Many of the heights along the railroad are surmounted by ruins of ancient Etruscan towns, some of which are visible from the train. This is the country that was peopled by that mysterious nation that was forced to succumb to its stronger southern rival. I visited a museum of Etruscan antiquities in Florence and was much astonished at the height of civilization which the articles indicate. We are trained to the comfortable egotism that four thousand years ago men were ignorant savages, two thousand years ago they were about half emerged from that state and now we have attained the limits of the possible and have all the arts and all the inventions that can proceed from the human brain. We think Socrates was a pitiable fellow because he never rode in a steamboat and we cannot conceal our contempt for Xenophon because he did not transport his ten thousand by a military railroad. Some of our ingenious friends are figuring on the book of Daniel to prove that the universe is to pass away during the existence of the present generation. Surely, they reason, when man reaches such a high stage of development as we have, it is time for the the world to return to its original elements. Everyone, whether he be learned or unlearned, finds his self-conceit in the present immensely less after visiting the museums of antiquities at Naples, Rome and Florence. There one obtains a worthier idea of the greatness of the older nations in every sense.

The train proceeded on its way and we finally saw the island of Elba, Napoleon's land of exile. The outline of its mountainous surface stood out boldly against the sky and seemed very beautiful, but it was all too small a sphere for the ambitious genius of Napoleon. He who had overturned monarchs like ninepins could not be content to rule an isle over which one could walk in a day.

At the last station before Leghorn, I should have changed cars, as the trains from Rome run directly northward without touching that city. I paid no attention, however, to the cries of the porters and as a consequence soon had the mortification of seeing the spires of Leghorn vanish in the background. After a quarter of an hour the train rolled into the depot at Pisa, and the officials demanded my fare if

I remained there but said I could return to Leghorn and they would ask nothing. This latter generous offer I gladly accepted and an hour later I was in Leghorn, none the worse off for my mistake.

This little episode will not be understood by Americans without some explanations. The Italian railways have a system of collecting tickets which is peculiar to themselves. The office is not opened until half an hour before the departure of a train and without a ticket one is not admitted to the waiting-rooms. A more inconvenient system could scarcely be devised. If one goes to the station before the office is open he is compelled to stand in a little anteroom, that is crowded with loafers and poluted with the vilest tobacco. If he is weary, he must solace himself with consulting the time tables for the hundredth time, or take a lesson in language from begrimed posters which announce a long departed excursion train. When the ticket is finally secured one is admitted to the waiting rooms. But who can sit down in a quiet frame of mind during the few minutes before the train goes? I have observed everywhere that the passengers fling their valises upon the cushioned seats and stand in impatient expectation of the unlocking of the door leading to the platform. When this is opened there is a grand scramble for the places in the carriages. The tickets are sometimes examined on the way, but not always. The conductor looks much like a brakeman on a coal train in hot weather and belongs to an entirely different species from the gold chained, diamond ringed, fashionable gentry who collect the pasteboards on an American railroad. When one alights at his destination he still has his ticket but this is taken by an official at the gateway which leads to the outer world. Should one from any cause wish to continue his journey he is compelled to walk completely around the station to find the ticket office, as the exit and entrance are always at opposite ends of the building.

The busy commercial city of Leghorn presents all those varied scenes of activity which are familiar to the Americans, but she has neither treasures of art nor relics of antiquity to attract those who are seeking the special characteristics of Italy. She has buildings that are pleasing but not extraordinary. She has immense harbors and some few statues on her public squares. Her streets are admirably paved with broad, smooth slabs of stone. Beggars are a rarity within her gates. But these virtues are scarcely sufficient to detain the traveler for any considerable length of time. Several hours were all that I cared to spend, more especially because the inevitable rain had begun to fall. I know I have overlooked many of the wonders of Italy, but I have seen something more than any of my predecessors —I have seen it rain in nearly every large city on the peninsula. In the past eight weeks in Italy, the sky has been as cloudy for the most of the time as it ever is in one of our prosy Northern countries. A German journalist observed last week that the May poets sang according to the calender, and not according to the weather. From my experience I am tempted to say that those who glorify the ever blue Italian sky derive their inspiration from tradition, and not from the reality. But this I will not insist on.

The country traversed by the railroad from Leghorn to Pisa is low and flat and intersected by numerous canals from the Arno. Beyond Pisa the route to Florence runs close to the river, and the scenery gradually increases in beauty. On each side rise the mountains with their bright green mantles of grass, their white villas and their shapely cypresses. The valley between these two barriers has a vegetation that seems to be of tropical luxuriance. The peculiar style of Italian farming conduces much to cause this effect. The fields, which are planted with grain, are intersected with rows of fruit trees, which are connected with each other by big vines. These three kinds of vegetation growing at the same place form a beautiful scene, such as one never finds in the grain districts of northern lands.

It was still raining when we arrived at Florence, but I managed to get around considerably in spite of the fury of the storm. I was three days in the city. The last two were very cold, although it was the latter part of May in that land which we dream is the eternal home of sunshine. Everybody who had an overcoat put it on, and those who were not so fortunate buttoned their coats up to their chins and ran shivering along the streets, seeking shelter from the wind behind the buildings.

Florence has a location which I admire very much. It lies on both banks of the broad and rapid Arno, although the greater part is on the right side of the stream. Upon the left the hills press close to the river, and the observer from the opposite bank has a varied view that is very pleasing. At his feet flow the foaming waters. Beyond lie the bright-colored houses, and above these the fresh-looking gardens and groves of cypresses stretch away to the summits of the hills. High over all the distant peaks of the

Apennines stand out, capped with snow and enveloped in a canopy of clouds. If one ascends one of the heights on the left bank of the Arno he soon obtains a splendid view of the city and the adjacent portion of the valley. So that whether as a part of the landscape or as a standpoint of observation, the hills are an advantage to the beauty of Florence.

Everyone is favorably impressed with the Tuscan capital, especially if he has just left the filth and wretchedness of Southern Italy. The streets are well paved, the houses are of pleasing exterior and the people have an honest and obliging character. Beggars are seldom seen and even the needy and deserving are said to have the same pride as northern nations, which restrains them from that unmanly resort except in cases of extreme necessity. The people have a polite bearing which reminds one of the French. The shopkeepers do not fail to thank one even for the smallest purchases.

The Piazza della Signoria has maintained its rank from the earliest times to the present as the center of life in Florence. Here the zealous reformer Savonarola and two other monks were burned at the stake in 1498. The square is now adorned with a fountain and an equestrian statue of Cosmo I. and is bordered by some of the most famous buildings in the city. Upon one side stands the old palace, whose rough walls and battlements, and lofty, slender tower form a strange but impressive spectacle. Upon the adjoining side of the square is situated the Loggia dei Lanzi, an open portico filled with some valuable specimens of statuary. In the corner between these structures is the entrance to a long, narrow court which is surrounded on three sides by the lofty building which contains the far famed collections called the Galleria degli Uffizi. A broad arcade extends around the court and the outer side of its columns are embellished with statues of famous Tuscans. It is but necessary to mention a few of their names to show what a great part this province has played in the history of the world. Among them are Dante, Petrarch, Boccaccio, Macchiavelli, Guicciardini, Giotto, Michael Angelo, Donatello, Leonardo da Vinci, Galileo and Amerigo Vespucci, the godfather of our land. Enough of genius is here to make Tuscany a sacred place, whatever her future may be.

The Museum is not so extensive as that at Naples, nor does it contain as valuable treasures as the Vatican collection, but it is nevertheless one of the finest in the world. Its ancient statues comprise such famous pieces as the Niobe groups, the Thorn Extractor, the Scythian Knife Grinder, and the Medici Venus. Besides these there are dozens of the master-pieces of Raphael, Michael Angelo, Titian and the other great painters of Italy. Even the artists of the Dutch, German, French and Spanish schools are well represented. At this season the halls are thronged with northern visitors, and one is surprised when he meets a native, instead of the opposite being the case. In traveling now one often sees the same persons in the city that he met a few days before several hundred miles away. I found a company at Ravenna which I had previously seen at the Palace of the Doges at Venice. Some Germans whom I met in the Albanian Mountains near Rome I saw ten days later riding through the streets of Milan. So it is with many others.

A covered passage leads from the gallery of the offices across the old bridge to the collections in the Pitti Palace, which stands on the opposite bank of the Arno. The building is one of the largest, most peculiar and most impressive in Florence. It is built of immense blocks of unsmoothed stones, and its simple massiveness seems to disdain all resort to the flimsy ornaments of ordinary structures. It was begun as early as the middle of the fifteenth century, but was not completed until the eighteenth. At present it belongs to the crown, and is used by the royal family whenever they reside at Florence.

The collection of paintings yields to few in the world in rank or value and perhaps to none in the magnificence of its halls. The ceilings are decorated with frescoes whose subjects form the titles of the rooms. Gilded chairs with velvet cushions are conveniently arranged for the accommodation of the visitors, and each apartment contains rich tables of lapis lazuli, granite and jasper. The walls present such an array of masterpieces that I was of course perfectly bewildered. There are a great many Madonnas by Raphael in the collection, and these attract crowds of copyists. I am usually as uncritical as Mark Twain, and think that the bright new copy is better than the old smoky original, but even I could see the enormous difference between the expressions of the masterpieces of Raphael and those of the imitations. The physiognomies of his Madonnas are widely varied, but he breathes into every face a soul of tender love mingled with sadness, which his copyists seek in vain to produce. Their striving after the sublimity of the original often results in a ridiculous caricature.

The Cathedral of Florence is one of the largest and finest examples of the Italian gothic architecture. The immense structure, with the exception of the facade, is entirely covered with black and white marble. In our rich country we can hardly afford to buy a piece of that expensive material of sufficient size to mark the spot where our bodies pass to their original elements, but in this land of paupers we find the churches embellished with acres of the costly stone. The facade of the Cathedral was formerly covered with frescoes but these have long since faded away, and in April 1860, King Victor Emmanuel laid the foundation for a marble front. The work has proceeded but slowly and though twenty years have elapsed, the scaffolding is still up and the project is not fulfilled. Marble makes a fine appearance when new but it becomes sadly discolored with age. When one admires a building of that material he thinks more of what it once was than of what it is. Even with magnificent St. Mark's at Venice a good deal of charity is necessary to enable one to overlook the disfiguring stains that mar its appearance.

There are thousands of people who have heard of the Baptistery doors at Florence and yet know nothing more about their existence. The reference to them in speaking of the bronze portals of our National Capitol has no doubt done much to cause this. The Baptistery, or Church of St. John the Baptist, is an octagonal, dome-covered stone structure standing just opposite the Cathedral. It was begun in the sixth century and subjected to various alterations at different periods. It is covered with marble like the Cathedral and its three famous double doors of bronze were executed in the fourteenth and fifteenth centuries. They were designed by Andrea Pisano and Lorenzo Ghiberti. The former spent twenty-two years on the one that is from his hands. The door facing the Cathedral by the latter artist is universally considered the best. The designs of all of them are on biblical subjects.

A short walk from the cathedral brings one to the church of St. Lorenzo. The facade has never been completed and the ragged-looking wall of ugly bricks gives no hint of the magnificence that is within. The main division of the church possesses nothing to distinguish it from the hundreds of other rich churches which one sees in Italy, but the New Sacristy and Chapel of the Princes back of the high altar are sights that are far from being common. The former contains two monuments of the Medicis by Michael Angelo, which are considered his best works. Beneath the portrait statues of the dukes are the famous pairs, Evening and Dawn, Night and Day.

Adjoining the sacristy is the burial chapel of the Dukes of Medici. It is octagonal in form and covered with a dome. The walls are of marble, and produce a magnificent effect. Around the walls are ranged the sarcophagi and statues of the princes. The gorgeous decorations in gilt, fresco and mosaic are of a richness that could scarcely be surpassed. The family is said to have spent four and a half millions of dollars on the construction of this chapel, and if I may be allowed the irreverent sentiment, I think they showed themselves a set of fools in doing so. It is my conviction that the quicker a man passes respectably into indistinguishable dust the better it is for him. Wherefore should one wish to have his carcass preserved through hundreds of ages like the Egyptian mummies? Some impious traveler will drag you out after a thousand years to decorate a museum and amuse silly clowns with your grinning ghastliness. Or wherefore should one heap stone on stone in vain endeavor to keep his dear ashes from mixing with the common clay. Perhaps your fate will be a repetition of that of Agrippina, wife of Germanicus, whose funeral urn served the louts of the middle ages as a measure for corn. Time has proven the falsity of Egyptian philosophy and daily proclaims in unmistakable tones that the main object of a man's life should not be the erection of his tomb.

In the cloisters to the left of the church is situated the Lorenzian Library, which is the oldest and most valuable in Florence. I had some difficulty in finding my way through the passages, but finally succeeded in getting to the right place. After passing up a beautiful flight of steps I entered the door. Why is this the library! thought I; It looks like a church. An aisle passes through the middle of the hall, and upon each side are seats with high backs of dark colored wood, which look exactly like pews. Before each bench is a rack which forms a part of the next seat in front, and upon this lie the precious manuscripts attached to chains. The volumes are concealed by dark cloths, so that there is nothing in the general appearance to distinguish the hall from a Protestant church. The light came dimly through the windows, as seemed quite appropriate. The few silent readers paid no attention to me, but my footfalls echoed harshly within the walls. As I walked along and glanced at the names of the manuscripts that are registered on the sides of the seats, I felt a sense of awe for the ancient lore that is treasured in those time stained pages. Indeed I felt that I myself was an unwarranted intruder of our later age upon a field that is not of us. I half expected to see a tonsured monk rise in wrath from some dark corner and expel me from the sacred precincts with a malediction in ponderous Latin. But no such phantom appeared to disturb my meditations, yet when I again reached the busy street I could not help thinking that it was in truth a different age from that represented within the cloister's walls.

In a narrow lane not far from the great square there is a house which is held in all honor. It is but a few yards broad and towers up to the fourth story out of all proportion to the size of its base. Notwithstanding these unfavorable characteristics the town has been so much interested in that little house that she has caused it to be repaired in order to aid in its preservation. And well she may pay it such homage, for here the immortal Dante was born. It is too late for Florence to render full reparation to her wronged and exiled son. It matters little now to him or to his fame whether the Tuscans bow in adoration or remain as unjust as were their fathers. But still, as the past cannot be undone, the Florentines do well to cherish his memory and seek to add one leaf to the laurel that is his crown.

To the lover of literature all other places in the city dwindle into insignificance when compared to the church of Santa Croce. It was built in the fifteenth century but the facade was not completed until 1863. The marble looks clean and bright and gives one an idea of the beauty which the cathedral must have had when it was new. On the square before the church stands Pazzi's colossal statue of Dante which was inaugurated May 14, 1865, the six hundredth anniversary of the poet's birth.

> "In Santa Croce's holy precincts lie
> Ashes which make it holier, dust which is
> Even in itself an immortality.
> Though there were nothing save the past, and this,
> The particle of those sublimities
> Which have relapsed to chaos:—here repose
> Angelo's, Alfieri's bones, and his,
> The starry Galileo, with his woes;
> Here Macchiavelli's earth returned to whence it rose."

Think what emotions one has when he stands by the great columns of the church and reads such names on the monuments as Michael Angelo, Alfieri, Macchiavelli and Galileo! Westminister Abbey is of course a more extensive and more impressive resting place of the great than Santa Croce but there is no other place in Italy which deserves to stand in higher honor.

CHAPTER X.

GENOA AND THE BIRTHPLACE OF CHRISTOPHER COLUMBUS.
—TURIN AND LAKE COMO.—BACK IN AUSTRIA.—
TRIESTE AND ITS ENVIRONS.

TRIESTE, June 7th, 1880.
From Florence I went to Genoa, stopping at Pisa to see the famous leaning tower, the cathedral and the Campo Santo, and at Spezia to see the beautiful bay where Shelley was drowned.

The envious Tuscans long ago were accustomed to say that Genoa had "seas without fish, mountains without trees, men without faith and ladies without modesty." Without either affirming or denying the truth of the bitter assertion, I am able from experience to add one more to the category of its wants, and hereby affirm that the city has hotels without fleas. Some five or six weeks ago I was rash enough to express a doubt as to whether Italy was so infested with vermin as travelers would make us believe. I admit that it may be possible to visit the country without any unpleasant experience, but to do so it is necessary to keep away from the streets and parks. Running as I did through all the narrow lanes and filthy quarters in order to see the various shades of native character, I soon had abundant proof that the tales of the travelers were not invented. The endless herds of beggars and goats keep the thoroughfares of the cities fairly alive with colonies of the creeping or rather the jumping world. As soon as the foreigner appears in the streets every single flea abandons the particular pauper from whom he has derived his rations and joins in the general stampede toward the stranger, crying at the top of his voice, "fee, faw, fum, I smell the blood of an Englishman." It makes even the boldest turn pale when he hears the multitude grinding their teeth in eager expectation and sees them coming on in gigantic jumps, as closely arrayed as the armies of loafers who went to the Black Hills. They climb over one as quickly and readily as the fabled rats did in the old mouse tower on the Rhine, and if they do not pick one's bones as clean as the rodents did those of the wicked bishop, the escape should be classed among the unexplained facts of history. I could tell of personal combats as bloody, if not as glorious, as any that were ever fought on the plains of Troy.

Having thus happily spent the night at Genoa, I took the morning train upon the railroad which runs along the coast toward France. The views from the cars were very pleasing, as the blue expanse of the sea was always in sight. At the station at Cogoleto I disembarked. The natives stared at me wonderingly, as it is not common for even American people to visit where Christopher Columbus was born. Cogoleto is a small fishermen's village of a few hundred inhabitants. It consists of one long street, which winds in an uncertain way along the coast and is bordered on both sides by houses. The beach presented the usual array of stranded boats and drying nets, and at the mouth of a little creek near by the women were engaged in hammering, and rubbing and wringing the soiled linen of the village. After leaving the station I entered the narrow, serpentine street and soon found a house with a long inscription in Latin, which announced with many rhetorical flourishes that it was the birthplace of the great Columbus. The building has four stories, and is painted in bright colors, according to the custom of the country. The ground floor is at present occupied by a small provision store, while the upper stories are used as dwelling apartments. Upon applying to the woman who stood behind the counter of the shop with the request to be allowed to see the house, I was directed by her to a stair-case leading to the second floor. Upon rapping at the door of the middle room I was admitted by another woman to the apartment, in which she said the discoverer of the New World was born. It is an irregularly shaped room with rather meager furniture. A broken model of a ship, which stands on top of a cupboard, was, perhaps, constructed in honor of the immortal navigator. After passing through several rooms, which exhibited all the disorder of a slovenly house on Monday, I reached a sort of a terrace upon the side next to the sea. The few flowers along the railing made it the pleasantest place I had seen in the building. The village is small and the house is mean, but there lies the illimitable sea, whose inexhaustable treasure of wonders was sufficent to awaken the genius of Columbus and make him long to see the great world, which lay beyond the blue line of the horizon. Genoa has erected a large monument to the memory of the great discoverer, and I think it would be well if American cities would follow its example.

After returning to Genoa I took the afternoon train to Turin. The first part of the journey was through the mountains, so that I enjoyed a number of beautiful views. Just before reaching Alexandria the plain at Marengo could be seen, where Napoleon won his hard-fought battle eighty years ago. The remaining portion of the ride was dusty and disagreeable, and I saw that I had escaped one evil by the rainy weather which had hitherto followed me.

The city of Turin is, perhaps, the only one in Europe built perfectly regular. I have not seen any place yet on the continent which is so thoroughly American in its appearance. The streets are broad and the more important ones are traversed by horse cars. The houses have a pleasing exterior, beggars are scarce, and the hack-drivers are quite subdued in spirit. Yet for all this, Turin is not a modern city. Her plan is said to be essentially the same as that of the colony which was established there by Augustus.

The principal street is a very fine avenue extending from the mediæval castle to the banks of the Po. The buildings on either side are provided with arcades, like those of Bologna, but they are far grander than their model. I wonder that this style of architecture which is so convenient for business is not more universally adopted. At the extremity of this main street is an exterior square and magnificent bridge over the river. Immediately beyond is a church in imitation of the Pantheon. To the right stands a hill surmounted by a monastery, from which a splendid view of the city is obtained. To the left far in the distance, rises a loftier peak, which is crowned by the burial chapel of the house of Savoy.

I made the usual round of the sights at Turin. I visited the museums, churches and monuments and saw a few things that I remember and thousands of others which I have forgotten.

There is no other feature so marked in Turin as the number of her public statues. Nearly every street of importance is adorned with one, and when seen from a distance through the long rows of houses they have a very impressive effect. Many of the monuments are no doubt insignificant as works of art, and some of the subjects have a mere local importance, but there could be no worthier way of ornamenting the city. There is a bit of romance connected with one of these statues which deserves to be recorded. It represents but a common soldier yet he proved himself an uncommon man. On the 30th of August, 1706, the citadel of Turin was hard pressed by the French invaders. The hostile grenadiers had successfully advanced to the very gates, where the private Pietro Micca sprung a mine and perished with the enemy, but saved his country. The statue represents him stepping forward at the critical moment torch in hand. His fist is clenched, his face is firmly fixed and his eyes seem to fairly burn with the intense enthusiasm which led to his sacrifice. The cautious policy of our everyday life tends to imbue us with a selfish cowardice, but it is all in vain. Some hero arises and shows us how one can forget his individual passions when animated by a great mission. His deed quickens our sluggish pulses, we forget our cold calculations on advantage and disadvantage, and our irrestrainable admiration testifies that we are better than we think. The citizens of Turin have never forgotten him, whom they affectionately call the "Soldier Miner," and a century and a half after he had perished their gratitude was still so strong that a monument was erected to his memory.

I left Turin by the early morning train for Milan. The country, through which we passed, is flat but very fertile. The farmers were engaged in cutting hay and the fields were very fragrant. A pleasant breeze neutralized the unusual heat of the sun and wafted about the agreeable odors of the freshly mown meadows. The discomforts of railway traveling were so completely avoided that the journey seemed more like a carriage ride through the smiling fields.

We passed a great many rice farms during the morning. This is the season when they are kept under water to the depth of about half a foot. We saw hundreds of acres that were thus submerged. Of course this is only possible in the valleys along the rivers. The fields are intersected in all directions by a net work of dams by means of which the water is evenly disposed of and a constant current maintained.

The only place of historical interest along the line between Turin and Milan is the battle-field of Magenta, where the French and Italians defeated the Austrians June 4th, 1859. The snowy peaks of the distant Alps were visible during a considerable part of the journey, but they seemed like a long white cloud as the fog hid their bases from sight.

Milan, "the grand," at once impresses the stranger with its prosperity. There is little to remind one of the characteristics which the traveler thinks of as peculiar to Italian cities. The people look as clean, as well dressed and as wide awake as in any of the other towns of Europe. The streets are as crooked as they could well be if that had been the design of their builders, but in spite of this misfortune the long rows of magnificent buildings, do not fail to have a pleasing effect.

The Milanese consider their cathedral the eighth wonder of the world. It is the third largest church in Europe, St. Peter's at Rome and the cathedral at Seville ranking first and second. The exterior is adorned with about two thousand statues in marble, which give the building an appearance peculiar to itself. Many of these have a merit which is more than mediocre, for such masters as Canova have contributed to the number. When one thinks of the time and labor which were necessary in preparing these ornaments, he will be able to form some idea of the vastness of the undertaking. Whether the immense structure be viewed from the square below or from the roof and tower above, it alike impresses the beholder with its grandeur. Should the visitor undertake to examine the details, weariness will at length force him to desist and acknowledge that this is indeed one of the wonders of the world. The interior is in keeping with the magnificence and greatness of the exterior and even the fact that one has seen St. Peter's does not lessen the awe that he feels when standing under the lofty arches which lie so far above him.

There are a number of other churches in the city which present something of interest. A few of them are the only existing remains of the old town which was destroyed by Emperor Frederick Barbarossa. The refectory of the suppressed monastery near the church Santa Maria delle Grazie attracts the most visitors, as it contains Leonardo da Vinci's world famous fresco of the Last Supper. The picture is so badly preserved that it conveys little more than a general outline of the figures, each of which has a strongly marked individuality. The details of the faces have so completely faded away that the copyists draw largely on their imaginations in painting the picture. The consequence is that the expressions of the countenances on the copies rarely agree. But notwithstanding these drawbacks, the fresco is a very popular subject for reproduction among the artists and at the time of my visit I counted ten full copies and four or five of the head of Jesus.

At the north-western verge of the city stands the beautiful Arch of Peace a fine imitation of the old Roman structures of similar character. It was begun by Napoleon in 1804, as a termination to the Simplon road across the Alps, but long before it was finished, the Emperor had lost his throne. The decorations were then altered and the arch was dedicated to Emperor Francis of Austria. This change reminds one of the fate of the columns of Trajan and Marcus Aurelius at Rome which were purified of their heathen uncleanness by the popes and are now surmounted by statues of Saints Peter and Paul.

I left Milan by the north bound evening train and after a half hour's ride arrived at Monza. I went at once to the cathedral which contains the famous iron crown which was used at the coronation of thirty-four Lombard kings and in later times on similar occasions by Charles the Fifth and Emperor Napoleon. "It consists of a broad hoop of gold adorned with precious stones, round the interior of which is a thin strip of iron, made from a nail of the true cross brought by the Empress Helena from Palestine." On the walls of the chapel in the church which contains this interesting relic Napoleon, Ferdinand I. of Austria and Victor Emmanuel have erected tablets to commemorate their coronation.

The following morning I resumed my journey northward and arrived at Como in time for the early boat on the lake. I took a ticket for Bellaggio which is situated at the junction of Lake Lecco with Como and is considered the finest point in regard to scenery.

The scenery on Lake Como is considered the most beautiful in Italy and has been a favorite theme of the poets from Virgil to Bulwer. The expanse of water is scarcely broader than a river and its general appearance reminds one of the Rhine. The hills here assume the size of mountains whose summits are often barren wastes, and the bright colored villas take the place of the moss grown castles which border the German stream. Instead of the northern vineyards one sees here groves of the dark green walnut and chestnut, sprinkled with the gray tinted olive.

At Bellaggio I found a goodly number of foreigners and a long church procession in ecclesiastical tinsel. I walked over the hill and obtained a splendid view of Lake Lecco, which I thought little inferior to her more extensive rival.

On returning to Milan from Lake Como, I embarked at noon upon the through express train for Venice. If I had been beginning my tour of Italy, I would have at least stopped at Brescia, but I was sated with the sights which the smaller towns afford and so concluded to make no further halts. When I first entered the carriage I found two young Englishmen who had come over the Simplon from Geneva for a few days' look at Northern Italy. Several minutes later four American young ladies came and took the remaining portion of the apartment.

The country intersected by the railroad is a fertile plain, with little to interest the observer. In the distance to the north the Alps were visible, but otherwise the scenery was quite monotonous. The Englishman, who sat next to me, borrowed my guide book and loaned me the latest copy of the London Telegraph. As I had not read a newspaper since I had left Florence, I was soon so absorbed in the telegrams and leaders of the daily that I neglected the landscape altogether. The time passed rapidly, and I was completely surprised when the train emerged from a tunnel and the beautiful Lake Garda was revealed to us with the bright green mountains which surround it. Toward the south we could see the gently rising hills where the French and Italians won the bloody battle of Solferino over the Austrians, June 24th, 1859.

Finally, when the sun was low in the western sky, the spires of Venice appeared in the distance amid the blue waters of the Adriatic. Not every one experiences the same satisfaction in the half ruined palaces and stagnant canals of Venice, and many have the image which the poets have created in their minds rudely shattered by some of the unexpected features of the reality. On the wharf before the depot one hears many exclaim in disappointment: "Is that the grand canal!" There is an element of the disagreeable in everything, and the traveler who leaves his imagination at home, will find little pleasure in viewing even the grandest spots on earth.

I paid another visit to St. Mark's in the evening, and early the following morning went to the church of the Frari, at the opposite end of the city, which contains two tombs that command general attention. In the left aisle is the monument of the famous Canova, which was erected from a design which he himself had made for a mausoleum for Titian. It consists of a pyramidal vault of marble, with bronze doors which stand slightly ajar. A veiled figure is represented as about to enter, and is followed by a group with inverted torches. The design is quite unique and forms a pleasing change from the everlastingly recurring style, which consists of a large sarcophagus with a sitting female figure at each side, who stares steadily at nothing. In the opposite aisle of the church is the monument of Titian, which is surmounted by a statue of the master.

Later in the morning I took the train for Trieste which brought my Italian tour to an end. Near Cormons we crossed the frontier into the Empire of Austria and stopped at that station for the custom house inspection. The officer passed my knapsack without asking me to open it and I made haste to shake off the last reminiscence of Italy by getting rid of the paper money which I had on hand. While I am speaking of this subject, I will make a few explanations. One never sees silver or gold coin in circulation in Italy. They use paper notes for sums above half a franc (ten cents) and for anything less, copper is the medium of exchange. On account of the petty system of giving small donations for every service which is the custom of Italy, the traveler is compelled to carry a mass of copper which is heavier than is convenient. If one does not give a nickel in America, he gives nothing, but a cent in the eyes of the officious Italians of the lower class is not a sum to be despised. In Naples the changing of small amounts is a regular trade and at every corner of the business quarter one sees the petty bankers with their heaps of copper.

Italy, with Spain, Belgium, Switzerland, Greece and a few smaller States, belongs to a money union which has adopted the French system. This fact gives grounds for the hope that the civilized world may one day have a common coinage, just as it is confidently expected that weights and measures will attain the same simplicity. It would be no insignificant triumph of trade if the money stamped by one nation could circulate the world over, and thus abolish the inconvenient systems of exchange which now embarrass the transactions of commerce.

Trieste has a beautiful situation on a large gulf, which is formed by an amphitheatre of hills. The scenery is inferior to that at Ancona, Naples, Spezia or Genoa, but one can by no means consider it insignificant, even after having seen those places. Charles the Sixth declared the city a free port in 1719, and she at present carries on a heavy trade with all parts of the world, and especially with the Orient. Fifteen thousand vessels enter and leave the haven annually, which shows that she merits her title of the " Southern Hamburg. " It is the intention of the government to abolish the privileges of Trieste as a free port in 1882. Of course this will cause many articles to become dearer in the city, but it is argued that a great many manufacturing establishments will locate here, and thus compensate for all losses. As everything which passes into the interior is now subject to the same duties as foreign articles, this has effectually prevented the opening of such industries in the city.

The inhabitants of Trieste are almost as heterogeneous as those of Alexandria, Egypt. The Italian element is the most extensive, but German is spoken also by the majority of the tradesmen. Among the foreign nations represented here more or less are the Greeks, Armenians, English and Americans. In addition to these there are many transient visitors from all parts of the Orient. One sees some quaint costumes in the streets. The most common of these consists of a fez, short jacket, broad Turkish knee-trousers, white stockings and high shoes. Among the rarer Orientals are a few Turks whose long red robes and turbans make them look as though they had just arrived from the Golden Horn. The Greeks and Servians have each a magnificent church, and one frequently meets their priests, with their long black robes and tall rimless hats. I went last evening to the Greek church to hear the chants in the native tongue. The officiating priest was a mysterious looking person, to whom the masses might quite naturally ascribe a knowledge of the invisible things.

There are a number of handsome new buildings in the city, and one of the finest of these is the Town Hall, which also contains the room used by the Landtag, or Provincial Assembly for Istria. As all the seventeen Legislatures of the empire were opened yesterday, after a recess of a year and a half, I went to the hall to witness the ceremony that took place there. The honorable members who were dressed in silk hats and broadcloth, pushed their way through the admiring crowds of small boys and loafers, and ascended the grand staircase, while the sentinels and liveried lackies made their salutes with all due deference to the great dignities. We who represented no constituencies, climbed the small back stairway without ceremony and found places in the gallery. The Assembly chamber is elegantly finished, although of somewhat small proportions. At eleven o'clock the thirty-six members arose in their places to welcome the imperial Statthalter, or Governor of the Province, who entered in full military dress, and took his seat on a small platform to the left of the Speaker's desk. The Landeshauptmann then took the chair and delivered an address in sonorous Italian. I could not understand the speech, but he laid his hand several times on his heart and looked toward the ceiling, and I felt much moved. After three cheers (a hoch) for the Emperor, the Governor made a brief response, bowed and looked infinitely gracious, and the Assembly adjourned.

A brief stay at Trieste is sufficent to show that the majority of the steamers which enter and leave the port, belong to the Austrian Lloyd Company. Their vessels ply to all points of Eastern Italy, Dalmatia, Greece, Turkey, Asia Minor, Palestine, Egypt and India. Much of the wealth of the East thus flows to Trieste, and vast additions are now being made to her harbor. The Lloyd Company owns many buildings in the city, but the docks where the vessels are built and repaired are about three miles from here, near the village of Servola. A finely shaded road leads thither and enabled me to visit them yesterday, even during the midday heat. The shops, of course, contain many wonderful machines, by which iron is shaped and cut like wax, but I think the men there would be somewhat surprised if they could spend a few hours in such gigantic American establishments as one finds at Springfield and similar places. The Europeans may laugh at our follies and twit us for our pompous ignorance, but they have had to cross the Atlantic to learn how human toil can be lessened in more ways than one. There were some twelve or fifteen steamers undergoing repairs at the Lloyd docks, and the guide told me that the company owned seventy-seven vessels, and the number was being constantly increased. Upon my asking if the laborers were all Italians, they said that they had some of every nation except the French. I thought I would test his statement and asked him if they had any Americans. He answered that they had one, a machinist, but he was away with a steamer.

On one of the principal squares of Trieste there is an admirable statue of the ill-fated Emperor Maximilian of Mexico. Before he set out on his fatal expedition to America he was a Rear Admiral in the Austrian navy, and lived for a long time in this city. About six miles toward the north, on Point Grignana, which projects into the sea, stands Palace Miramar, which was once the Prince's home, and is now considered the most delightful spot in the vicinity of Trieste. I walked out there this morning, and left amply repaid for the exertion.

The palace is built of the limestone which is quarried in endless quantities in the neighborhood, and looks as fresh and beautiful as if it had been finished yesterday. It stands at the water's edge, and the broad stone terrace next to the sea commands a fine view of the city and gulf. Everything is fitted up in princely magnificence. The park abounds in shaded walks and quiet retreats. Fountains play unceasingly, cooling the air and soothing the senses with the babbling of the falling streams. Statues end the vistas of the long-ivied arbors; sweet-smelling flowers fill the air with fragrant odors, and rare plants from many climes attract the eye and engage the mind. What a world of beauty! What a realization of the paradise of which we dream!

CHAPTER XI.

A TRAMP OF THREE HUNDRED MILES IN THE AUSTRIAN MOUNTAINS.—THE ADELSBERG CAVES.—GRATZ.—OVER THE SEMMERING PASS.—VIENNA.

VIENNA, June 29th, 1880.

I have long talked about the great foot journeys which I was going to make, but they have always been so far in the future, that my friends have perhaps come to doubt whether the plans would ever be fulfilled. Under these circumstances I felt that I must try a tramp from Trieste northward in order to vindicate my ability to walk. A person, who has ever boasted of his bravery, is forced by his pride to make as good a show of spirit as possible when circumstances put him to the test. Perhaps a little of this feeling assisted me in mustering up my courage to encounter the fatigues of a foot journey through the mountains. Be that as it may, I shouldered my knapsack last Thursday morning and started to find the road from Trieste towards Vienna. I chose a turnpike which crosses the railroad at Divazza, about twelve miles out, so that I could take the train if my spirit failed me.

As I proceeded I came to the dreary limestone wilderness of the Karst which stretches across the province of Istria from Gorizia to Fiume. Until late in the afternoon my path was through this desolate region. White crag rises over crag and deep, rough sided fissures everywhere abound. A meager growth of grass among the rocks and a few fertile spots in the valleys are all the inroads which the vegetable world has been able to make in the stony desert during the ages of time.

From the summit of the hills I had a beautiful farewell look at the blue Adriatic and the city of Trieste. The bay was dotted with sails and the waters were gleaming in the morning sun. Railroads are of inexpressible convenience but they have robbed us of much that is agreeable. The dusty tourist of to-day sees little of the country he passes. He never experiences that exultant feeling with which the weary pilgrims of the highway behold the distant sea from the mountain tops. I met a Bohemian "Handwerker" in Trieste who told me of the joyful surprise he had when the blue gulf suddenly came in sight as he reached the summit of the hills. I must confess I envied him. I have seen many seas and lakes and the Atlantic, but the circumstances of the first view were never pleasant enough to leave a lasting impression. I would willingly exchange all the pleasure I felt at arriving at a sea by a railroad for a share of the rapture with which Xenophon's ten thousand were thrilled when the Euxine appeared in sight.

My knapsack rested uneasily on my shoulders and I often stopped to rest, while the troops of brown faced market women strode by with huge baskets on their heads, exhibiting no signs of fatigue. Americans may think that I ought to have felt some shame at being surpassed so easily by female pedestrains, but the brawny peasant women of Europe may well dispute the assertion that they are the weaker sex. I certainly would not venture to enter the lists against them to maintain the superior strength of the masculine portion of the human race. The market women walk sometimes ten or twelve miles to Trieste with a great load of vegetables or fruit and return the same morning. The farmer's wife and daughters work in the fields and accomplish as much and as severe labor as men. If it were yet the fashion for lovers to carry off their brides by main force I suppose an unwelcome suitor could be as easily repelled by the stout maidens in a conflict of muscle as they are by the gentler means of the present.

At noon I reached Divazza and while enjoying my dinner in the open air before a country inn, I concluded that my courage was not exhausted and that I would continue my tramp still farther. The Italian language is here superceded by a dialect of the Slavonic. Later in the afternoon I found a solitary laborer by the roadside who answered my German greeting in the same tongue. The dreary Karst had evidently made him hungry for companionship and he immediately began to enter into a long conversation with me by inquiring where I had come from, where I was going and what profession I had. After he had been enlightened on these points he wanted to know if I spoke Krainerish I assured him that I did not speak Krainerish and might have added that I did not speak Cherokee, or Choctaw, or Modoc. If I learn a few civilized languages, I shall do well and do not care to meddle with any of the barbarous dialects of out-of-the-way people.

Toward evening I entered a beautiful valley bordered

with pine covered hills, and walking became more interesting although I was very tired. At Prewald I passed the lofty peak of Nanos, which is frequently scaled by pleasure seekers. I was too weary to feel any desire for such an undertaking and continued my journey. At nine o'clock I reached a village with the name of Hrasce which indicates the language of the people. I sought lodgings in four inns in vain and at the fifth and last was told that they had no rooms. I sat sometime there being too exhausted to think of the unpleasant state of affairs. Finally one of the servants interceded in my behalf and the inhospitable landlord explained that they were not allowed to take in strangers without a passport. I quickly informed the suspicious wretch that I had the necessary article, and a room was immediately found, although he had solemnly and repeatedly assured me previously that there was none in the house. This is the first time I have used my passport except to identify myself at the banks. I made twenty five miles during the day which will do for a beginning with fourteen pounds of baggage.

The next morning I walked six miles farther to Adelsberg where the famous limestone caves are situated. They were known in the middle ages, but it was only in 1816 that it was discovered that they were very large. Having paid the fee at the ticket office and procured two guides, I walked to the entrance which is three quarters of a mile from the town. A well shaded path leads thither and the opening is closed by a neat iron gate. The caves are controlled by the government and the affairs are administered to the satisfaction of everybody. Smooth, solid walks have been made throughout the entire length of the grottoes and strong railings placed wherever a fall of a few feet could be possible.

Just below the opening to the grottoes the river Poik plunges into the very heart of the mountain and continues its subterranean course for several miles. In the next valley it emerges and then after passing through another range of mountains in the same way, it reappears in the plain beyond. In my subsequent journey I saw both of these portions of the stream. Such strange phenomena are not unfrequent in this country.

The river appears in the cave a short distance from the entrance and after that it is entirely concealed. After the guides had prepared the lights we started in, the roar of the stream growing gradually louder until we reached the "dome," where the water is crossed by two natural and one artificial bridge. This is the most sublime part of the grottoes. The eye can scarcely distinguish the vaulting far overhead, and from the impenetrable darkness below comes the unceasing sound of the flowing stream. There is enough of the terrible in the place to fill one with awe as well as wonder. Farther on the fantastic formations of the stalactites and stalagmites began to be seen. There are many beautiful columns of marvelous whiteness. Some have a massive size while others are as frail as glass. Man has found shapes sculptured in the limestone here which resemble a hundred different objects in the upper world. There are trees, flowers, and plants ; there are animals from the lion to the tortoise ; there are banners and curtains, pulpits and thrones, sarcophagi and cemeteries. Indeed there seems to be no end to the fantastic variations which are assumed by the rock.

One large chamber with a lofty dome is used on Pfingstmontag as a dancing hall. Hundreds and hundreds of candles are employed on that day in lighting the grottoes and thousands of people assemble from far and near to witness the magnificent spectacle.

The guide said that the entire distance which we walked was five English miles. We were between two and three hours in accomplishing the trip. As at the Mammoth Cave white, blind fish and insects are found far from the light of day.

After seeing the grottoes I again set out to continue my walk northward. The dreary limestone wastes disappeared and the scenery became more beautiful as I advanced. Green, pine covered hills and broad, fertile valleys followed one another in constant succession, affording a constant amusement for the mind and relieving the weariness of the walk. I stopped at a toll house in the afternoon to get a glass of water and the keeper, according to the custom of the people, at once asked me of what country I was. After I had satisfied his curiosity, he said that Americans came very seldom along that road, with which observation I readily agreed. These are the first toll gates which I have seen in Europe.

At dark I arrived at Loitsch thoroughly tired in every limb. I visited all the inns but could not find a bed anywhere. They seemed to have only one apiece and I came too late to secure that. In desperation I went back the second time to one landlord, who appeared more gracious than the others, and begged him to fix a place for me in some way. He accordingly made a couch upon a bench and some chairs in the public room and upon these I managed to spend the night. I would have appreciated his kindness much more if there had been a few less fleas in the blankets.

I continued my tramp the next morning until nearly noon when it began to rain and I improved the time by visiting a shoe shop at Ober Laibach for repairs. I found that the master workman could speak German and he began a long conversation with me by asking where I had come from. Nothing could exceed his astonishment when he learned that I was from America. His brother had emigrated to New York and died there and he was naturally much interested in the country. There seemed to be no end to his questions about the trade and customs in our land and when I left him he heaped well wishes upon me as only Germans are able to do.

Late in the afternoon I came to the plains of Laibach and soon reached the city which is beautifully situated at the foot of a range of hills. Toward the northwest the snow clad peaks of the Julian Alps stand out prominently against the sky, while upon every other side mountains of lesser height limit the distant view. Laibach has about 23,000 inhabitants and abounds in fine parks and promenades. The principal square is well shaded and is called Congress Platz, to commemorate the asssembly which was held in the city from January to May, 1821, to take measures against the insurrection in Naples. On one side of the square is a large bronze bust of Fieldmarshal Count Radetzky, who once owned the palace Tivoli near the city which is now one of the most popular places of resort in the neighborhood. I was sitting near the statue watching the easy good nature with which the people of all classes enjoyed themselves together when an elderly gentleman came and took a seat beside me and without much effort opened a conversation. When he heard that I was on a tramp, he related some of his own experiences years ago before the days of steamboats and railroads. After a pleasant chat he showed me the post-office and gave me some other information in the most accommodating manner possible. This almost universal social and obliging spirit makes the Germans so beloved by strangers.

After parting with my newly made acquaintance I set out to walk a few more miles and shortly after dark stopped for the night at the village of Jeschza on the banks of the Save. After a fruitless search for a bed I was compelled to be content with a couch on a bench similar to the one of the previous night. The points of resemblance were but too well carried out, for the fleas were as numerous as the beggars in Venice. But this was not all, for the topers were noisy over their beer and their pipes smoked like the funnel of a steamship. After they had finally departed I was just about to go to sleep when two gendarmes came in to get a drink and see what guests there were in the house. I was too drowsy to notice whether they tried to read my passport or not, but if they did it is not probable that their puzzled minds got any farther than the picture of Liberty and the eagle. The gleaming bayonets and shining barrels of there muskets were the formidable appearances which followed me into the land of dreams.

The next morning I crossed the Save, which seemed about the same size as the Danube at Ulm. At noon I stopped for dinner at an inn at Lukovitz. The landlord asked me where I came from, where I was going and what business I had. When I told him the name of my native land, he exclaimed in utter disbelief : " What would an American want in this poor county, when everything goes better over there?" I finally succeeded in convincing him of the truth of my statement and he then regarded me as a sort of wonder.

In the afternoon I entered deeper into the mountains. Toward evening I came suddenly to the summit of the watershed between the Sann and the western streams and was surprised by a magnificent view of a beautiful green valley enclosed by a circle of hills. The pleasure of the moment was so great that I felt that pedestrianism deserved all the praises it has received, although at some other moments I had doubted the fact.

After the usual preliminary search for a place to sleep in the evening, I was once more obliged to take my chances for the night's rest upon a bench. Fortunately but one flea and one bummer put in an appearance and neither of them was active enough to keep me awake after having walked twenty-six miles during the day. The next morning I entered the valley of the Sann and in the afternoon passed through Cilli, an active little town commanded by a picturesque ruin. My course led next northward and I was again in the midst of the mountains when I was overtaken by rain and darkness. As I turned a curve in the road, I saw a company of men approaching in the distance. The foremost one wore a long mantle, knee-trousers, and sandals and had his feet and ankles swathed. I recognized the outfit at once and concluded to air my stock of Italian by greeting the strolling musicians in their native tongue. Accordingly I wished them a "buon giorno," to which they replied in a similar way, being overjoyed to hear their own language. If the conversation had gone no farther than this I would have come off in good style, but they immediately began to ask me about the road in Italian and it is needless to add I was swamped in a moment.

That night I slept on a bench with nothing but a little sack of straw to relieve the hardness of the boards. The next morning while continuing my tramp, I met a little girl, who muttered something in her Slavonie dialect, came and kissed my hand and then passed on without another word. This is an unusual experience for a republican and it occupied my mind for some time afterwards. She could not have thought that I was a prince, for my clothes showed unmistakable signs of pedestrianism. Nor could she have supposed that I was a clerical dignity, since those reverend gentlemen do not run around the country with knapsacks on their backs and their trousers turned up. So it must be forever a mystery to me whether that little Styrian peasant girl took me for a pope or a king.

At noon I dined at a little country inn far from the influences of civilization. After dinner the landlady began to catechise me as usual and was immensely astonished when she heard of my native land. I amused myself and startled her by relating a few of the wonderful things of the country across the sea. It has been one of my recreations during my tramp to find some landlady who does not know German well enough to notice my mistakes, and whose meager amount of schooling has been supplemented by a miscellaneous mass of misinformation derived from stray vagabonds, and then set myself up as a sort of oracle from an unknown clime and tell long accounts of America amid boundless applause from my ignorant hearers. This particular woman asked me if our continent was not toward the morning sun. After I had told her the nearest way was toward the west (evening sun,) she wanted to know how long it would take to go there afoot. I then revealed the fact that there is a great ocean in the world, to which she listened with unfeigned surprise.

That night I found a decent inn which pleased me so much that I staid over the next day in order to rest. The following morning I set off much refreshed and at nine o'clock crossed the broad Drave and entered Marburg, a market town of considerable size. In the afternoon I reached the valley of Mur, in which I afterwards walked many miles. At night I had a serious time in finding a place to sleep. One landlord offered me a place in his barn which I refused. Another, at ten o'clock in the evening, said it was too late and shut the door in my face. I had given up in despair when I found a good inn and soon forgot my troubles.

This experience made me disgusted with tramping but the next morning I visited an old ruined castle near Wildon and my dislike was moderated. From the tower the famous astronomer, Tycho Brahe, made many of his observations.

Gratz, the capital of Styria, lies on both banks of the river Mur in the midst of a plain of considerable size.

The mountains rise in every direction a few miles from the city and afford an unlimited field for pleasure seekers. In the center of the town stands a solitary peak, called the castle hill, which was once strongly fortified and undoubtedly led to the foundation of Gratz. The Austrian Major Hacker with 500 men successfully repelled the attempt of Macdonald with 3000 French troops to take the stronghold during the Napoleonic wars. After the treaty of 1808 the walls of the fortification were destroyed and some years later the hill was covered with a net work of paths and the summit turned into a miniature park. It is nearly four hundred feet high and the prospect is such as one rarely sees. The view embraces the well cultivated valley intersected by the Mur and the varied array of mountains which form the most distant resting place of the eye.

Gratz was formerly one of the cheapest places to live in Europe, but the secret got out and the people now complain that the prices are as high as anywhere else. The city has long been a favorite retiring place for pensioned military and civil officers, so that quite a colony of veterans has been formed. The town has some beautiful parks, several statues, a bust of Schiller and a few interesting old buildings. Without being particularly remarkable either in the light of history or art, Gratz produces an agreeable impression on the stranger, and leads him to regard it as a pleasant place for study or rest.

My plans only allowed me a day in the city and so I set off again toward evening with my knapsack on my back. My pedestrian efforts in Krain and Southern Styria had indeed been attended with much that was very disagreeable, but for all that I was glad when I was again in the open country. I walked steadily along until I reached the place where the valley became narrow and the scenery seemed much like the Rhine. Just beyond the picturesque ruin of castle Goesting I sat down on a stone pile to rest and enjoy the romantic view. While I was reading a few pages from one of Goethe's dramas a peasant came along and began a conversation with me, which was fortunately possible, as the people from Gratz northward are all German. He supposed I was a student, and stopped to warn me that the solitary place was somewhat dangerous and said that a man had been shot at four times a few weeks previous while passing. European assassins, as is well known, are poor marksmen, but I concluded to move on. The valley became narrower and the scenery was very imposing. At one place it was necessary to run the railroad for some distance under the highway, as the space between the cliff and the stream is insufficient for both.

A little before dark I drew near the village of Kirchenviertl, where extensive paper mills are located. I found the inns north of Gratz much better than those farther south. The character of the landlords, however, was subject to many variations. Those I met during my tramp were in general either contemptably servile or as inhospitable as brutes. One would shut the door in my face while another would treat me as though I owned him, body and soul. The Austrian newspapers display considerable independence of spirit, but the lower classes have an awe for the titled land owners, such as cannot be conceived of by the self-respecting laborers of America.

During the next day after leaving Kirchenviertl I visited the ruined castle Pfanberg, which stands on a wooded peak near Frohnleiten. It is rarely touched by pleasure seekers and the wild vegetation grows on undisturbed. It was once a strong fortress with double walls upon the verge of artificially hewn precipices, but large trees now stand among the battlements and the forest birds build their nests without fear in the long deserted towers. I climbed over heaps of loose rubbish, peered into dark vaults and wandered through the ruined halls trying to call up in fancy the mailed knights and fair ladies of the dim past. But the frescoes in the chapel are sadly faded; the ancestral tombstones lie in scattered fragments, and the rank weeds grow in the court where the warrior said his farewells ere he went forth to battle. The current of life has gone down into the valleys and the ruined castles stand like abandoned wrecks of other years.

The two following days proved so stormy that I was compelled to spend most of the time in reading at the country inns. The villages of lower Austria are in general much cleaner and more pleasing than those of Germany. The majority of the houses have roofs of thatched straw and some have rude religious paintings on the front wall. Every village has a public shrine at the wayside with an image of Jesus on the cross, the Virgin Mary, or something similar. The greater part of these are horribly executed, as they are undoubtedly of local workmanship. We think of Christ as having been a perfect example of normal physical development, but the provincial image makers give him a wasted, mishapen form such as would only be fitting for one who has been consumed by age and all manner of disease.

In addition to the frescoes of the house fronts the pictorial art manifests itself in the signs of the stores. Whether the people are unable to read or not I do not know, but the merchants everywhere hang out paintings representing the articles they sell instead of enumerating them in printed characters. The inns have rarely any other sign than a green twig or a bunch of long shavings. These facts seem to indicate a meager amount of education among the people, but I hope it is otherwise.

I continued my tramp as best I could with the frequent rains. At Bruck the road left the Mur and thence followed the banks of its tributary, the Muerz. But as the ascent of the mountain chain became steeper this stream was left behind. It was toward evening when I reached the highest part of the Semmering Pass. The southern side is by no means extraordinary. The scenery is beautiful, but I thought it equaled by other summits which I had seen during the journey. The sun was already below the horizon when I took my farewell look toward the south. A purple mist lay on the valley of the Mur which extended as far as the eye could reach between two mountain walls. Golden fringed clouds ended the vista, and with this glorious sight I bade adieu to the land of Styria.

That night I slept at the inn on the summit, 3,910 feet above the sea, and for once I had no objection to a German feather bed for covering. The next morning I set off to descend the northern slope. Here I found the fine scenery that I had looked for in vain upon the southern side. There was a constant succession of sublime views of woodland, valleys and peaks. In the distance the snowy summit of the

Schneeberg rose high over all, while on the opposite side of the valley I could see the railway with its bold bridges and tunnels. After an hour's rapid descent I reached the market town Schottwien, which consists of a single street running through a narrow gorge. A wall at each end of the place has been all that was necessary to defend the town.

Some distance farther on I came to the banks of the Leitha in the broad valley of which I walked for the rest of the day. The last nine miles between Neunkirchen and Wiener-Neustadt were the most monotonous which I found in all my tramp. The road is perfectly straight and passes through a dense pine forest which is uninhabited.

Wiener-Neustadt is a pleasing city with a goodly number of parks, an interesting old church and a castle in which Emperor Maximilian is buried. He was born here, and was not permitted to rest under his gorgeous monument in the church of the Franciscans at Innsbruck, although that was his last wish.

Having now reached the plain of Vienna I ended my tramp and took the train to the national capital. I had walked nearly three hundred miles and suffered a great many discomforts, but for all that I consider it a pleasant journey and know I have seen much that I could not in any other way. I have come through a country where farming is done by hand, and where a laboror gets ten and fifteen cents a day in addition to very poor board. I have learned that we Americans know little of economy and if we suffer in one way it is because we squander our substance in another. In the far future our country may be in as pitiable a condition as Europe is to-day; but for the present America is emphatically the best place for the workingman. It is there, and there alone, that possibility holds out the golden apples of success before every man, and if he be bold and strong and true he will win.

CHAPTER XII.

VIENNA.—ITS CHURCHES AND MUSEUMS.—THROUGH BOHEMIA.—PRAGUE.—DOWN THE ELBE TO DRESDEN.

The capital of Austria impresses one at once with its size. In no other city that I have yet visited in Europe except Rome and Naples have the distances between the different quarters seemed so long. The population numbers over a million.

I always supposed that Vienna was on the banks of the Danube, as Cincinnati or Louisville border on the Ohio. But the fact is the city is about a mile from the river and is only connected with it by a canal which cannot be entered by vessels of ordinary size. The Danube here is a broad stream with a very swift current and has little resemblance to the upper part which I saw at Ulm.

The church of St. Stephen forms the heart of Vienna, and from the square before it the streams of life and trade circulate through all the outer districts. The edifice itself is a large Gothic structure, which dates from the beginning of the fourteenth century. The interior contains, in addition to the usual ornaments, the handsome monument of the insignificant Emperor Frederick III. and the tomb of the famous Prince Eugene, whom history ranks as one of the greatest generals the world has seen.

Among the other places of worship is the Votive Church

which was built to commemorate the Emperor's escape from the hands of an assassin in 1853. Its richly decorated interior has just been finished, and the seventy-eight finely painted windows command universal and enthusiastic admiration. If the European nations in general were accustomed to build such edifices every time their sovereign escaped from a murderous knife or ball, I think ecclesiastical architecture would develop to an extent surpassing that of any previous age.

In one corner of the new Market Place stands a little church, which possesses an interest which is not attached to prouder edifices. Under the building is the burial vault of the imperial house of Habsburg. A flight of steps leads down to the place where the crowned heads repose. One is surprised at the lack of ornament. Plain copper caskets cover the floor in every direction, and only a few have any other than a simple tablet. The oldest Emperor who lies here is Matthias, the founder of the vault, who died in 1619. The last one is Ferdinand the First, who died in 1875. Among the others are Empress Maria Theresa, Empress Marie Louise, wife of Napoleon I., and her son, and the late ill-fated Emperor Maximilian of Mexico. Nearly a dozen imperial rulers sleep in this plain vault while the busy world moves on in the street above. The stream of humanity is dull of memory, and those who cease to be abreast with the current are immediately cast aside and forgotten.

Vienna has numerous collections of various kinds, which rival even those of Munich. The chief gallery of paintings is in the Palace Belvedere, which stands in the midst of a large park in the south eastern quarter of the city.

In the lower palace Belvedere is a museum of Roman and Egyptian antiquities and a collection of mediæval arms and armor. The former contains a number of busts and statues which one can by no means neglect even though he has seen the treasures of Rome, Naples and Florence. The museum of armor and similar curiosities is one of the most interesting in Vienna. It was brought hither in 1806 from Amras Castle, near Innspruck. Among a thousand other things which I cannot name are the battle-axe of Montezuma, Inca of Mexico, suits of armor worn by Charles V., Maximilian I., Philip II. and the Duke of Alva. Besides this magnificent collection there are also two other museums of arms, both of which present much of interest. In the one belonging to the city there is a glass case which contains the skull of the Grand Vizier Kara Mustapha, who led the Turks at the siege of Vienna in 1683. After he had been driven back by the Polish King, John Sobieski, he was strangled by order of the Sultan for his want of success. The wretch was pursued by fate even after he had suffered death at the hands of his friends. For when Belgrade was taken by the Austrians under Prince Eugene his body was exhumed and his skull, shroud and the cord with which he was executed were brought to Vienna by the victorious army. Thus the bones of the unfortunate Turk are exposed to the curious gaze of the common herd in the very city which he vainly strove to take. What melancholy changes time brings to us poor mortals!

The other armor museum is in the Imperial Arsenal, a large building south of the city. The ground floor contains a number of marble statues of distinguished heroes. A broad flight of steps ascends to the Austrian Hall of Fame, a large salon with a dome which is decorated with frescoes of battle scenes. The museum has a large collection of armor, some of which belonged to the various German Emperors. One suit was worn by Prince Eugene. The most interesting article, however, for Protestants is the coat which Gustavus Adolphus wore at the battle of Lutzen. The holes through which the fatal bullets passed are still visible. One feels a thrill of awe when he contemplates the garment which has been made sacred by the past sufferings of the heroic champion of liberty and progress. And then, too, one thinks of all that might have been if the Swedish King had lived.

The Imperial Palace is an extensive but irregular pile of buildings, inclosing several courts and exhibiting different styles of architecture. Besides the parts used as the residence there are other portions of the structure which are occupied by collections of various kinds. In the eastern wing is the imperial library, which contains 400,000 volumes and 20,000 manuscripts. The main building is adorned with frescoes and elegantly finished. In some special cases are preserved a number of rare editions and articles of historical interest. Charlemagne's prayer book and Tasso's Jerusalem in his own writing are among the things which can be named. The most important treasure in a historical view is the Peutinger tablet, a road map of the Roman Empire of the latter part of the second century.

On the opposite side of the court is a collection of coins and antiquities which is very interesting. It contains a magnificent array of gems and gold ornaments and the seal of Alaric, the King of the Goths. But the most important collection in Vienna, as far as wealth is concerned, is the treasury of the imperial house. When I reached the entrance at the appointed hour I found a large crowd already assembled; so great is the eagerness of the people to see the immeasurable riches of the crown. The collection comprises the memorial gifts which the sovereigns have received as well as the treasures which are purely ornamental. In the first room are some curious old herolds' garments embroidered with gold. Next is a lot of intricately wrought watches and clocks. Then comes a number of crystal and gold vessels of all sizes and designs, some of which cost fabulous sums. In a room toward the right is a collection of articles which have a historical importance; the insignia of the old "Holy Roman Empire," crown, scepter, imperial apple, coronation robes and relics, the insignia of Napoleon I., as King of Italy, and a talisman with horoscope which once belonged to the superstitious Wallenstein. In one corner stands the costly gilded silver cradle in which Napoleon's child, the King of Rome, formed his first impressions of this world. In another room stands a large glass case which is always surrounded by an eager throng of visitors. The light flashes upon a thousand diamonds, for the treasures have an immeasurable value. There are the crowns of the Emperor and Empress and the scepter and imperial apple, all glittering with gems. Then there are badges of the different orders. Leaves and flowers and ribbons lie there, all made of the sparkling diamonds. The largest gem of the collection is the Florentine diamond which once belonged to

Charles the Bold of Burgundy. After the Swiss had defeated him at Murden, a peasant is said to have found the treasure and sold it to a merchant for fifty cents. It weighs one hundred and thirty-three and a third carats. The grand cross of the Order of Maria Theresa is composed of five hundred and forty-eight brilliants with a twenty-six carat diamond in the center. Around this array of inestimable wealth the crowd pressed continually, eager to gaze at the stones which only kings and fairies can possess. Perhaps some envied the Emperor, but it is not likely that any of us will ever see another such a fabulous treasure.

Like all European cities Vienna has a goodly number of statues and parks. The fortifications of the inner town have been leveled and transformed into boulevards. In the broad plain between the city and the Danube there is an immense forest-like park called the Prater, which is a favorite resort of all ranks of the Viennese, from the chimney sweeps to the Kaiser. I went out there on Sunday evening and found the Germans in their glory. The principal avenues were lined with all conceivable kinds of wonders under canvas, from a phonograph to a trained flea show. Beer was flowing as fast as the current of the Danube and masticated pretzels were following the deluge into the limitless abyss which the German calls his stomach. Some of the more sentimental were sitting under the protecting shadows of the old trees and murmuring sweet words to the willing ears of the fair. I have little sympathy for the ruling passions of the Germans, and do not think that the summit of human happiness is to be found in the bottom of a beer glass, nor that the greatest joys are to be drawn through an ancient pipe whose odors are foul enough to poison one who has ever breathed the pure atmosphere of nature. But still I think it would be well if Americans would imitate the periodic picnic excursions which every family in this country makes to some convenient park or grove. Perhaps then the serenity of the outer world would tend to cool the feverish blood in our veins and calm the nervous impetuosity which makes us the slaves of our aims in life.

Vienna's cemeteries are situated just outside of the city in all directions. I made a long excursion afoot from the southeastern gate around to the northwestern, visiting the most important of the burial grounds and some other places of interest. At some distance from the gate of St. Mark is the cemetery of the same name, which contains the grave of the great "Tonmeister," Mozart. In the midst of a wilderness of wooden crosses I found the monument which was erected in 1859 on the spot which is supposed to be the composer's resting place, although the fact, alas! can never be known with certainty. The chapter of the miseries of the learned is so long that one may well wonder that those who slave for public pleasure do not revolt and demand a share of the gold of the dullards who enjoy the fruits of their labors. Mozart died at Vienna in the prime of life, worn out by labor and disappointment. The physicians called the disease by several long names according to their different opinions, but it is probable that the chief ailing was not within their sphere of observation. The composer's savings were meager, and to avoid expense a public grave was taken at the cemetery. The few friends who followed the body hither, however, turned back at the city gate on account of a violent storm, and unattended the great tonemaster was laid to rest among the hundreds of obscure dead. When the disconsolate widow visited the cemetery afterwards there was a new sexton, who could tell her nothing of the grave of her husband. At such terms great men win their fame!

The monument represents the mourning Muse of Music with the half unrolled scroll of Mozart's last work, the requiem, which proved, indeed, as he said, to be for himself. A few trees shelter the spot, and all around stand the wooden crosses like a field of grain. Every foot of ground has its tale of woe, but none can be sadder than that which tells of the melancholy fate of genius.

A walk of a half hour brings one to the Matzleindorf cemetery, which is just south of the city. It contains the grave of the composer Gluck. A small, pointed monument marks the spot and bears a short inscription in testimony of his honest discharge of the duties of life.

From here I walked out to the well-known mperial summer palace of Schoenbrunn. Napoleon occupied it in 1805 and 1809, when he entered Vienna, and in 1832 his son died in the same room which he had used. The extensive park is laid out in broad walks and stands always open to the public. In one corner is a small Roman ruin and the "beautiful fountain" which gives its name to the palace. There is something royal in a majestic row of tall trees which cannot be imitated by wealthy upstarts. The reverend shade of an artificial forest, like a gallery of dusky ancestral portraits, is an unimpeachable evidence of princely blood.

After seeing the statue of Emperor Maximilian of Mexico

at the adjacent village of Heitzing, I turned toward the north and in an hour reached the suburban town Wæhring. I went immediately to the cemetery and soon found the graves of two other famous composers, Franz Schubert and Beethoven. The monument of the former consists of a sort of canopy supported by two columns, which cover a bust of the lamented master. The inscription says, "Music buried here a rich possession, yet still finer expectations," for the composer was but thirty-one years old when death claimed him for his own. The monument of Beethoven is a large pointed column bearing a golden butterfly and a lyre with the simple inscription, "Beethoven." Yet that single word is sufficient, for who has not heard of the deaf composer?

I next proceeded over the hills to the Kahlenberg, a lofty mountain which rises near the Danube and commands an extensive view. As the weather was somewhat misty, I did not climb to the top, but rested on a grass plot which afforded an excellent prospect. Far to the right I could see the mountain chain extending toward the Semmering Pass. Before me lay the sea of spires and roofs of the imperial capital. Farther to the right was the forest of the Prater and among the trees rose the dome, which is almost the only relic of the buildings of the great exhibition of 1873. Next toward the north flowed the broad stream of the Danube, which is crossed by five great bridges. Then from the river the plain stretched toward the east until it was lost in the mists of the evening. This is the famous Marchfield, the battlefield of history. Here Ottakar, King of Bohemia, overthrew the Hungarian invaders, and here, too, he lost his crown and life in battle with Emperor Rudolph, of Hapsburg. Here Napoleon was repulsed at Aspern, and here he drove the Austrians back at Wagram. Here were blood and death and glory. Here sword clashed against sword, and bayonet against bayonet ; here cannon and musket poured forth murderous volleys at human targets ; here men became fiends and hewed one another to atoms, killed without mercy, and died lamenting that they could no longer destroy. As the last rays of the setting sun fell on this scene of horrible memory I descended the mount and returned to the city.

I left Vienna, on Saturday morning, by the Franz Joseph railway. We crossed the Danube some distance above the city, and then entered a region where low ranges of hills alternate with the valleys of small streams. The fenceless hills are destitute of houses. The country has no large cities and few places of historical interest, and the only thing that I have to record concerning the journey is the fact that I saw a gravel train with a large crowd of women and girls, who filled the office of shovelers. I have seen the so-called weaker sex pulling wagons, working in streets, harvesting hay, hoeing corn, and performing similar feats, but this is the first time that I have found them employed in building railroads. They did not seem at all troubled at having such a task, but were merry enough to sing.

Prague has a beautiful situation on both banks of the broad Moldau, and is surrounded by hills of various heights. After a short walk from the depot, I passed through the powder tower, which was once a city gate, and entered the old town, which presents quite an antique appearance, with its narrow lanes and quaint old buildings. A short distance farther I came to the square before the town hall, which, like many similar places in European cities, has a part in tragic history. After Tilly had defeated the Protestants on the White Mountain, in the beginning of the Thirty Years' War, twenty-seven of the captured leaders were executed in the square with various degrees of cruelty. The officers first cut off the University rector's tongue and then his head. They nailed the town secretary's tongue to the scaffold and then strangled him. This bloody act of the 21st of June, 1621, is not, however, the only event which stains the place, for after Wallenstein was defeated at Lutzen, he vented his rage by causing eleven of his higher officers to be put to death here, " for cowardice on the battlefield."

The Charles bridge, which is the most interesting relic of antiquity in Prague, was built in the fourteenth century, and is entirely of stone. A lofty tower stands at each end, which once served as a means of defense. The bridge has been the scene of bloody struggles during the Thirty Years' War and the conflicts with Frederick the Great. Over each pier there are ancient statues, which contribute to give the structure a quaint appearance. In the middle of the bridge stands a crucifix, whose pious inscription but serves to mark it as a monument of the shameful persecutions which were enacted in the name of Christianity: " Thrice holy, holy, holy to the honor of Christ the crucified. Erected from the fines of a Jew, who was reviling the holy cross, by a very worthy royal Tribunal Appellatorium, 1606."

A short distance beyond the crucifix a tablet designates the place where St. John Nepomucenus was thrown into the river in 1383 by command of Emperor Wenzel because he refused to devulge what the Empress had confided to him as her confessor. The legend says that his body floated for some time upon the Moldau, while five bright stars formed a nimbus around his head. The faithful do not have any difficulty in believing the story, and they touch the spot with their fingers whenever they cross the bridge. And yet more, many thousands from Bohemia, Moravia and Hungary make a pilgrimage hither every year, and the saint's monument in the cathedral is built of three thousand pounds of silver.

From the bridge a street leads past a fine monument to Field Marshal Radetzky up to the Hradschin, or ancient royal palace, which stands upon a hill in the northwestern part of the city. It is a very extensive building of indifferent appearance, enclosing a number of courts. From one of the windows next the town the imperial governors were thrown by the Protestants in 1618, and thus began the Thirty Years' War, which desolated vast districts, destroyed thousands of cities and villages, and caused the death of a million human beings.

In one of the courts, enclosed by the wings of the palace, is the cathedral, a Gothic edifice, which is far from being completed. It contains some interesting monuments, one of which marks the resting place of a number of German Emperors and Bohemian Kings.

I next crossed the Moldau and visited the Judenstadt or Jewish quarter. The streets are narrow and the houses of uninviting exterior, but the spirit of that wonderful people drives through every difficulty and accumulates wealth in the strangest sorts of ways. In the midst of some shops where old shoes, cast off clothes, scraps of iron and the like are bought and sold, I was quite startled at seeing a large steel engraving of the familiar face of U. S. Grant staring at me from the door of a dealer in rubbish. Perhaps the eyes pleaded with me as an American to rescue him from such a place, but I was hard-hearted and let him stay. And so the poor General's picture is doomed to hang for an indefinite period in the shop of a vendor of the odds and ends of human goods.

The Jews form a considerable portion of the population of Vienna and Prague, and one often sees some strange figures. In Vienna they have a peculiar costume among the men, which consists of a long dark coat reaching below the knees, which they wear over the usual garments which are worn by the Gentiles. In addition to this they let their beards grow long and train a curl before each ear, which gives them a quaint appearance. One meets hundreds of such men, who look as though they were thoroughly versed in the mysteries of prophesying and dealing in old clothes. Involuntary gestures, long seasons of solitary meditation and incoherent mutterings of the lips are the palpable indications of superhuman knowledge.

In the midst of this busy Jewish quarter is their cemetery which dates from the earliest times of Prague. It is no easy task to find one's way through the narrow alleys but I finally accomplished the feat and entered the ancient ground. It is a scene not to be met with everywhere. Thousands of half-hewn stones stand close together, having one side covered with long inscriptions in the Hebrew character. Some of the monuments have rude signs of the tribe to which the deceased belonged, such as two hands for a descendant of Aaron. Then there are heaps of smaller stones which friends bring to commemorate their visit and do honor to the dead. The cemetery is a strange spectacle, but looks too much like a wilderness. All the European burial grounds have such crowded rows of monuments that the visitor is always oppressed by the consciousness of man's insignificance. But under the green trees of an American cemetery death seems like a natural sleep and the eternal beauty of nature consols us in our sorrow.

After spending the day among the interesting old buildings of Prague, I left by the train toward Dresden. I intended to make a foot journey through the mountainous district near the frontiers of Bohemia and Saxony, and therefore took a ticket to Lobositz, a small town at the beginning of the narrow part of the Elbe valley. As the train rolled out of the Prague depot I obtained a passing glimpse of the Ziska Mountain, where the famous one-eyed Hussite general won a victory in 1420. After a short distance the railroad leaves the pleasant valley of the Moldau and crosses a wide level tract of country, which extends to Lobositz on the Elbe.

It had been raining very hard during the day, and when I left the train I found the roads so muddy that I concluded to wait until the next morning, and even entertained serious thoughts of abandoning my projected tramp. I spent the night in a tolerable inn which put on fashionable airs and had a name of the Golden Eagle or Green Tree, or something similar, I have forgotten just what. When I awoke I had only courage enough to determine to walk to the next station, and so set out in an uncertain frame of mind.

The road was not quite so bad as I had feared, and I soon reached a slight hill not far from the town which is surmounted by a monument. Lobositz is one of the many places in Europe which have gained a name in history from the battles which were fought in the neighborhood. The only claim which Lobositz has for immortality is the fact that Frederick the Great defeated an Austrian army near the town, Oct. 1st, 1756. The monument commemorates a subsequent visit of Emperor Joseph II. to the spot.

A short distance farther on I entered the narrow valley of the Elbe, which is already a considerable stream. Like the Rhine the romantic region is disturbed by a railroad upon each bank of the river. The hills are covered with vegetation and dotted with houses, but vineyards are very rare. I have had a good opportunity to appreciate the comparative smallness of the German speaking portion of the Austrian Empire. From Trieste to Gratz I met a number of Slavonic dialects, and was shut off from all intercourse with the people. Then a few hours ride northward from Vienna brought me again in the midst of a language which I could not understand. Add to this the fact that the Hungarian language begins a short distance east of Vienna and one can then appreciate what a small portion of territory is occupied by pure Germans in the Austrian Empire.

I enjoyed my solitary walk down the Elbe so well that I did not stop at the first station. The river craft which I saw consisted mostly of large flat boats, but occasionally some neat little steamers came along to enliven the scene. I would have been well enough satisfied with my tramp, but it began to rain furiously later in the morning, and all the romantic past vanished. At noon I stopped at the Anker Inn at the village of Wannow and liked the location so well that I staid two days. The house stands near the water's edge, and at a little wharf before the door the diminutive Elbe steamers land every few hours. A short distance down the stream upon the opposite bank rises a lofty projecting rock —the "Lorelei of the Elbe"—which is crowned by a most picturesque ruined castle called Schreckenstein. Far in the distance across the long sheet of water I could see the bridge and steeples of the little village of Aussig. All around one obtains pleasing glimpses of rock and foliage in endless variety. In the solemn stillness of the twilight I sat and watched the towers and battlements of the old castle over the stream until I drifted back into those strange days of chivalry when life was one long poem, and the privileged lords almost escaped the prosaic jars of our rude world.

The fact that I am an American did not awaken as much curiosity in the inn as usual, for two lady artists from the great Republic have recently made some long visits at the house, so I was not regarded as a particularly rare animal. The little steamers had pleased me so much that I concluded to abandon my tramp, and embarked on the second day upon the John Penn for Dresden. The scenery of the Mittel Mountains seemed very pleasing as we glided along but I saw nothing as beautiful as Schreckenstein which I could not forget. At the group of villages near Bodenbach the hills approach closer to the river and become higher and more rugged. This is the beginning of the district called the Saxon Switzerland.

Some time after this we reached the frontiers of Saxony

and at 6 p. m. steamed under the stone bridge at Dresden. I felt quite glad to cross the line once more into Germany after an absence of three months and a half among the Italians and Austrians. While I would not say a reproachful word against the noble and intelligent spirits which those nations unquestionably have, still I know from experience that the Germans in general are more friendly toward strangers, and welcomed with pleasure the hour that brought me once more among them.

CHAPTER XIII.

THE BEAUTY AND ART TREASURES OF DRESDEN.—OVER THE PLAINS OF SAXONY.—LEIPZIG.—LUTZEN.—WITTENBERG.—BERLIN.

BERLIN, July 22d, 1880.

The traveler who approaches Dresden by the river is at once impressed with the gayety and magnificence of the famous capital. When I landed from the steamer early in the evening, the long stone bridges and broad quays were thronged with people, and everyone seemed in that pleasing state of exhilaration which is fitting for those who live among the choicest treasures of art. A green-covered remnant of the old city wall is still standing along the river and its summit has been converted into a most agreeable promenade, which the natives call the Bruehl Terrace. After depositing my baggage in a hotel, I returned to this inviting walk and was more than usually pleased with the surroundings. The river is crossed by three massive stone bridges and lined with churches, palaces and dwellings, which combine to give a worthy idea of the architecture of the city. The surface of the stream is covered with bath houses and small water craft.

A short distance from the terrace is the royal palace, a large irregular edifice, which was founded in 1534. In a suite of rooms on the ground floor there is a collection of jewels and curiosities, called the Green Vault, which is similar to the imperial treasury at Vienna, though of less value. The array of statuettes, vases and trinkets of rare and costly materials is perfectly bewildering. The curiosities of the collection are Luther's and Melanchthon's rings ; a diamond of five and a third ounces weight ; a ladies' bow ornamented with six hundred and sixty-two diamonds; the largest onyx known, seven inches in height ; and a curious model representing the court of a grand mogul at Delhi with a hundred and fifty-two movable figures in gold and enamel.

The picture gallery, which has made Dresden such a familiar name in all quarters of the globe, is situated in a large imposing building of unnamable shape called the Zwinger, which was erected in the beginning of the last century.

The gem of the picture gallery is Raphael's Madonna di San Sisto which is one of the most famous paintings in existence. It is placed in an apartment by itself and is continually surrounded by throngs of admirers. Some few lean back sagaciously and point out the place where the master could have improved his work, but the picture has enjoyed the homage of many generations and most people are not rash enough to doubt its excellence. It was purchased for the Dresden gallery in 1753 for forty-five thousand dollars.

In the Johanneum, which is not far from the Zwinger, there is one of those historical museums which I think the most interesting and instructive which the European capitals possess. Besides a very fine collection of furniture, utensils, trinkets, arms and armor, representing the various periods, there are also a number of articles which have a peculiar value on account of their history. One case contains Luther's sword and goblet. I think that it is quite natural that the Germans should hold the reformer's drinking cup in all honor, for they never tire of repeating his famous maxim, "who loves not wine, wife and song, remains a fool his life long." I heard it sung with unlimited applause at a Sunday night revel last winter and the singer was encored until he was exhausted. My German friends have solemnly said it over to me as a fearful warning to mend my ways and the other day I heard a toper in a country inn quote it for the edification of another who appeared slightly backward at the beer mug. Luther's theology is not received in every part of the Fatherland but every genuine German can without scruple subscribe and swear to his maxim, "who loves not wine, wife and song, remains" a fool his life long."

In the quarter of the city on the opposite side of the Elbe is the Japanese Palace, which contains a few collections of various kinds and the royal library of 500,000 volumes, 2,000 specimens of early typography, 4,000 manuscripts and 30,000 maps. I was not guilty of coveting any of the jewels in the Green Vault, but among these treasures I am afraid I broke one of the commandments pretty badly. So we are by nature and I cannot say that I am more rational than the others. I smiled with pitying contempt when I saw a costly but useless trinket upon which some wretch spent a quarter of a century of work, and yet when I look at the musty volumes that are unread and forgotten, I sometimes doubt whether the laborious authors have accomplished more than the man who devoted his space of life to the carving of a toy. But then let every one tramp in his own chosen tread-mill, and if he thinks it is heaven do not try to undeceive him. " Where ignorance is bliss, 'tis folly to be wise."

In a little street back of the Japanese Palace there is a three-story building which ought to be held in honor by every true lover of the muses. Here once lived Dr. Christian Gottfried Koerner ; here one famous poet was born; and here dozens of Germany's greatest men have met on terms of closest friendship. In June, 1874, when Schiller was in Mannheim writing for the theater, sick in body and still sicker at heart, he was surprised to receive an elegantly embroidered pocket-book with four portraits and letters from Leipzig. That packet was from Dr. Koerner, and his encouragement brought new life to the poet and began a friendship that was only terminated by the cold hand of death. In the following year Schiller went to Dresden, where his new found friend had settled, and was received with open arms by his admirer. The kind hearted doctor aided him in escaping pecuniary want and he soon recovered his mental and physical vigor. The years 1786 and 1787 he spent at his friend's house in writing Don Carlos and parts of other works. "I have now finally attained," he wrote to a friend, "what my most ardent wishes aimed at. In the midst of our dear ones here I am lifted up as though in heaven." During the summer months he composed in a little house in a vineyard a short distance up the Elbe. It is a pleasant hillside close to the river, affording excellent views of the stream and adjacent fields and is now thickly dotted with villas. In 1801 Schiller visited his friend the second time and was equally delighted. Among the others who were on intimate terms with the Koerner family were such famous men as Goethe, Nicoli, the Humboldts, the Schlegels and Novalis. In the year 1788 when the unfortunate Mozart was on one of his journeys he became acquainted with Dr. Koerner and " Aunt Doris, " the Doctor's sister-in-law, drew his portrait in pencil.

In the midst of such refined surroundings Theodore Koerner, the famous poet, was born, September 23, 1791. He grew up in those painful days of Napoleon's tyrannical rule and all his aspirations were directed toward the redeeming of his Fatherland. When the nation awoke in 1813 and all classes rushed to arms, the poet laid down his books and seized the sword. With hundreds of students and men of mental power he donned the black uniform of Luetzow's Volunteers, and fought and sang like a true poet. A few hours before his death he wrote a song to his sword, his iron bride. On the 26th of August, 1813, he fell in the battle near Gadebusch, 19 miles from Schwerin. A small volume contains all that Koerner wrote, but the book continues to be popular, and has appeared in a dozen different forms. The Germans love the man too well to forget the poet. Dresden has erected a large statue to his memory, and modern painters have given him a place in those battle pictures which adorn the galleries of the capital. Theodore Koerner's name will live as long as the nation preserves the memory of the tyranny of Napoleon and the rising of the people in 1813.

Over the door of this remarkable house are two medallion portraits of Schiller and Koerner, cast from a cannon captured in the last war with France. The three front rooms on the ground floor are used for a museum of articles relating to the distinguished persons connected with the house. The collection comprises a large number of autographs of prominent characters in the Napoleonic wars and the most varied kinds of mementos of Theodore Koerner and his father's family. There are the watch, ring, vest, epaulets, and officer's sash which the poet wore when he fell. And then, too, they show the fruitless amulet which his sweetheart hung around his neck to ward off the hostile bullets. The library-room contains a large number of books relating to Schiller and the Koerners and the cases and desk which belonged to the doctor. A large quantity of manuscripts of Theodore Koerner are shown, some of them dating from his earliest years. One almost believes that they have every scrap of paper on which he ever wrote. The chief custodian is completely absorbed in his charge and buys or begs the minutest relics of his dear poet as though they were diamonds. It is nearly a monomania with him, and of all the similar museums on earth I think he has the most complete. Over the door of the house is the quotation from Goethe's Tasso : " The place a noble man has trod is sanctified : after a hundred years resound his word and deed to the grandson again."

After three days' stay in Dresden I felt ready to move on toward Leipzig and accordingly embarked on an Elbe steamer for Meissen, which I reached in a few hours. It was market day and the squares and narrow streets were filled with peasants and their baskets of fruit and vegetables. The country people of Saxony have no picturesque costume to make them remarkable, but their honest, cheerful faces leave a good impression upon the stranger.

Meissen is one of the oldest towns in Saxony and looks rather quaint even to-day. Upon the Castle Hill there is a group of old buildings, the most imposing of which is the cathedral, which was founded in the thirteenth century. It is one of the most pleasing of the smaller structures of that kind which I have seen. Upon entering the church one first passes through the Princes' Chapel, which is the burial place of the ancestors of the present royal house of Saxony. The most of the tombs are covered with large, smooth slabs of bronze or brass, in which life-size portraits are carved together with the inscriptions. The audience room of the cathedral has a simple grandeur of column and vaulting that one cannot soon forget. The custodian showed us a few curiosities and then led us to a point in the rear of the cathedral, from which we had an extensive view of the Elbe valley and the distant hills.

The old castle of the fifteenth century adjoins the church, but I did not stop to visit it. An ancient bridge with battlements leads from the Castle Hill to the Afra-Fels upon which there is an old abbey which was converted into a school in 1543. In the last century Gellert and Lessing were among the pupils. The institution was governed upon monkish principles and pious meditation and Latin occupied most of the time. This rigid monastic life would have been oppressive to many but it proved congenial to the spirit of the young Lessing, who was destined to regenerate German literature. He found endless pleasure in the miscellaneous reading of his leisure hours and all through life he looked back with wistful gaze at the happy years which he spent at Meissen.

I next descended the hill, passed through the quaint old town and took the steamer down the river to Riesa. The following morning I went by railway to Leipzig, the "little Paris," as it was called in the last century. As soon as I left the station I entered a park-like square adorned with statues and bordered by extensive buildings. A short distance farther are the theaters and famous university. After seeking for Goethe's house in vain, I went toward the market square where I obtained a glimpse of Auerbach's famous cellar. Every street seemed to be full of book-stores for there are about three hundred in the city besides the eighty large printing houses. The publishers in all parts of Germany have branch offices in Leipzig and the trade has no equal in Europe. During the Jubilate Fair, dealers from a distance throng here and the industry has reached such an extent that the book-dealers have their own exchange.

These great fairs occur three times a year, and the trade comprehends various articles, but especially furs, leather, cloth, woolen ware, glass and linen. They are attended by thirty or forty thousand merchants from all parts of Europe and the East. The value of the annual sales is said to reach the enormous average of fifty millions of dollars.

After the fairs, books and university, Leipzig is perhaps best known to fame on account of the bloody four days' battle of the allied armies against Napoleon, which began on the 16th of October, 1813, and ended on the 19th, when the French started upon their retreat to the Rhine. The scene of this "battle of nations," (Voelkerschlacht), as the Germans call it, was in the extensive plain southeast of the city. I left the Grimma Gate toward evening to visit the famous spot. The ground rises very gradually from Leipzig and forms a slight elevation two miles south of the city. Beyond this the plain seems nearly level, although a nearer view discloses some minor irregularities. The highest part of the ridge lies near Thonberg in the midst of cultivated fields, and is to-day called Napoleon's Hill, because the Emperor watched the decisive battle of the 19th from that spot. The summit is planted with trees and flowers and surmounted by a monument. A square pedestal bears a bronze cast representing a three-cornered hat, sword, map and field glass lying upon a cushion.

Immediately adjoining the monument is a small shed, where nourishing drinks are sold to the patriotic pilgrims who come hither in crowds upon Sundays and holidays. There is perhaps no monument of any consequence in Germany which has not a restaurant near at hand. An atmosphere of tobacco smoke and a mug of beer seem to sharpen a German's appreciation of the beautiful and put him in a suitable frame of mind to meditate upon the heroic deeds of his forefathers. If the dealers in these delectable articles were alive to their interests they would be assiduous students of history and untiring advocates of the erection of numberless monuments.

From Napoleon's Hill I continued my walk southward. As it became thoroughly dark I reached the village of Probstheyda, which was the center of the French position. As it was already late I stopped at the inn for the night. The following morning I walked some distance farther to the monument to the memory of Prince Schwarzenberg, the leader of the allied armies. It is a simple rectangular block of granite, with an inscription recording that it was erected by his widow and his three sons. It is surrounded by a grove laid out in walks and the custodian exhibits a few bones and balls from the great battle. They were very insignificant in comparison to those at Waterloo but it is a rule with relics that the supply is in exact proportion to the demand. If the Germans wished it, I suppose the English work-shops could supply them with as many and as varied "genuine" mementos of the conflicts as they do for Waterloo.

A few steps beyond this is an elevation called the Monarchs' Hill, from a tradition that the three rulers of Prussia, Russia and Austria stood there when they received news of the victory of the 18th. It is marked by a plain pointed monument of iron, and, I will add, is fortified with a restaurant.

The Grimma Gate, through which I returned, is the place where the allies first forced their way into Leipzig on the 19th. A neighboring square, where they made their first stand, is marked by a monument of balls that were found in the city and environs. When the French left the town arrangements were made to blow up the bridge over the Elster after all had passed, but the man who was charged with this duty became confused and set fire to the explosives too soon. By this fatal mistake the entire rear guard was cut off, and either fell into the hands of the enemy or perished miserably in the stream. Prince Poniatowsky leaped his horse into the river, but the current carried him down and he was seen no more. Two monuments in the western part of the city mark the spot where the bridge stood and the place where the unfortunate prince was drowned. There have been few more terrific conflicts than this battle of the nations which the German historians are wont to compare to that victorious repulse of foreign tyranny which the tribes made under Herman in the Teutoburg Forest in the spring time of the northern race.

" Where is the village of Lutzen?" I asked a railroad official as I dismounted from the Leipzig train at Durrenberg station.

" It's no village—it's a town," was the short reply.

" Well, where is it and how far is it?" I asked further, for I was going to Lutzen, and whether it was a village or a town was a matter of minor importance. " It's in that direction," returned the man in uniform, pointing toward the southeast, "and it's six quarters of an hour if you march well."

Upon further inquiry I learned that I had come too far by railroad and would have to go back a few miles over the the ground I had just passed. This was not very welcome news, as I am not such an ambitious pedestrian as I was in Southern Austria, and shall not undertake any more three hundred mile walks very soon again. The July sun is not at all stimulating and photographs and books are accumulating so fast on my hands as to make my knapsack "swell wisably," as the lamented Weller would say. There is nothing better than a good volume of some favorite author to drive away weariness and home-sickness and make one forget the beery and smoky atmosphere of the country inns, but when I plod along the hot and dusty roads with my pack on my back I feel decidedly of the opinion that books have a specific gravity that is not equalled by lead.

But it was nearly seven o'clock in the evening and I had a distance of "six quarters of an hour" to walk and the best thing that I could do was to set off and show that I could "march well." The country for miles around Leipzig is a plain that exhibits but very slight undulations of the ground. It presents many advantages for a fair conflict and has been the scene of more great battles than any other region in Germany.

The waving fields of golden grain looked peaceful enough as I left Durrenberg. The lazily revolving fans of the numerous windmills supplied the place of trees in the landscape. Interspersed among these stand the lofty and slender chimneys of the coal mines which dot the country in every direction, emitting constant streams of smoke as though the forge of Vulcan itself was busy at work under this quiet plain.

I had not proceeded far until a shepherd told me of a nearer way which led through a number of rustic villages. The houses of these little communities are surrounded by great fences but the hearts of the noble Saxons stand open toward strangers. I knew how to appreciate the kind greetings which I received from old and young, for I felt the contrast which it made to the hard, unfriendly stares and sullen answers I had met with in Austria. The toddling infants lisped their good evening! to me as I passed and the same cheering words were repeated by the stout toilers and by the aged veterans whose husky voices were as undefined as the babes.

The plain in this neighborhood contains a sort of turf, the preparation of which gives occupation to many villagers. When it is first brought in, it is scarcely distinguishable from dark valley soil. They then mix it with water and knead it with their feet, as the Swabians tread their grapes. After this process is finished it is moulded into blocks like bricks and left to dry in the sun. In every hamlet I saw groups of both sexes working at the turf with feet and ankles stained as black as midnight.

I suppose I did not march well for the golden hues of the beautiful sunset had left the sky and it was nearly nine o'clock when I reached Lutzen, whose two church towers I had seen from afar. I was soon eating bread and butter and terrific country cheese in the inn of the three lime-trees and enlarging my knowledge of Lutzen. I was told that the town had about four thousand inhabitants and had remained true to the results of the battle, for there are not more than a couple of hundred Catholics in the place.

The following morning I set out to view the battle-field in company with a middle-aged merchant who considered an American worthy of his attention. The scene of the famous conflict was in the plain toward the north and east of Lutzen and the monument is fully a mile distant. The importance of the battle for the preservation of German Protestantism and free thought can hardly be overestimated. For though their strongest champion, Gustavus Adolphus, perished on that day, and though the result by no means ended the horrible war, still the Catholic power never recovered completely from the blow and the conflict marks a turning point in history.

On the evening of the 5th of November, 1632, Wallenstein lay with the imperial army before Lutzen, waiting for the Swedish king to attack. The same night Gustavus Adolphus led his troops in the field opposite the enemy and both sides prepared for the battle of the morrow, upon the result of which rested the fame of both generals and the welfare of their causes. Wallenstein had made a feeble sort of intrenchment by deepening the ditches along the highway, which he defended by a battery. This proved the main point of the conflict, and the guns were repeatedly taken and lost. When morning dawned a thick fog hid friend and foe, and not until 11 o'clock did the battle at length begin. Gustavus knelt in prayer before the ranks, and then the army sang Luther's famous hymn to martial music : "Ein' feste Burg ist unser Gott." With cries of "God with us!" they advanced to the attack and were fiercely met by the imperialists, whose watchword was "Jesus Maria!" Hither and thither swayed the tide of success. The ditches were crossed and re-crossed. The slain lay in heaps. When Gustavus returned from a victorious charge upon the left wing of the imperialists he heard that his own troops were giving away at another quarter and hastened to the rescue. But his near-sightedness led him too close to the enemy, and a ball shattered his arm. The king became faint and requested his companion, the Duke of Lauenburg, to conduct him quietly to the rear in order that his army might not loose spirit. But as they were doing this another ball entered the king's back and he fell from his horse. The imperialists plundered the corpse and the cry soon passed along the Swedish ranks that the king was dead. Like fiends they rose up, burning for revenge. The enemy gave way before their irresistable rage and were thrown into disorder. The imperialist powder train took fire and the terrific explosions increased their bewilderment. A disastrous retreat seemed unavoidable when the furious Pappenheim dashed up from Halle with eight regiments of cavalry. He turned the scale for a time, but soon fell mortally wounded and night left the battle undecided. Under cover of the darkness the imperialists retreated and the field and artillery remained in the hands of the Swedes. Nine thousand dead covered the plain.

Such is a brief outline of the battle of Lutzen, the most famous of the Thirty Years' War. After a walk of about a mile we came to a little park by the roadside which contains the monument. It consists of a granite block covered by a large Gothic canopy of iron. The vaulting is painted blue and perforated with star-shaped openings through which the light shines making it seem like a portion of the sky. A stone in the rear of the monument bears the inscription in German of older date : "Gustavus Adolphus, King of Sweden, fell here in battle for spiritual freedom, November 6th, 1632." My friend told me that the place was visited by a great many Swedes and that memorial services were held here every year which were attended by large numbers of the neighboring people.

After returning to Lutzen I walked three miles toward the south to the village of Gross-Goerschen, where the fierce battle between Napoleon and the allies took place, May 2d, 1813. As I did not see anything but an iron cross covered by a canopy my enthusiasm was sensibly diminished when I returned from the six mile walk under the mid-day sun.

I have never yet been treated with such distinguished honor as I was at the inn of the three lime-trees at Lutzen. Thousands are wearing themselves away physically and mentally in order to attain the dear satisfaction of being lionized, and yet if they would pack their effects into a knapsack and come over the ocean they could enjoy that pleasure at less expense. Every interval in the dealing out of beer the landlord devoted to conversation with me, and whenever a fresh lot of topers came in he would say in much the same tone that the menagerie exhibitors use : " This is an American ; he was born in America ; his parents are still in America ; and he is going back to America. Gentlemen, this is an American." Then followed universal admiration and numberless questions. I was finally compelled to tear myself away, for otherwise I should have spent many hours in " waiting just a little longer." The landlord gave me directions as to the shortest way across the fields, asked me to write to him and bade me a solemn farewell.

I walked six miles to Corbetha station, but did not have enthusiasm enough to go five miles farther to Rossbach, where "old Fritz," with 22,000 men, defeated a combined force of 60,000 French and German troops, on the 5th of November, 1757. I contented myself with looking across the plain and thinking of those doggerel verses in which the people celebrated the result :

"And when the famous Fred'rick comes,
And pats upon his trousers,
Then run the royal regiments,
The French and their carousers."

As there was no train in the evening I walked six miles to Merseberg and went the following morning to Halle.

After spending a couple of hours there I again entered the train and rode across the monotonous country toward the Elbe. Late in the afternoon we passed the river and stopped at the station at Wittenberg, where I dismounted.

My course in Europe has been somewhat erratic, but there are a few places which I wished to visit especially, and Wittenberg is among the number. If all the great past in German history was blotted out, if modern Tetzels still sold drafts on the grace of God unopposed, Wittenberg would nevertheless be a name forever famous, and its connection with Hamlet would preserve its memory to the latest generation. But Wittenberg was not destined to exist through the ages like a geographical name in a Homeric oration. It has woven itself into the vital interests of our race, and will ever be remembered and blessed as a signal post in the eternal progress of the human mind. However much the principles then set forth may be modified, the child will not forget the parent and free man will ever look with thankful hearts toward Wittenberg, where the sturdy pioneers struck boldly and manfully to vindicate the right of individual thought.

The city at present contains 12,500 inhabitants and lies about a quarter of a mile from the Elbe. Down to 1875 it was a fortress of the empire and the large earthern walls and ramparts are almost entirely preserved. The broad ditch has degenerated into an ugly morass which cannot be beneficial to the sanitary welfare of the people. The road from the station crosses the trench upon a solid embankment, and enters the city by the Elster Gate. Immediately adjoining the wall upon the left is a large building called the Augusteum, now a theological seminary, which contains the portion of the old Augustinian monastery which Luther used as a private dwelling. I entered the main door and crossed the inner court to the wing opposite the entrance, which bears the memorial tablet, recording the fact that "Dr." Martin Luther lived and worked there from 1508 to 1546. It is remarkable with what tenacity the Germans persist in prefixing the academical title to the reformer's name. When one is venerated in English we designate him by a single, simple word, feeling convinced that there is no danger of his being lost in the crowd. "Mr." Moses scarcely startles us more than "Mr." Shakespeare or "Mr." Milton. Doctor Johnson is the only person in our literature, whom I can think of, who has been coupled with a college title, and that is undoubtedly because Boswell has preserved the conversation of his contemporaries.'

When Luther came to Wittenberg from Erfurt in 1508 to take the chair of philosophy in the university, he lived in the monastery, and after the reformation had changed the order of things, the Elector of Saxony presented him the house for his own use. The custodian shows several large halls which have been restored in the ancient style, and which contain a number of portraits of distinguished men of that century. One of these apartments is destined to contain the Luther Museum, in which the scattered mementos of the great reformer are to be collected.

From here the custodian conducted me to the family apartments which are in the second story and face the courtyard. After passing a small ante-room, we entered the principal chamber which was the scene of the various domestic as well as the intellectual labors of the reformer. The ceiling, wainscot and floor are all old, and the entire apartment bears a strong resemblance to the main room of the peasant's house of to-day. The windows contain the original panes, which are small and round like the bottom of a bottle. They are so imperfect that it is impossible to see through them, but this want is supplied by little doors which may perhaps be better designated as peep holes. By one of the windows there is a rudely constructed double chair in which Luther and his Catharine sat face to face in the sweet hours of leisure. In the center of the room stand the large family table with sliding top which served for the varied needs of household economy. In one corner is a large stove made of tiles which bear reliefs representing the apostles and allegorical figures from designs by Luther himself. In another room, which is much smaller, there are some relics of the reformer. Besides a couple of the inimitable drinking cups, there are some specimens of embroidery by his wife, one piece representing his portrait. On the wall hangs a full length picture of Luther which was printed from a wood engraving by Hans Lust, the first printer of Wittenberg, who also published the first editions of Luther's translation of the Bible, and his other writings.

This interesting suite of rooms has attracted a great many visitors. October 14th, 1712, Peter the Great inspected the historic place and wrote his name on one of the doors in Russian. The spot has been covered with glass and the characters are still visible. The Czar wanted to take Luther's glass goblet with him as a memento, but it was refused, and so he dashed it to pieces. This is certainly a very characteristic anecdote. The fragments are still exhibited. I found the names of a great many Americans in the register, and among the others were Minister White and his wife. Two other fellow-country men were visiting the place at the same time with me and so it seems that Wittenberg enjoys a fair share of the attention of Americans.

A few houses beyond the Augusteum stands the dwelling of Luther's companion and assistant, Philip Melanchthon. It is a tall, narrow edifice with antique gable and quaint windows. An inscription records that Melanchthon lived, taught and died there.

A few steps farther brings one to the building that was once used by the famous University which Elector Frederick the Wise established in 1502. The encouragement and protection, which Luther received from the students, facilitated his work and they deserve a place in the regard of posterity. In 1817 the University was incorporated with that of Halle and the building is now used as an infantry barrack.

In the square before the old town hall stands Schadow's statue of Luther and Drake's statue of Melanchthon, each under a Gothic baldachin. The former is considered an excellent representation and the pedestal bears Luther's words: "If it is the work of God, it will stand ; if it is the work of man, it will fall."

In the southwest corner of the square stands the dwelling house of the famous Lucas Cranach, the painter, who has immortalized the features of Luther and many of the Saxon princes. He died in 1533.

The last building toward the west upon the left side of this principal street is the old castle church which was erected in the fifteenth century. Luther preached here frequently before the conflict with the Pope and upon the double doors of wood which opened out upon the street he nailed his ninety-five theses which were so much in accordance with the spirit of the times (Zeit-Geist) that they spread immediately throughout Germany and changed the current of future thought. This was on the 31st day of October, 1517, the birthday of the reformation. During the bombardment of Wittenberg in 1760 the famous doors fell a prey to the flames. In 1858 King Frederick William IV. caused them to be replaced by metal doors bearing a copy of the theses in the Latin original.

In the church opposite these doors are the graves of Luther and Melanchthon. They are marked by small tablets of bronze which lie a few inches below the level of the pavement and are usually covered with wooden lids.

Monarchs too have stood by this grave and even enemies of the reformer have felt a worthy respect for the dead. When Charles the Fifth captured the city in 1557, during the Schmalkalden war, he asked to see the grave of the brave man who had met him without fear at Worms and resisted him throughout his life. As the monarch stood in solemn silence before the narrow tablet which covered the ashes of his enemy, that conscience-forcer and thousand-murderer, the Duke of Alva came forward and asked that the heretic's bones be dug up and burned. Then the Emperor turned to that fiend—and Charles the Fifth never was greater than in that moment: "Let him rest in peace," said he, "I make war with the living, not with the dead." If the Duke of Alva had had one drop of noble blood in his veins he would have slunk away to some dark corner where the sun could never shine.

The pulpit from which Luther preached is still preserved and is used at the present day. Before the altar are the tombs of two Saxon electors, covered with large bronze reliefs. One marks the resting place of Frederick the Wise, who was Luther's patron and friend. Just outside of the Elster Gate to the left of the road leading to the station, stands a tall oak surrounded by a small park. A tablet records that Dr. Martin Luther burned the papal bull of excommunication on that spot, December 10, 1520. This act placed an impassable gulf between him and Rome. I spent the rest of the evening of my visit in walking down to the Elbe, and rambling through the meadow. When it became dark I returned to the quiet town and sought a hotel. The next morning I came on to Berlin.

The traveler who walks through Berlin's famous street Unter den Linden for the first time, must ever be impressed with the magnificence of the German Capital. At the western extremity of the thoroughfare stands the stately Brandenburg Gate, an imitation of the Propylae at Athens, which is surmounted by a car of victory, that was carried off to Paris by Napoleon in 1807 but recovered in 1814. From this point the broad avenue extends toward the east with two fine rows of lime-trees in the middle from which it derives its name. On each side rise palaces, dwellings and grand hotels and at the crossings of side streets one obtains glimpses of long lines of glittering shops which extend away as far as the eye can reach.

At the western end of the avenue of lime-trees stands Rauch's great equestrian statue of Frederick which is regarded as the finest monument in Europe. To the right is the plain palace of the Emperor, and back of it the royal library. To the left are the academy and university buildings. And then before one stretches out a long square and the view is terminated in every direction by numerous statues of warriors and palaces and public buildings. Critics may find fault with the details but every stranger is sensible of the magnificence of the combined effect. Although Berlin has such rivals as Dresden and Munich everyone must acknowledge that she is a worthy head of the empire.

As one advances farther and crosses the bridge over the Spree, which is adorned with statues, he obtains a view of the old royal palace upon the right and the grand colonnade of the museum upon the left. Statues of famous generals rise in every direction, for this is the Walhalla of a military nation. Where one finds one monument to a private person he meets a dozen to soldiers. Lessing and Kant have a place in the groups on the pedestal of the statue of Frederick the Great but it is at the rear part, which is very characteristic.

The old royal palace is an immense rectangular edifice of dingy appearance which is like many similar structures the result of the labors of several centuries. It has two broad courts and several lofty gateways, which give some idea of the pompous stiffness of the "good old times." The palace is used now principally on grand occasions and its magnificent salons form one of the chief sights of Berlin.

The old museum contains a collection of antique sculptures upon the ground floor and a gallery of paintings upon the floor above. The new museum stands just back of the old one and is connected with it by a gallery which passes over the intervening street. It is magnificently arranged and the walls are covered with frescoes, some of which are masterpieces of art. The upper floor contains a very full collection of casts from famous sculptures of all ages. The ground floor contains a fine ethnographical museum which affords a good idea of the civilization of India, China and Japan. Next to this is a collection of northern antiquities which have been found at different places in Germany. From these the specialist can form an acquaintance with the habits of that sturdy race which resisted the progress of the proud Romans.

But by far the most valuable and interesting collection is the Egyptian museum, which is one of the best of the kind in Europe. It owes its existence mainly to the labors of the famous Egyptologist Lepsius who brought most of the articles with him upon his return from his scientific researches in the land of the Pharoahs.

The Berlin University is established in a large building nearly opposite to the dwellings of the Emperor and Crown Prince. It was formerly the palace of Prince Henry, brother of Frederick the Great and was presented to the University in 1809 by Frederick William III. It is of the approved style of palaces, and consists of three wings which form the three sides of a rectangular court, leaving the fourth side open toward the street. It requires but a glance to determine that the place is now a university for the students are always standing around the doors, like bees about a hive.

Berlin is without doubt the worst police ridden town in Germany. Perhaps the proximity of Bismarck had some influence in causing this. In order to look at the books in the public reading room of the royal library one is compelled to exhibit his passport. I have been in a good many libraries but this is something new to me. One is treated better by the librarians even in Austria, that benighted land where every country inn keeper and cross-road policeman has the right to demand a passport.

I never had any disagreeable experience with the antiquated use of passports in Germany until I came here. I have a room in a private family and was compelled to take my passport to the police headquarters when my arrival was reported. The officer questioned me closely as to how long I was in Vienna and other points which I have touched during my travels. Under similar circumstances in Austria, Italy or other parts of Germany one is only required to state his name, age, residence and profession to his landlord who reports them to the police. I am thoroughly convinced that the freedom of moving around is not the least valuable liberty which we enjoy in America.

The Prussians may without dispute claim that they have come nearer than any other nation to reducing man to a machine. The ambition of everyone is to get a place where he will have a fixed monotonous task, that requires no enterprise, but which affords a regular salary and a pension. These men seem to think a uniform the natural garb of the male portion of the human race. Not merely the thousands of soldiers have a military appearance, but men of many different classes. I suppose if a Prussian were to awake some time and find himself in citizen's dress in a free country he would be more astonished than the drunkard who was washed and put into the duke's bed and when he awoke from his stupor was treated like the duke himself and told that he had long been sick.

In traveling about I find a great many little variations in the customs. Each one laughs at the expression of his neighbor but I accommodate myself to each as it comes. For instance the Austrian never says adieu or anything similar. When he parts with friend or foe he always says, "I recommend myself," as though one would think any better of him because he recommended himself. Many, many years ago, when Berlin was smaller and the waters of the Spree were clearer, the natives were accustomed to say to each other at the eating hours, "blessed is the meal time," or some similar greeting as is peculiar to the eupeptic Germans. But in these latter days the matter is shortened and the people merely say "meal time," taking for granted that it is blessed. When I go to the restaurant for dinner, my fellow-boarders look up from those immense fruit dishes which they misuse as beer glasses, and say "meal time!" And then like a Roman in Rome I say "meal time!" just as though everyone after a European breakfast was not distinctly conscious that the hour for dinner was at hand.

CHAPTER XIV.

FROM GERMANY TO SWEDEN.—ACROSS THE BALTIC.—STOCKHOLM.—A TRIP TO UPSALA.—SWEDISH LIQUOR LAWS.

STOCKHOLM, SWEDEN, August 9th, 1880.
I left Berlin after an eighteen days' visit, by train for Stettin, where I embarked on the steamer Tilsit for Stockholm. We started at one o'clock, but it was almost dark when we reached the sea. The Oder expands at its mouth into a large lake called the Haff, which is separated from the Baltic by two extensive islands. After spending a couple of hours in descending the river and crossing this body of water we entered the channel between the two islands and finally reached Swinemuende, a town at its outlet, where an hour was consumed in taking on freight. The lighthouse lantern was already burning as we at last steamed out into the Baltic, and the pilot with his little boat dropped into the rear.

The Tilsit is a small vessel, and the officers and crew have not that supreme contempt for the rest of the human race which is characteristic of the sailors on the Atlantic. As night came on a portion of the men and some of the passengers formed in groups in the friendly warmth of the funnel and then began the usual inquiries of Germans as to whence, whither and why. When one speaks with a sailor on the ocean he almost invariably finds that he has circumnavigated the globe a dozen of times, and made numberless other voyages, but these Baltic seamen have never passed the Skager Rack and know as little of the mysteries of the Atlantic as the veriest backwoodsman in America. When it came my turn to inform the German assembly where I had come from, the old weather-beaten tars shook their heads in wonder and said, "My, how a man can travel in the world!"

The first night at sea passed quietly enough and when I awoke the next morning we could see the little island of Bornholm which at present belongs to Denmark. Later we saw Oland but Gothland was too far to the east to be visible.

On the afternoon of the second day the islands on the coast opposite Stockholm came in sight. After taking a pilot on board we entered the inlet which leads to the Swedish capital. All around us lay innumerable little islands of primeval granite. Not a rent nor upheaval could be detected in the adamantine substance. Millions of years have chipped small fragments off here and there and the glaciers and floods of the ages have worn away the angles until all has a rounded outline, but the dark colored granite bears the grim look of eternity. A stunted growth of pine has found root in the shallow depth of soil that has lodged in the hollows but is insufficient to conceal the dusky rock. Upon the outermost headland lies a mean little village which is peopled by pilots, fishermen and government officers. After passing this we went for miles without seeing a human habitation. The channel sometimes broadened into a lake, while at other places there was scarcely room to pass. But everywhere the scenery was the same. All around us the low granite islands with their fringes of pine terminated the view. Although the weather was pleasant the scene wore a look of winter which almost made one shiver. At such a place, under the influence of these peculiar surroundings one could easily become enwrapt in dreams of Thor and Wodin and all the gods of the northern heaven.

Stockholm has an exceedingly beautiful situation. Some call it the Swedish Venice, while others think it has some resemblance to Geneva. One of my German friends designated it as the Northern Naples. The channel which connects Lake Malaren with the sea is at this point bounded on each side by long hills of naked rock, and bears a number of islands of considerable size. The city was founded upon the islands, which afforded protection from hostile invaders, and gave access to the extensive harbors. After the early wars had been succeeded by more peaceful times, the city expanded upon the mainland in each direction. At present the city has two characteristic features. The divisions upon the mainland are built upon hillsides, and may be said to resemble Naples or Genoa, while the part between these two, which lie upon the islands, reminds one of Venice.

On the evening of my arrival I left the Stettin steamer in company with a German from St. Petersburg, and after finding a hotel, we set out to look at the city.

A short walk from the wharf brought us to the Royal Palace, which is an immense building, enclosing a court, but not very striking in style. Beyond this a bridge leads to a small island, from which the most famous places in the city can be seen. The well-known poet, Tegner, thus describes the scene : " How grandly do the tower, heroes' statues, palace and temple of the muses reflect themselves in the stream, and evening red over the Riddarholm, where, beneath marble, Sweden's honor sleeps."

Another bridge connects this island with a square on the main land which bears a monument to Gustavus Adolphus. A short walk brought us to another square, upon which stand statues of Charles XIII., the last of the Holstein line, and Charles XII., "the madman of the North." At another square where there is a statue of the famous chemist, Berzelius, we found a cafe that was thronged with visitors. It seems to me that the national traits of character have been changed completely. From the time of Charles the Twelfth back into hoar antiquity where the clear sunlight of historical fact disappears and the investigator is guided only by the dim and treacherous gleam of tradition and fable, back through all the ages the Swede distinguished himself as one whose only delight was in battle. Heaven was reserved for those alone who died a violent death, and the sluggards who waited till disease consumed them were to go to the land of fog which was the abode of evil doers. Whoever attempts to read the Swedish history must be confused by the long array of kings who won the throne by murder and perished in turn by the knife of the assassin. It is like the bloody finis of the Niebelungen Lied or like the horrible crimes of the first royal house of France. Later the warlike Swedes under Gustavus Adolphus stemmed the victorious career of Tilly and Wallenstein and under Charles the Twelfth defeated many times their number of Saxons,

Danes and Russians. But to-day the Swedish soldier is a very mild looking man, and the most of the people, far from being quarrelsome, are on the contrary very polite and friendly.

One of the characteristics long held as belonging to the Swede is the love for strong drink. In later years efforts have been made to alleviate the bad effects of this appetite, and they are said to have been in some measure successful. The districts of the country have what we in Ohio would call local option; that is, a majority can prohibit the sale of spirits. If the trade is not entirely abolished, recourse is had to the Gothenburg system by which a company is empowered by the authorities to buy all the licenses and control the entire sale. The officers of these companies have independent salaries, and the receipts, less the expenses and five per cent. interest, are handed over to the civil department, which expends them in caring for the paupers and infirm who are the victims of drink. Thus the community is relieved of one great burden and the vice is made to pay the expenses it causes. The system was adopted in Stockholm in 1877.

On a headland opposite the royal palace stands the National Museum, a large building which contains a number of very fine collections which do honor to the Swedish Capital. The picture gallery contains about thirteen hundred paintings, which represent the various national schools, and are particularly rich in works of modern artists, whose subjects are taken principally from life among the peasants. Though these may have little artistic merit, most people will find them more interesting than many of the dusty works of the old masters. It seems to be a characteristic of our age to seek the poetical and beautiful in every day life instead of aping the worn out toggery of Greece and Rome.

Next to the picture gallery are two collections of armor and clothing worn by Swedish kings. The former is insignificant compared to the similar museums at Vienna, but there is enough of historical interest attached to the royal costumes to make them important in the eyes of the visitor. After a hurried look at the array of faded finery one reaches a case which contains some articles of clothing which were worn by Gustavus Adolphus and the blood stained sheet in which his body was wrapped after the battle of Lutzen. In the middle of the room stands the horse which he rode when he fell. Art has preserved the famous steed, and he looks almost as animated as he did on that eventful day.

In a case opposite these articles are some suits which belonged to Charles the Twelfth. There are a few relics of his stay at Bender as the guest of the Sultan. But the chief claim upon the vistor's interest is the costume which he wore when he fell in the trenches before Frederickshald, November 30th, 1718. The queer looking blue coat, yellow vest and trousers and long boots are all preserved, and in the black hat one can see the large hole through which the bullet passed which caused his death.

I lingered some time looking at these relics of Sweden's heroes, and then went down to see the historical museum, which is the most valuable in the building, as it is the most complete of its kind in the world. I do not suppose that any nation has a better exhibition of its various industries, from the earliest times to the present, than Sweden possesses here. First comes the flint period, which extended from the remotest times down to about a thousand years before our era. The articles of this age are very similar to those which antiquarians gather in America, and represent the earliest devices of the human brain. Next comes the bronze epoch, when utensils began to be made of metal. This period began about a thousand years before Christ, and lasted until the beginning of our era. The articles are more varied, and display greater skill. Man is beginning to subdue the outer world, and instead of being a stranger, he became the lord. Then comes the iron age, which began in Sweden about the first year of our era. The evolution of human ingenuity creeps gradually forward. The Swede feels stronger, and commerce begins. Coins from many European nations testify to the distances traversed by the venturesome Northmen. Other relics from the middle ages bring the historical survey down to the present time. Were I a Swede, I would be as proud of this museum as any nobleman is of his ancestral record. It is something to be able to trace the progress of our fathers from the crude efforts of the flint period to the myriad sided industry of the present day.

The most sacred place in Stockholm in the eyes of the Swede is the Riddarholm Church, which contains the tombs of the Kings and great Generals. The building is not remarkable in appearance, although the spire is quite prominent. It stands on a little island from which it takes its name. The interior of the church is of the usual form with recesses upon each side which serve as burial chapels. Regular service was held there down to the year 1807.

The oldest tomb is that of King Magnus Ladulas, who died in 1290. In the first chapel to the left of the altar rests the body of the most famous Swede, Gustavus Adolphus. His remains are deposited in a large sarcophagus of green marble.

Opposite the chapel of Gustavus Adolphus is that of Charles the Twelfth where the bones of the "madman of the North" repose in quiet. A recent perusal of Voltaire's excellent history of that monarch had made all the incidents of his eccentric career familiar to me, and I regarded his tomb with an interest which was scarcely exceeded by that which I felt for Gustavus Adolphus. I could not help thinking of the contrast between the paltry heaps of dust which lay inclosed in that marble casket and that wild being who forced a peace from the Danes, defeated myriads of Russians at Narva, and dethroned a Polish King. It is a common thought, but it is one which everyone feels when he stands before a hero's tomb.

The church contains the graves of many other Kings and Queens, but they are hardly as well known to fame as the Great Gustavus and Charles the Twelfth. Among them are the patron of literature, Gustavus the Third, Bernadotte, the founder of the reigning dynasty, and all the last Kings. All of the chapels and the main body of the church are covered with tattered flags and drums, which are trophies of Swedish victories over the Danes, Prussians, Saxons, Poles, Austrians and Russians. The church is opened for visitors three times a week, but the interest seems to be so great in the place that it is constantly thronged with strangers and patriots.

For a person who stays but a few days in Sweden an excursion to Upsala is so convenient that most people are able to make it. Two means of communication are available, the steamer and the railroad. I went there by water and returned by the train. We left Stockholm at 9 in the morning, but it was half past three in the afternoon when we reached our destination. The scenery was somewhat monotonous, but very characteristic of Sweden. Bleak granite hills and cheerless forests of pine were all that could be seen for miles. The steamer passed through a chain of long and narrow lakes that are connected by channels which sometimes are scarcely passable. Many hours went by before we saw a cultivated field, but the neighborhood of Upsala looks much more hospitable. Before reaching the city we left the lake and ascended the narrow river Fyrisa which is not wider than an Ohio canal. The steamer went very slowly and the time seemed unusually long.

There was an excursion party on board and we all went together to the cathedral, which is a large edifice in the French style. Back of the altar is the tomb of Gustavus Vasa who threw off the Danish yoke and founded the independent Kingdom of Sweden. To the right of the altar is the sarcophagus of Erick the Ninth, the national patron saint. He was one of the founders of Swedish Christianity and converted the heathen temple at Upsala into a church. He was finally defeated and slain by the Danes in 1160. Not far from his tomb is the sarcophagus of John the Third, who murdered his brother Erick the Fourteenth. Under the organ loft in the back part of the cathedral lies the body of the celebrated naturalist Linnaeus.

Upsala is very famous now as a university town, and the library contains the only existing fragment of Bishop Ulphilas' Gothic translation of the Bible, which dates from the fourth century. As this is almost the whole source of our knowledge of that language, which is the basis of the German, the manuscript has an inestimable value. Every history of Germany or German literature has something to say of it, and I wanted to see it more than anything else in Upsala. My vexation was boundless when I found that it was impossible to see the manuscript for either love or money.

I solaced myself as much as possible by climbing the castle hill with a Danish student, where we had a fine view of the plain. Upsala was once the residence of the kings and the stronghold of paganism. From the elevation by the castle we could see the three large hills at Gamla Upsala, which are supposed to be tumuli of the Kings. They bear the names of three Northern Gods : Thor, Wodin, and Freyr. After seeing these relics of ancient Sweden we went to the station and took the evening train to Stockholm. I spent the time very pleasantly in talking with two Englishmen, much to the astonishment of our fellow-passengers.

CHAPTER XV.

ALONG THE FINLAND COAST.—THE SIGHTS OF ST. PETERS-

BURG.—THE GREAT CHURCHES.—THE FORTRESS OF

SAINTS PETER AND PAUL.—TYRANNY OF THE CZAR.

St. Petersburg, Russia, Aug. 20th, 1880.
When I left Stettin for Stockholm I intended to go from the latter place to Christiana, Norway, by rail and then return to Germany, via Copenhagen, by steamer. I was so far from expecting to come to St. Petersburg that I had not the slightest desire to enter the domains of the Autocrat of all the Russias. I supposed that it would be difficult to cross the frontiers and that the strict police regulations would be unendurable to a republican. The men on the steamer had a sort of indefinite idea that I was going to see everything in the world, but when they asked me if I intended to visit St. Petersburg, I replied in a very decided negative. But among my fellow passengers from Stettin was a German who has been for twelve years a resident of the Russian capital, and in conversing with him I was convinced not only of the possibility but also of the desirability of a trip to St. Petersburg. When he left me on the second day that we were in Stockholm my plans were so far changed that I told him I would probably follow him by the next boat. Accordingly I made prepartions to leave the

Swedish capital on Tuesday, August 10th. The very first step that I took was indicative of an entry into a different atmosphere. In order to be able to buy a ticket one is compelled not only to have a passport but also to have the vise of the Russian consul. Thirty-five years ago in the good old times a similar measure was necessary everywhere in Europe and this formed one of the principal inconveniences which Taylor encountered on his first series of travels.

When I bought my ticket my passport was taken by the agent and I was told that I would get it again in St. Petersburg. Promptly at the appointed time on Tuesday evening the steamer Finland cast off her lines, slowly turned around and then started on her course. The passengers on the steamer waved their handkerchiefs to their friends on the wharf who answered with the same enthusiasm.

I remained on deck until twelve o'clock but up to that hour we were still in the group of islands which border the Swedish coast. The officers of the boat seemed to be in good humor for they sent up a number of rockets without any other apparent object than to please the passengers. The following morning I awoke at four o'clock and found that we were still running between low granite islands but they were the Alands and we were already within the Russian empire. If one looks at the map of the northern part of the Baltic Sea he immediately supposes that a considerable distance of the passage from Stockholm to Finland would be out of sight of land. But we passed the narrow stretch of open water between the Swedish coast and the Alands by night and during the entire trip from there to St. Petersburg we had land in sight. The sea was as smooth as the most quiet river and even the most sensitive stomachs had no cause to rebel.

Toward noon the channel of a river lay before us and a sailor who was standing on deck near me told me that we were not far from Abo. Upon talking with the seaman I found him a good specimen of his class. He was born in northern Finland, and when very young he ran away from school and became a cabin boy on a ship. He has been fourteen or fifteen years from home, but has never returned although he was once at Abo where he attended a nautical school. At last a year ago he began writing home and now he was on his way to pay his first visit. He said he had written a letter home from India a few weeks before but that his return was entirely unexpected. No one would know him and he would perhaps go and ask his parents for lodging like a stranger. He said he had been in nearly every country on the globe. "Were you in South America?" I asked, he answered yes, and then told me how he had seen the bombardment of a town in the Chilian war. "Were you in India," I asked again. "Oh yes!" he answered and related something about the queer native temples. And so it was with almost every country I could think of. He had been there and was able to tell a little of customs of the people he saw. He had circumnavigated the globe a half dozen times.

As we steamed up the river the town of Abo gradually came in sight. The channel is bordered upon each side by a chain of hills and the town is built upon the slopes, being divided into two parts by the stream. Abo was the capital of Finland and seat of the university until 1827 when the town was nearly destroyed by fire and has never completely recovered. It has at present a population of about twenty thousand.

If the physical character of a country were to determine its nationality one might say that Finland should still belong to Sweden. Both lands have the same appearance on the coast, bleak granite hills with a sparse growth of pine. The official language of the country is Swedish, but even in Abo one begins to see the traces of Russian customs. The first novelty that met our eyes was the appearance of the droskies or carriages that were standing on the wharf. The drivers wear long coats which reach to the ankles and are gathered about the waist by a sash or belt. A low, broad hat of peculiar shape completes the outfit which is very Russian. The droskies are open and have room for but one person. The horses are hitched to the vehicle in a manner that is universally prevalent in this country There are no traces. A short strap binds each shaft to the collar and to keep the shafts spread and prevent them from pressing on the sides of the horses a stout wooden bow is used which passes over the neck of the animal. The Russians call this very practical but a more clumsy arrangement could scarcely be devised.

Abo lies at sixty degrees and twenty-six minutes north latitude and is undoubtedly as near to the pole as I shall ever ago. But notwithstanding this, the weather was, I believe, the warmest I have encountered in my travels. As the steamer lay six hours at the wharf I could think of no more comfortable way of putting in the time than by taking a bath in the river. This would have been far from pleasant upon the same latitude in Greenland.

Toward evening we left Abo and again entered the maze of granite islands. Early next morning we arrived at Hango and at noon we reached Helsingfors where another halt of six hours was made. This city is the capital of Finland and the seat of the university. The coast is fortified for miles on each side of the harbor and six monitors and a few other war vessels were lying in the roads. The two most prominent buildings in Helsingfors are the Greek Catholic Cathedral and the Senate House. Both stand upon elevations above the city and make quite an imposing appearance. The church has five towers resplendent in gilt which glitters in the sun. The Senate House is not so gorgeous, especially upon nearer examination, but still looks very well from a distance.

Finland is quite distinct from Russia, the Czar being but a grand duke. It has a different coinage and a representative system like that which Gustavus Adolphus gave to Sweden. It is considered the best administered province in the empire. The people have a more pleasing character than the Russians and ninety-eight per cent. of the population are Protestants.

In the evening our steamer turned her head once more toward the sea and we soon passed the monitors and forts bristling with cannon. The next day at noon we reached Viburg where I spent the two hours of our stay in walking around the walls and looking at the hideous old castle.

The following morning we passed Cronstadt, the advance guard and sea haven of St. Petersburg, and the two hours later we reached the city. Fog and rain made the outlook anything but encouraging. The gilded spires, which at other times have such a splendid appearance, were lost in the mist. But finally the weather improved and after our passports had been carefully examined and duly stamped we were allowed to go ashore and form our first impressions of the city.

St. Petersburg lies on both banks of the Neva in a low plain which has the double disadvantage of being subject to inundations and difficult of drainage. The gilded spires of its Greek churches made an imposing appearance in the distance, and one's expectations are not disappointed upon a nearer approach. Its streets are as broad as those of any city in America, and its houses are in general well built. It is intersected by a number of canals and the Neva and its branches afford good water communication with the different parts of the city. The main river is crossed by two fine iron bridges and two bridges of boats. Below all these lie the larger steamers and sailing vessels which navigate the Baltic. Above them are the river craft, the lumber rafts and the flat boats which are used to bring down a cargo and are then sold for fire wood.

The most prominent features of a Russian city are the gilded spires of its temples, and the uppermost characteristic of the people is their religion. When I left the Stockholm steamer I crossed the lower bridge, upon which stands a Greek shrine which cost millions of roubles. Every minute one sees the natives bowing before the image. They cross themselves three times and bend their bodies profoundly while doing so. The better classes perform this act of devotion very unobtrusively, but the peasants bow until their heads almost touch the pavement, while their long, straight hair flies in the wind, making with their uncouth garb a very strange appearance. Every house and shop in Russia has a shrine and burning lamp near the door and strangers always bow and cross themselves before they address the inhabitants. I am acquainted with a German whom I met in Stockholm and he told me that his Russian visitors always look around the room for the shrine and upon failing to find it they bow anyhow. He further said that some of his German acquaintances keep images and lamps near the door in order to accommodate the natives.

The Russians have an irresistible thirst for whisky, and I have never seen so many drunken men in any city as in St. Petersburg. On Sunday or a holiday, and the later comes as often as the former, one sees the streets thronged with staggering people. They rarely, however, display any warlike spirit, but hug and kiss each other in a very loving style. Russia must be the cheapest place in the world to get drunk, for the people get the most insignificant wages, and yet indulge in that luxury oftener than the princely paid American laborers could afford. Among my acquaintances here is one of our fellow citizens, who is by no means addicted to temperance principles. I have frequently gone with him into the doggery on the corner, and have there observed that the natives always uncover their heads, bow and cross themselves in adoration of the shrine over the bar just before they drink a four-finger glass of whisky. A German remarked to me that they will go to church and worship the images with all the unction of a saint, and then rob the contribution boxes. Of all the countries which I have yet visited, I think Russia lies in the thickest fog of superstition.

The south side of the Neva, near the center of the city, is bordered by a row of buildings which form the chief feature of the capital. The middle one is the immense winter palace which the Nihilists have made quite notorious. There is nothing now visible to indicate that an explosion had ever taken place. The palace faces the river upon one side, and upon the other looks out upon a square in which rises the Alexander column commemorating the events of the Napoleonic wars. It is of Finland granite, and is said to be the largest monolith in existence.

Upon the east side of the winter palace, and connected with it, stands the hermitage which was built by Catharine the Second, and now contains the chief art treasures of St. Petersburg. These include some very valuable paintings, and some ancient and modern sculptures. I went one morning to look at these, but they would not admit me without a passport. As the police were at that time sitting upon mine, I could not accommodate them. Two days later I went with a sealed declaration from my landlord that my papers were all correct, and upon this evidence I was at length admitted. The halls are elegantly fitted up, and in any other city would be crowded every day with visitors. But the hand of despotism is upon the throat of Russia and I felt really glad when I was out of her imperial halls, even though they are filled with choice specimens of art.

The finest church in St. Petersburg is the magnificent Isaac's, which is loaded with georgeous ornaments. Each side has an entrance and a colonnade of Finnish granite monoliths. The edifice is surmounted by four small towers at the corners, and an immense dome in the center, all being covered with gilt.

The Kasan Cathedral is second in elegance in the city, and is an imitation of St. Peter's at Rome. Even the circular colonnades have been reproduced, though all upon a smaller scale. The interior is decorated with the usual style of pictures which one sees in a Greek church, and besides these the walls are hung with captured flags. Opposite the altar hang twenty-eight keys of cities that were taken by Russian arms.

Although these two churches are undoubtedly the most magnificent in the capital, still the church of Saints Peter and Paul is the most interesting. It stands within the citadel, which was founded by Peter the Great, and which lies almost opposite the Winter Palace. It contains the tombs of the imperial family since the foundation of the city. The sarcophagi are nearly alike, being all of plain white marble. To the left of the altar lies the body of Peter the Great, the founder of the modern Empire. I have visited the hut in Holland where he lived as a common laborer, and I have stood at the grave of his opponent, Charles the Twelfth, of Sweden. So it was with more than usual interest that I viewed the last resting place of the greatest Czar. The Russian nation owes much to Peter the Great, but the evils which it at present suffers perhaps originated in him too. He devoted his life to the instruction of his people, but he and his successors persisted in treating them as children. If such is to be their condition it were better to have left them in ignorance so that they would never have known of their thraldom. Since I have been in St. Petersburg the " third section " or secret police service has been abolished. The papers are loud in their eulogies of the magnanimity of the Czar, but it seems to me like a man who owes you a million dollars claiming honor for paying you ten cents. I have talked with a number of settlers in Russia, and the universal opinion is that the government is rotten from rind to core. An English book-seller told me emphatically that any handful of men picked up on the street at random would form a better administration than the present one. The world is too old for an unlimited despotism, and Russian tyranny must bend or break.

CHAPTER XVII.

VISIT TO COPENHAGEN.—"THE PLATFORM OF THE CASTLE OF ELSINORE."—LUBECK.—HAMBURG.—BREMEN.—TRAMP IN THE TENTOBURGIAN HILLS.

On Friday, August 27th, I left St. Petersburg by steamer and reached Lubeck, Tuesday, August 31st. At four o'clock on the afternoon of the next day, I embarked on the Danish steamer Najaden for Copenhagen. After descending the uninteresting Trave, which required a couple of hours, we reached the open sea. Night soon came on, and there were no waves of consequence enough to disturb our slumber. About seven o'clock the next morning Copenhagen appeared rather suddenly before us, and a few minutes later the steamer was lying at the custom-house wharf. I opened the little satchel which hung from my shoulder and showed the examining officer the contents (two books, a piece of soap and a clothes brush), and he at once allowed me to pass without contributing anything to the revenues of the kingdom.

The streets of the capital were rather quiet, as the Danes, Swedes and Russians do not get up very early in the morning. The city has a dingy appearance, and most of the thoroughfares are as crooked as a cow path. The people have a different physiognomy from the Germans, and bear almost as close a resemblance to the Swedes as their language.

I walked about without caring much whither and happened upon a number of statues in the public square and finally came to the Christiansborg Palace which is the residence of the reigning sovereign. It is a large square building whose exterior is not particularly attractive. Back of it stands a gloomy looking edifice in imitation of the ancient Italian tombs, which contains the most valued treasures which Copenhagen possesses. It is the far famed Thorvaldsen Museum. The rectangular structure encloses an open court in the center of which lies the grave of the great Danish sculptor whose masterly chisel has contributed to the adorning of every civilized land. A few vines grow above his head and his name is engraved on the curb stone which surrounds them, but all is severely simple. Yet I doubt if a hero in this wide world reposes more royally than does this same artist here. For in the halls around him are models and copies of all his works, forming a collection which is the pride of every Dane and an object of admiration to every stranger. Never was a tribute more fitly paid to a man of genius than this, and the example might well be followed by other lands. Many of the sculptures were already known to me from having seen the originals in my travels.

Besides these models and copies the museum also contains Thorvaldsen's private collection of paintings and antiquities and his library and furniture. Among the pictures I found many of Italian life and as the dirt and fleas were many miles away, I admired them very much. Thorvaldsen was eighteen years in Italy and some of the paintings represent scenes in which he figures.

The second wonder of the Danish capital is the museum of northern antiquities, which is the finest of its kind in existence. It contains about forty thousand articles, arranged in chronological order and representing every department of northern civilization from the earliest discovered relics down to the middle of the seventeenth century. I thought the similar museum in Stockholm almost unsurpassable, but this Danish one is much finer and fuller. The articles are arranged in five periods : The flint, down to B. C. 1500 ; the bronze, down to A. D. 250 ; the iron ; the mediæval, from about 1030 to 1536 ; and the modern, down to 1660. Perhaps the most interesting is the bronze period, which shows that a higher civilization existed in Scandinavia two thousand years ago than we are accustomed to believe. The weapons and utensils have an elegance of finish which could scarcely be more than rivaled at the present day. Even at that remote period these northern barbarians, whom we think of as bearded heathen, had reached such a degree of refinement that they had invented razors. The intelligent attendant at this department told me that a gentleman had made the experiment of shaving with one of the bronze razors, and had shown that it was just as possible to do such a thing now as it was two thousand years ago, when Sheffield was still a howling wilderness, and Wade & Butcher had never been heard of.

A number of grave mounds have been opened, and in some of them skeletons were found encased in wooden coffins. The well-worn black burial robes are still preserved and give a favorable idea of the skill in weaving at that period. In some of the coffins they found little boxes, which among other articles, contained some combs. Perhaps some young gallant took this precaution in order to be able to arrange his disordered locks after the long journey into the next world, in order to meet with becoming dignity his lady love in the golden halls of Walhalla.

On the morning of the second day I set out to make a little excursion into the northeastern part of Zealand. As I unfortunately had not time enough to take the steamer on the sound I was compelled to go by rail. The road makes a long curve into the country and passes by several small lakes. I had expected to find the land flat like Holland, but it is rolling, and one sees hills of considerable size. After a pleasant ride of two hours, we arrived at Helsingor, which was the limit of my journey. This is a commercial town of eighty-five hundred inhabitants, and is situated at the narrowest part of the straits between Denmark and Sweden. I passed through the place, merely glancing at the old town hall and went direct to the old fortress of Kronborg. This consists of a large building with quaint gables, which is surrounded by strong walls and moats. Its guns command the entrance to the Baltic and were once the means of collecting the unjust toll which Denmark levied upon all vessels passing through the sound. In 1857 this usurped right to tax ships was renounced in consideration of seventeen and a half millions of dollars, which was paid by the Baltic Nations.

On the side of the fortress next to the Straits, there is a flag battery, where the national colors are constantly displayed. Visitors are admitted to this point, which commands a good view of the Sound, with its numerous sails, and the hilly coast of Sweden on the opposite side. This battery is said to be "the platform of the castle of Elsinore," where the ghost appeared to Hamlet. I spent the few minutes spare time I had in watching the surf from the North Sea breaking upon the beach, and then I returned to Copenhagen. After climbing the Round Tower by its winding cause-way, and obtaining an excellent view of the ugly red roofs of the city, I embarked upon the steamer Ellida for Lubeck. The next morning, after being delayed five hours by the fog, we reached that place, and so I finished my brief excursion to Denmark.

Whether one approaches the city of Lubeck from the Baltic or by the railway, the lofty spires of its churches apprise him from afar of the nearness of the town, and indicate even in the distance that it possesses an unusual style of architecture. The place has been a free city since 1226, and was one of the chief founders of that great Hanseatic League, which united eighty towns beneath its banners, and did so much in elevating the common people of Northwestern Europe. It had factories in the great world market of London, as well as at Novgorod, on the borders of the wilds of Russia. Its armies conquered and garrisoned Southern Sweden and Denmark, and so far broke the spirit of Danish tyranny that the League obtained the proud privilege of ratifying the elections of the Kings. When one works in the profession of his choice, wealth, in the broad sense of the word, is the measure of worth, and so it came that these free cities abounded in able men of enlightened minds and broad sympathies, who were munificent patrons of literature and art. All the Hanseatic towns have succumbed to the times and been incorporated in other territories, except Lubeck, Hamburg and Bremen, which have succeeded in preserving their independence down to the present day.

The churches of the city are built of brick in a massive style which has been much imitated in the neighboring region. The finest of these edifices is the immense church of St. Mary which was erected by the citizens to outrival the Cathedral of the Bishop. The interior is adorned with elaborate monuments to the men who faithfully served the city. A grave in the church of St. Mary formed doubtless no small part of the ambition of a native burgher.

The walls are adorned with some paintings of artistic value and a few that are interesting from their quaintness. Back of the high altar is a very curious astronomical clock which attracts numerous visitors at noon when figures representing the emperor and electors appear. I went there at the appointed time, and found quite a miscellaneous crowd assembled. There were some honest burghers' children, a few Englishmen with red faces and foggy voices, and a half dozen "Handwerker" with immense canes, rusty garments and unshaved faces. We all congregated in the chapel back of the altar and watched the indicator on the dial. Finally a whirring noise from the bowels of the machine announced that the business had commenced. After a few preliminary groans a figure at the top of the clock hammered twelve on a bell, and then the emperor and the electors came forth in single file from one side and disappeared on the other. As each one passed the figure of Christ, who was enthroned in the center, he turned toward him and bowed, which salute was acknowledged by a motion of the hand in token of benediction. The whole performance scarcely occupied a minute. The clock was constructed in 1565, and repaired in 1860.

Almost adjoining the church of St. Mary is the old town hall, which was built in 1444. True to the German custom there is a wine cellar under the hall which dates from the same period. The vaulting is very curious, and the chimney piece in the apartment where bridal festivities were held contains the warning inscription : " Many a man sings loudly when they bring him his bride ; if they knew what they brought him he well might weep."

From Lubeck I went to Hamburg, which is the largest of the three free towns of the German Empire. The place has two distinct divisions, which are as different from each other as they could possibly be. The quarter adjoining the river is intersected by narrow alleys which almost rival the lanes of Naples in filth. The houses have an immense number of windows, and this fact together with their lofty gables, make them resemble the buildings of Holland. The people seem almost as noisy as the natives of Naples. The other quarter is magnificently built in modern style, and borders upon a lake called Binnen Alster, which is always enlivened by numerous sailboats, little steamers and groups of swans. The place seems more like a fashionable watering place, where pleasure is made the object of life, than a portion of a great city which is one of the largest ports in the world.

The city is intersected by numerous canals, which contribute toward giving it a Dutch appearance. The river is covered with sea-going vessels and river craft, and presents one of the busiest scenes of the kind which one has an opportunity to witness. The port is entered and quitted by about fifty-five hundred ships annually.

In the churchyard at Ottensen, which is a suburb of Hamburg, is the grave of Klopstock, the poet, who was born in 1724 and died in 1803. The inscription on his tombstone, written by his wife, modestly calls upon Germans to approach the grave of their greatest poet. Critics are by no means indifferent to the merits of Klopstock, but few would place him upon an equal rank with Lessing, to say nothing of Goethe and Schiller.

On Monday morning I continued my journey to Bremen where I found nothing to interest me particularly, except the antique buildings at the market place and a few statues scattered about the city It is a clean and comparatively quiet place and the river contains but few boats. It is indebted for its importance to its harbor of Bremerhaven, which is situated at the mouth of the Weser, thirty-eight miles from Bremen. Its shipping is not half so extensive as that of its sister city. Both Hamburg and Bremen flourish principally from their commerce with our country and they will continue to be familiar names to every American as long as they are great channels through which our republic draws additions to its population from Scandinavia, Denmark, Germany, Switzerland and Austria.

I went from Bremen to Herford and as there is not yet a railroad in the direction in which I wished to go I prepared to try a tramp again. I cannot say that I felt particularly spirited for I had lost my umbrella the night before and was not prepared to encounter either sun or rain. I may remark here that I have seen and heard of a great many people who lost umbrellas, but I believe there is nobody on record who has found one.

After making some precautionary inquiries as to where I could board the diligence if I gave out I slung my old knapsack over my shoulder and took the turnpike toward the Teutoburgian Hills. It is seventeen "good" miles as the Germans say, from Herford to Detmold and I expected to be able to reach the latter place by evening without much exertion, relying upon my Austrian record. The road leads through a fertile country which is cultivated, but scarcely has beauty enough to reward one for the fatigues of a long foot-journey. Next year the railroad will be finished which is now in process of construction, but I shall not have any use for it next year and so that is poor consolation. I walked about eight miles when it began to rain and as it was about noon I stopped at an inn by a tollgate to investigate the condition of the pantry. I did not find anything but the inevitable "Butterbrod und Wurst," yet that helps to keep soul and body together. As the rain continued to fall until an omnibus came along at four o'clock which was bound in my direction, I concluded to ride for the rest of my journey. I had just seated myself down between an ugly old maid and a man who was smoking a horribly strong cigar, when the landlord came out of the door and shouted to the driver " Hey there ! that's a native American, he was born in America." My fellow passengers stared at me for the rest of the ride but that is something one soon gets used to in Europe.

At about six o'clock we rolled through the stony streets into the interesting city of Detmold. After depositing my baggage in a neat little hotel I started for a walk to see the place. Detmold is the capital of the principality of Lippe-Detmold which is not any larger than one of our counties. Notwithstanding its smallness it was as independent as any territory in Europe until the present German Empire was formed. Think of such a state exercising all the functions of government and it seems exceedingly ludicrous. One of our counties could raise an army big enough to annihilate the prince and all his subjects. Detmold has seven thousand inhabitants and is, I think, the finest little city of its size in Germany. The houses are very well built and the streets are broad, straight and clean. It is very quiet, but nevertheless has an air of a capital which suits it well. It seems very queer to go through such a little place and find the signs on the stores just like those of Munich, Vienna or Berlin. Nearly everybody seems to assist in supplying his majesty with necessaries and feel therefore authorized in putting the princely coat of arms over his door in glittering gilt and cultivating a metropolitan air. Here is the court barber, there the court bookseller and a little farther is the court clothier. And so it is all through the city. In the center of the place stands the residence palace, a structure dating from the sixteenth century. It has towers like an old castle and is partly covered with vines. The modern windows however show that it has been refitted to be comfortable as well as beautiful. Before it is a little park which is always open to the public. Sentinels pace to and fro at the doors and gates to guard his majesty from intrusion, or, as is more probable, to give the soldiers something to do. In the southern part of the city upon a broad avenue stands the new palace with its carefully kept garden. It looks beautiful but it is surpassed by many a merchant's house in America.

After spending the night in this agreeable little capital I set out in the morning with favorable weather to ascend the Teutoburgian Hills. This is supposed to be the place where the first German hero, Herman, Prince of the Cherusci, destroyed the army of Varus in the year 10 of our era. The Romans were decoyed into the depth of the forest by the Germans who then attacked them upon all sides with a rage that burned in every breast against the strangers who had robbed them of their liberty and were trying to seal the yoke upon their shoulders by destroying their native customs and laws. The fabled furies were not more pitiless than were these exasperated barbarians. But few escaped to tell the dreadful tidings beyond the Rhine and for years the foreign yoke was broken until discord entered the native ranks and the great Herman himself fell a victim to the jealousy of a rival prince. This heroic act coupled with the melancholy fate of his wife and child has made the Cheruscan Prince one of the most loved warriors in the German temple of fame.

Many years ago the sculptor Ernst von Bandel conceived the idea of erecting a colossal statue to Herman on the summit of the Teutoburgian Hills near the supposed site of his great victory. The artist devoted the greater part of his life to this task. The substructure was begun in 1838 and the completed monument was inaugurated August 16th, 1875. This was none to soon, for the artist died in the following year. It stands upon the Grotenburg, one of the highest peaks of the Teutoburgian Hills, being 1162 feet above the level of the sea. The statue represents Herman with one arm resting upon a shield while the other hand holds a sword aloft in the air. The height of the pedestal is one hundred feet ; the height of the figure fifty-four feet ; the height of the sword's point above the helmet, thirty feet, that is, one hundred and eighty-four feet in all. It is larger than the colossal Bavaria at Munich and the builder had the additional disadvantage of having to erect it on a hill. The cost was about two hundred and seventy thousand marks.

Paths have been constructed from Detmold which facilitate the ascent. The hills are covered with dense forests of pine. The monument is provided with an internal staircase and one can mount to a gallery at the top of the pedestal which commands an extensive view over the Teutoburgian Hills and the fruitful lowlands toward Herford. The statue itself can be ascended by internal stairs, but on account of the injury which the figure might suffer from their use the public is not admitted.

After having seen the monument I walked about six miles to the Externsteine which are a curious freak of nature. They are a group of five slender rocks which rise perpendicularly from the earth in a row to the height of from a hundred to a hundred and thirty feet. They look like towers, or, as some say, like gigantic teeth. Several of them can be ascended by steps and and afford a good view of the neighborhood. In one of the rocks there is a grotto thirty-five feet in length which seems to have been used as a chapel. On the outside next to the road there is a large relief of the descent from the cross which has been hewn from the solid rock. It is supposed to date from the year 1115. Near the pillars is a small lake with rowing boats which contribute to make it a pleasant place of resort.

I next walked between seven and eight miles farther to Bergheim which is a station on the railroad to Hanover. I found a very good inn there and liked it so well that I staid two days.

CHAPTER XVIII.

HANOVER.—BRUNSWICK.—TRAMP OVER THE BROCKEN.—
LOST IN THE WOODS.—GOETTINGEN.—CASSEL.

I took leave of the pleasant little inn at Bergheim, near Detmold, where I had spent two days and a half so comfortably and embarked upon the train for Hanover. The journey was through a beautiful valley bounded by green clad hills, some few of which still bear ancient signal towers as a reminiscence of the ruder times that are passed. We finally rolled into the station at Hanover which is a marvel of elegance and systematic arrangement. I deposited my baggage with the porter and set out to see the sights of the city.

In America we are so used to hearing Germans condemning each other's language as an abomniable dialect, that most people conclude that correctness in this particular is not to be found in any province of the Fatherland. But the matter is different here. Whether one go to Swabia or Prussia he will be told everywhere that the purest German is spoken in Hanover. This fact is as firmly settled in the Teutonic mind as it is that the best beer is to be had in Bavaria and the best wine in the vineyards on the Rhine.

A short distance from the station is the theater which is one of the largest in Germany. Not far from it is the Waterloo square which contains a column in memory of the eight hundred Hanoverians who fell in the last battle against Napoleon. Upon the west side of this stands a small open temple which protects a bust of the famous Leibnitz who is buried in a neighboring church. The house in which he dwelt is still standing and is one of the quaintest in the city. Hanover also boasts of having been the birthplace of the great astronomer Herschel.

The streets in the old quarter are crooked and the houses have an antique appearance. In all directions extend the handsome modern suburbs with their pleasant parks and broad avenues. Toward the north a broad road bordered by lime trees and foot paths leads to Herrenhausen Palace which was the favorite residence of the first two Georges of England After visiting the adjoining park I returned to the city and took the train to Brunswick. This is another ancient looking town whose streets were laid out before the straight line was considered a thing of beauty. Its walls have been transformed into promenades, but the city has not grown much beyond its old limits. The squares are adorned with statues of various Dukes of Brunswick and a new monument to the fallen in the Franco-Prussian war has just been erected.

Southeast of the city stands a monument which was erected in 1837 to the memory of Schill and fourteen sergeants of his corps, who are numbered among the martyrs of the Napoleonic wars. In 1809 when the conflict began between the French and Austrians, Major Ferdinand von Schill left Berlin with his regiment without the knowledge of the king in order to stir up a patriotic revolt against the tyranny of Napoleon. But in July the Austrians were silenced at Wagram and the full force of the foreign foe was turned against the ill-fated handful of Prussians. Schill retreated to Stralsund. The town was besieged, taken by storm and the gallant Major with the most of his corps fell in the defense. The fourteen sergeants that were captured were brought to Brunswick and shot and buried upon the spot where their monument stands. Schill's body was buried at Stralsund but his head was preserved in spirits at Leyden till 1837 when it was brought to Brunswick and interred beneath the same stone which marks the resting place of his companions in arms. Schill is enthroned in the German Valhalla together with Andreas Hofer, the Tyrolese mountain hero, and Theodore Korner, the warrior poet of Dresden.

A short distance from the grave of the patriots is the cemetery of the St. Magnus parish. Among the hundreds of obscure graves is that of the great "thinker and poet" Lessing, who died in Brunswick, February 12th, 1781. The house in which he expired is still standing. His grave is marked by a horizontal slab and an upright pillar which bears a bas-relief. The latter, as stated by an inscription, was erected by the ducal theater of Brunswick in 1874. Next February will be the hundredth anniversary of the great man's death but his grave his even now kept covered with blooming flowers. Though these may at last perish, the laurels which wreathe his brow in the temple of fame will remain fresh forever. He led in the main an unsettled and unhappy life and many of his works are but fragments of greater designs, but his service in improving the German language and cultivating a better taste in literature was invaluable. In addition to this he was a pioneer in free thought and one of the stoutest champions in the crusade against mediaeval intolerance.

Lessing's dramas hold their place unchallenged upon every German stage. The people seem to receive them as enthusiastically as if they were new. It is gratifying also to see that his merit is beginning to be appreciated across the Atlantic. In Prof. Hosmer's beautiful History of German Literature an excellent chapter tells the principal events of Lessing's life and paints the ruling traits of his character. Miss Frothingham's translations too are making the reading public familiar with some of his masterpieces. A short time ago that strong sentence as to the possession of absolute truth, which Sir William Hamilton quotes, was all that was known in England and America of the greatest thinker and poet of the age preceding Schiller and Goethe. I have in my hand a "universal" biographical dictionary which was printed at Hartford, Conn., in 1846. The learned author thereof was completely unconscious of the existence of Goethe, probably the greatest poet since Shakespeare, and he dismissed Lessing with the following notice which would be thought a literary curiosity in Germany:

"Lessing, Gotthold Ephraim, a German poet, in the time of Voltaire, published various things, but without judgment."

After the project of founding a national theater at Hamburg had failed Lessing accepted the position of chief librarian of the ducal library at Wolfenbuettel, a little town seven miles south of Brunswick. Here he remained until his death, poorly paid it is true, but enjoying an abundance of leisure time as well as having plenty of books.

After attending an excellent representation of Goethe's Faust at the ducal theater at Brunswick, I left for the Hartz mountains, stopping on the way at Wolfenbuettel. It was raining dismally and my first care was to find the library. It is situated in a commodious building opposite an old palace which is still surrounded by a moat. It contains about three hundred thousand volumes and eight thousand manuscripts. They have a few curiosities to exhibit. Among them are a couple of specimens of Tetzel's letters of indulgence, some manuscripts of Luther, his inkstand and, of course, his drinking glass. The museum or library in Germany which has not one of Luther's beer mugs is in equally as woeful condition as the cathedral which has not a piece of the true cross. If I see a few dozen more drinking vessels of the reformer I shall begin to call for the documents.

I spent some three hours very pleasantly in reading at the library. It seems to lack principally in modern literature and I asked in vain even for an encyclopedia of a recent date. Lessing's former residence stands next to the library. It is a small, plain house. Here he spent that happy year of his married life that was so soon clouded by the death of his wife and babe. The town of Wolfenbuettel is a drowsy sort of a place and I did not wonder that the great thinker sometimes grew tired of the monotony.

Taking the train I arrived at Hartzburg in the evening and prepared to make the ascent of the Brocken. It had been raining all day and as a couple of days' foot journey in the mountains lay before me, I was seriously afraid that I should be delayed. I did not waste any time in borrowing trouble, however, and after spending the usual hour in talking with the landlady about her cousins and her aunts in America, I betook myself to my bed of down, and slept as soundly as if my fate was not dependent upon the state of the weather of the morrow. When I awoke I was gratified with the sight of an almost cloudless sky and a brightly shining sun, which promised to speedily dry the roads and paths of the mountains.

After drinking my coffee and securing a lunch I turned my face up grade in the hope of reaching the summit by by noon. My beginning was not propitious, for I took the wrong road as soon as possible after leaving Hartzburg. A friendly teamster set me right, and then the ascent began in earnest. A steep road led me first up the Molkenhaus. Gradually the pine clad sides of other peaks came in sight. The dense forests of eternal green extended in every direction, grand yet gloomy. The trees were dripping with moisture, and I hurried on to avoid the chill. In an hour I reached the summit of the Molkenhaus, 1,625 feet above the sea. Here the trouble began. My guide book said to take the path direct toward the south. There were two which seemed to be parallel, and I took the better one which, of course, was wrong. The proper way descends on the left side of the mountain, and crosses the Ecker. I went down toward the right into the Radan valley. I went a couple of miles without the least suspicion that I was wrong. I finally noticed that the legends on the finger boards said nothing about the Brocken, or any of the intermediate points. A little later the path turned down the Radau in the direction in which I came. With the aid of map and compass I then found that a high mountain covered with a pathless pine forest was between me and my proper road.

Without delay I turned about and started up the mountain side. The slope was at about an angle of forty five degrees. The ground was rough, and I frequently crossed wet grass and moss. The dense branches of the closely standing trees made it damp and dark. It was very chilly, but I exerted myself so much that the perspiration fairly flowed in streams. Occasionally I threw down my knapsack and stopped to rest and meditate what a downright fool I was. I thought just then of a great many ways in which I could amuse myself better than by climbing mountains. I finally reached the Ecker, which I crossed on a log, but failed to find the right path. I followed a road toward the south, but it proved merely a path of the woodmen, which soon was lost in the trackless forest. From a little clearing upon a slight elevation I caught sight of a distant peak, which I at once concluded was the Brocken, and even thought I could see some buildings on the summit. I headed toward it, consoling myself with the belief that I was going in the right direction, even if I had not the luxury of a path. I have always thought of a mountain as a a pretty dry place, and had feared I would suffer from thirst for my appetite for water is about as insatiable as a German's is for beer. But it is different on the Hartz. The slopes are covered with a coating of moss about half a foot deep, which holds water like a sponge, and lets it gradually ooze out in the rivulets which furrow the mountains in all directions. The rains of the previous day had freshly charged this substance, and it was like wading in a pond when I fell into a patch of moss. To add to my difficulties, the trees became mere stunted bushes, whose matted branches were often an impassable barrier. And so I struggled along, slipping over rocks, sinking in the swampy moss, diving through low branches, which were invariably caught by my knapsack, sending a shower of pine needles and water down my neck.

After some time I reached a spot destitute of trees which afforded a good view of the country. A peak far to the east looked suspiciously like the Brocken, but there was no help for it, and I was compelled to ascend the mountain before me in order to find out where I was. A change came over the spirit of my trouble. The swamps and forests were left behind. My way led over a field of immense boulders. I leaped from one to the other, my knapsack always coming a couple of seconds after me and giving me a tremendous slap on the back. Deep under the rocks I could hear the sound of flowing waters, and the sides of the crevices were lined with beautiful fern. I do not know where I would have gone if I had fallen between the boulders, perhaps to one of the witches with which Goethe peoples the mountain. After jumping and climbing from rock to rock for some time, and being even compelled to use my hands occasionally, I at length arrived at the summit. Just before reaching it I started up a couple of deer in the bushes. After relieving myself of my knapsack, I scrambled to the top of one of the immense bare rocks which I had taken for houses. Holding on to the flag staff while the wind was whistling about my ears I could see over all the adjacent peaks and the smiling plain beyond. But far toward the east loomed up a still higher mountain, which, of course, was the Brocken. By referring to my map and compass I saw that I was on the summit of the Quitschen Berg. Between the two lies a deep and broad ravine.

It was half past one when I turned my face toward the Brocken in earnest. A sort of path aided me at first, but it soon terminated in a break-neck precipice. It required considerable leaping to get to the bottom of the valley and every jump accompanied by the uncomfortable reflection that I would have to toil up on the other side. Alongside the stream I found an excellent road which I thought would take me to the summit in comfort. But a few hundred paces farther it terminated in a burning charcoal heap. After crossing a little clearing I again entered the trackless forest. The low branches and heaps of rocks often barred the way and the whole side of the mountain was literally a swamp. I was thoroughly persuaded that Goethe made a good choice in locating the witches' revel on the Brocken. In many places the deep green moss covered the boulders and logs and ground with a thick coat like a rich carpet which was wonderfully beautiful. Although I was sprinkled with pine needles and mud, and although both shoes were full of water, I still had sentimental feeling enough to admire the magnificent scene. At length the trees became smaller and smaller as I ascended, and finally disappeared. Then the inn on the summit suddenly became visible, and my trouble was at end. I do not remember just now of anything so welcome since I saw land after the tedious days at sea. It was already four o'clock in the afternoon, and I had been moving since eight in the morning. This was double the usual time consumed in the ascent. After a little refreshment and rest I ascended the watch tower. The Brocken is 3,417 feet above the sea. As the country is flat in the neighborhood, the view is limited only by the curvature of the earth and the cloudiness of the sky. The towers of the Magdeburg, Leipzig, Erfurt, Cassel, Hanover, and Brunswick are said to be visible in clear weather. But few travelers see either these or the famous specter which is occasionally formed by the sun upon the mists, the mountain's shadow constituting the ghost. I was forced to be content with the general view of mountain and plain, which is grand. One of the watchmen on the tower, which belongs to the signal service, astonished the company by reading the time upon a church clock in a town far away at the base of the mountains. Another fellow took the glass, but failed to even find the tower. Finally a second saw the dial and confirmed the statement of the first one.

After satisfying myself I shouldered my knapsack and started to descend toward the south. In a little more than two hours I arrived at the forester's inn at Oderbruck where I stopped for the night. My tramp amounted to no more than twenty-two or twenty-three miles but it was a more gratifying journey than the distance indicates. Bayard Taylor slept at Oderbruck in May, 1845, when on his way to the Brocken. He got off the right path too, but I believe he came out worse than I did, as he was wet from head to foot from the snow.

I did not feel weary in the evening but could scarcely walk the next morning. I trudged slowly down to Andreasberg, then crossed a mountain and descended the beautiful Sieber valley. I reached Hertzberg at the foot of the Hartz at dusk, and was fortunate enough to find a train ready to leave for Northeim by which means I reached Goettingen the same evening. On the whole I do not think I can be particularly proud of my success as a mountain tourist.

Goettingen is a pleasant little city, but rather quiet in the absence of the students. Many houses bear memorial tablets marking them as the residence of various famous men when at the university, which now numbers about a thousand students and has large new buildings. The other curiosities of the city consist of a few monuments. It did not take long to see these and I left at noon for Cassel. This proved a delightful ride. The scenery was beautiful and the atmosphere gave the colors an oriental beauty. When about half way the train ran around a hill and disclosed to our view the quaint old town of Munden lying on the banks of the Fulda far below us.

We soon reached Cassel which is situated on an elevation by the Fulda. The valley between the town and the river is laid out in a large park which is much frequented. The promenade along the wall, which rises abruptly from this plain, affords a fine view of the expanse of lowland and the hills beyond. The atmosphere was very favorable and at sunset the tints of the landscape were richer than I saw under the much praised Italian sky. On this promenade is the magnificent new pictuie gallery building which shows how highly art is esteemed by the Germans. It is one of the foremost collections in the country. On the Friedrich-Platz stands the statue of Friedrich II., who sold twelve thousand of Hessian subjects to England for twenty-two million thalers to be used in destroying American liberty. The statue lay for some time in a stable wheie it had been thrown by the French but was at length restored to its pedestal. The contemptible tyrant will have need of something more than a monument to keep his name from infamy. If he were to return to this world he would be disagreeably surprised by two things. He would find the Hessians flocking to enjoy the blessings of the country which their forefathers as British hirelings sought to destroy, and he would see his own land in the hands of a descendent of Frederick the Great who presented Washington his sword as a mark of his esteem.

After looking about the city I went by rail to Castle Wilhelmshœhe which is situated at the base of a hill. Its park, which is one of the finest in the world, extends away to the summit. There are immense fountains, lakes, temples and statues, in fact everything that a tyrant could bring to minister to his pleasure. The work is said to have employed two thousand men daily for fourteen years and to have cost ten million dollars. The castle was inhabited by Jerome Bonaparte when king of Westphalia and by Napoleon III., when a prisoner of war.

After visiting the grave of the Swiss historian Johann Von Mueller I rode in the evening to Eisenach. The following morning, Sept. 18th, I visited the grave of the Low German poet Fritz Reuter, saw the house where Luther lived with Frau Cotta when attending school and the house where the great composer Sebastian Bach was born. I next ascended the hill to the famous Castle Wartburg, which picturesquely crowns the summit. It has been recently admirably restored and adorned and has the double interest of being historically important and of exhibiting a mediæval stronghold as it was in its best days. The Wartburg was founded by Ludwig the Springer in 1070. In 1206 Landgrave Hermann held the Sængerkrieg in the castle. This was a contest between the chief Minnesingers of that age. The wife of Hermann's son Ludwig, Saint Elizabeth is also a famous character in Wartburg history. The castle is ornamented with frescoes of the Singers' Contest and of incidents in the life of the saint. Of the latter Fetridge says: " In the castle is the picture of St. Elizabeth of Thuringen whose husband was hard-hearted as she was kind and charitable to the poor. On one occasion when she had her apron filled with food which she was about to bestow on the hungry, her husband caught her in the act; and, demanding what she had in her apron, she replied " flowers!" when, thinking to detect her in a falsehood, he tore open her apron, and low and behold! the bread and cheese were transformed into roses and lillies. She stands in the picture as if trembling for fear they will change again."

Luther after a pretended abduction was brought to Wartburg May 4th, 1521, by his friend Frederick the Wise and remained there until March 6th, 1522, engaged in translating the Bible. He raised mustaches and passed as a "Junker Georg." Cranach's picture of him in this disguise at Berlin is scarcely recognizable. The room which Luther occupied is kept almost unaltered. There one still sees the hole made by the ink-bottle which he threw at the devil. His satanic majesty does not ramble about as much as he used to, although the old people constantly tell us the world is more than ever devoted to him. Probably he has the rheumatism or else blistered his feet. A couple of centuries ago a man did not amount to much if he had not seen the devil a couple of times at least. Lecky says that "in the monastery of Wittenberg, Luther constantly heard the devil making a noise in the cloisters ; and became at last so accustomed to the fact, that he related that on one occasion, having been awakened by the sound, he perceived that it was ONLY the devil and accordingly went to sleep again."

CHAPTER XIX.

WEIMAR AND ITS FAMOUS MEN.—JENA UNIVERSITY.—OVER THE THURINGIAN MOUNTAINS.—COBURG, BAMBERG AND NUREMBERG.—BACK ONCE MORE AT STUTTGART.

STUTTGART, Oct. 1st, 1880.

From Eisenach I went to Gotha and then to Weimar where I spent two days in visiting the interesting points of the classic city. Weimar is situated in the midst of a gently rolling country, lying in a hollow so that the low hills seem like an irregular rampart a few miles away encircling the town. It is the capital of the grand duchy of Saxe-Weimar and numbers some sixteen thousand inhabitants. The narrow river Ilm, which centuries ago may have led to the foundation of the place, flows along the eastern side of the city, enlivening the pleasant park which covers its borders. New fangled improvements are here and there springing up; the wealthy are building modern mansions on the site of their ancestral halls; stations and similar necessaries of this boiling age are forcing in their way, but in the main the little capital has much the same appearance that it had in the golden days. Like all old German towns it consists of narrow, crooked streets, which connect a number of spacious squares. It is very quiet, for, apart from the lack of business, it is true that the Germans are much less noisy than the French or Italians.

I took up my quarters in a little inn but a few doors from Goethe's house, which is a plain, three-storied building opening directly upon the street and connected upon each side with the adjoining structures. I am afraid an irreverent person would call it an ugly house, but it has seen better days and the great poet filled it with collections of the choicest productions of literature and art. The genial Jean Paul wrote thus enthusiastically of his visit to Goethe : " His house, or rather his palace, pleased me ; it is the only one in Weimar in the Italian style ; with such a staircase ! A pantheon full of pictures and statues !"

Unfortunately the house is not accessible to the ordinary tourist, being still owned by his descendants. Though I could not enter, I, of course, looked with much interest at the dwelling of that great genius, who, as Byron said, "created the literature of his own country and illustrated that of Europe."

Goethe is numbered among the greatest of the human race, and he will retain that rank in spite of the occasional growls of egotistical Frenchmen and of disappointed fanatics, who, as Carlyle well said, are like the man who villified the sun because it would not light his cigar.

Schiller's house is about of the same size as Goethe's, and is not far distant. Being the property now of the city, it is open to visitors. One is shown the study and sleeping apartment of the poet, both of which, curiously enough, are at the very top of the house. There still stands the narrow bed upon which the afflicted Schiller breathed his last. It is now covered with wreaths. Near by are other articles of furniture, among which is the writing desk of the poet. Perhaps it was in that same little drawer, which one still sees, that Goethe found the decayed apples whose odor the sickly Schiller considered agreeable when composing.

A short distance from the house is the theater, a building of moderate size. I attended an opera one evening for the sake of the past. In front of the entrance stands Rietschel's finely conceived statue of Schiller and Goethe, representing them side by side peacefully holding the same wreath, a striking reproof of those wrangling critics who think the claims of one poet can only be maintained by disparaging another.

In the center of the city is the Stadtkirche, in which Herder preached. In front of it is a bronze statue of him, designed by Schaller, and erected in 1850 by "Germans of all lands." Opposite the northwest corner of the church is the parsonage, in which the restless poet-priest lived for some years. He was buried upon the scene of his labors. A simple tablet in the pavement of the church marks his grave, and bears his motto, "Licht, Liebe, Leben." The famous hero of the Thirty Years' War, Duke Bernhard, is buried near by.

On the south side of the city is the cemetery, which is the resting place of many famous men. The grand ducal vault is the most conspicuous object. It contains the remains of all the ducal family from the year 1662. Of course the most interesting is the sarcophagus of Karl August, the friend as well as the patron of the four great poets, who have made Weimar a familiar name throughout the civilized world. There are numberless sovereigns who are able to entertain men of genius, but there are few that can give them that appreciation and encouragement which is more valuable than their gold. But even the sarcophagus of Karl August must yield in interest to the greater dead. For in this same vault are placed the coffins of Goethe and Schiller, lying side by side as they were joined together in friendship and linked together in fame. There is no place more sacred in the eyes of the student of German literature than this. The devotion of the public is expressed by the multitude of wreaths which cover the coffins. It is remarkable how far away the familes of the two poets are interred.

In the Protestant Cemetery at Rome I happened to see the grave of Goethe's son while I was hunting for that of Shelley. In the cemetery at Bonn I visited the graves of Schiller's wife and second son.

While conversing with the attendant at the grand ducal vault I asked him incidentally where Goethe's wife was buried. He said nobody knew when or where she died, and added very decidedly that she was no wife for a minister. Donnerwetter! Do these Weimar people still think "Herr Geheimrath und Kammerpræsident" von Goethe greater and more respectable than simple Goethe the poet? And do they then really imagine that he owes all his glory to the fact that he was a nobleman and minister in this little principality, which is a trifle bigger than your hand? As for the statement of the attendant, it is false. Poor Christiana Vulpius Goethe died June 6, 1816, nearly sixteen years before the poet.

Wieland's house in the town resembles Schiller's somewhat. He has also a statue dedicated to his memory. It will be remembered that Wieland bought a farm once, and although, on account of embarrassment, it was afterward sold, he was allowed to be buried there. This estate is some six miles distant in the direction of Leipzig. I walked out one day over the pleasant hills. The grave of the poet lies on the bank of a rivulet amid the trees. A single stone marks the spot where lie Wieland, his wife and his friend Sophia Brentano. It is a suitable resting place for the fortunate poet, whose life was as tranquil as those of Herder and Lessing were stormy.

In the parks on the banks of the Ilm there are two modest summer dwellings which Goethe occupied at various times. Farther toward the north is the picturesque Grand Ducal Palace which contains a number of rooms ornamented with paintings of scenes in the works of the four great poets. On the adjacent Fuerstenplatz stands an equestrian statue of Karl August.

In the northern part of the city, not far from the railroad station, is the museum, a large building of sandstone It contains some very fine mural paintings, some statues, and a number of articles of interest in relation to the great characters who have made Weimar illustrious. I was particularly impressed by a little locket on which the artist had painted the eye of his sweetheart. Being always exposed to her tender gaze, how could the lover be otherwise than noble and pure?

Not far from the palace is the grand ducal library, which affords much that is interesting to the student. It contains some 170,000 volumes. Like all large European libraries, it possesses a sort of small museum of relics and curiosities. Among these are a model constructed by Peter the Great ; the cane of Frederick the Great ; a portion of the uniform which Gustavus Adolphus wore when killed ; Luther's monastic garments, etc., etc. The grand hall contains some excellent busts of the great poets, among which is Trippel's magnificent representation of Goethe in the prime of his life. It is the idealization of every manly trait, and is as handsome as Apollo.

The attendant who conducted me through the library was a mercenary old soul, and was continually trying to impress me with the immense value of everything in solid gold. As we descended the ingenious spiral staircase, which was constructed by a convict as the price of his liberty, the old guide laid his finger along the side of his nose and whispered that he would show me the great African traveler, Dr. Vergessenwer. We then passed an inoffensive looking man who was quietly examining some books. I did not make any signs of wonder, for the old sinner forgot to tell me how much he cost. Upon receiving his customary fee the attendant gave me some doggerel recounting the treasures of the library, and bade me an affectionate farewell.

Having thus visited all the wonders of Weimar I set out for Jena, feeling better satisfied than if I had visited a dozen dusty galleries. Indeed, Weimar has experienced the truth of those words of Goethe, that "it is advantageous to entertain genius ; if thou give it a guest's gift it leaves a finer one in return. The spot a noble man has trod is sancitified;

after a hundred years his word and deed resound to the grandson again."

Tuesday morning, Sept. 21st, I arrived at Jena from Weimar. This famous university town lies in the narrow Saale valley and is surrounded on every side by lofty hills. The old part of the city is composed of ancient houses intersected by narrow, crooked lanes. The outskirts present a more modern appearance, like the live bark around the old dried heart of a tree. The university buildings are on the northern side of the city. The celebrated scientist Prof. Hæckel has a large two story auditorium apart from the others. The promenade in the neighborhood bears a number of busts of various former professors. In every university town one sees tablets on the houses commemorative of the residence of famous students, but it is nowhere carried to such an extent as at Jena. Nearly every house of the better class is covered more or less with these memorial inscriptions which look like the patches on the face of a student of the fighting corps. Goethe visited Jena occasionally and Schiller became a professor of history at the university in 1789. The Germans do not seem to value his historical works for anything else than their form as they were not the result of personal investigation. Everything must be accurate to the letter or it does not pass review in Germany.

The battle of Jena which prostrated Prussia, was fought Oct. 14th, 1806, a short distance north of the city.

Having considerable spare time I ascended the adjacent mountain Hausberg which is a favorite excursion of the students. The summit was formerly crowned by a castle, of which only a tower remains which has been restored and provided with a staircase, so that one can enjoy a fine view now from the top. Love of nature is one of the chief characteristics of the Germans. The country in the vicinity of the cities is threaded with a net work of paths which are crowded with pedestrians of all ages and conditions on every fine Sunday. Towers are built on all the best summits where an extensive view is to be had. As for us Americans, indifference toward natural beauties seems to be our chief characteristic. Perhaps it is because we are still pioneers. America has fully as fine scenery as Europe if not finer, but we need to import some foreign tourists to make the fact known to us. Americans come over here, climb mountains because it is the custom and go into ecstacies over the prospect, but when they return to the States they seem to forget that we have hilltops, caverns and waterfalls, which have been waiting these millions of ages for somebody to appreciate them.

Tuesday afternoon I left Jena by the train up the Saale valley passing Rudolstadt, the former home of Schiller's wife, Charlotte von Lengefeld. I left the train at Saalfeld. The traveler from Jena to Coburg is compelled to take the long ride over the mountains of the Thuringian Forest by diligence, as there is no direct railway communication. At Saalfeld I found I could either leave at eleven o'clock in the evening or nine the next morning. Being in a hurry to reach Stuttgart I concluded to make the trip by night. The diligence was a clumsy vehicle but comfortable enough, except that it was bitterly cold. The horses crept slowly up the mountain side for a long time and then, quickening their pace, they ran along for hours in the gloom of the forest.

At the highest village in the mountains, half way toward Sonneberg, we stopped for a few minutes. After drinking some hot coffee I took another diligence, being the only passenger, and started down the valley. The moon shone brightly on the densely wooded mountains in quiet beauty. We rolled through villages catching glimpses of the numerous glowing glass-furnaces and about seven o'clock reached Sonneberg having made the thirty-two miles and a half in eight hours. I had to wait some time for the train ; then arrived after an hour's ride at Coburg

This city is especially interesting to the English from its connection with Prince Albert who was born at Rosenau four miles northeast of Coburg. The market place contains a statue of the Prince which was inaugurated in 1865 in the presence of Queen Victoria. The present ducal residence, the Ehrenburg, stands at the foot of a hill upon which is the ancient castle of Coburg, which has recently been restored. The old fortress was the scene of a siege during the Thirty Years' War and during the session of the imperial diet at Augsburg, in 1530, Luther resided here doing a great deal of translating and other literary work. It was during this time that he wrote his world famous hymn, "Ein' feste Burg ist unser Gott."

The castle, like the Wartburg at Eisenach, presents a large mediaeval fortress as it existed in its best days. The towers and ramparts are all complete, although the Prussian sentinel has taken the place of the armored warrior. The view from the walls is admirable. The principal building contains a fine collection of coaches, sleds, armor and similar articles. A number of elaborately decorated rooms are shown and among others one that was used by Luther. Of course they have one of his beer mugs. It is a wooden one, about the size of a small bucket. The castle contains some fine wood carving and a very large natural history collection. There are even a couple of live bears in a den under the windows of the principal building.

Thursday morning, Sept. 23d, I left Coburg for Bamberg the famous old city of Franconia. It retains many of its ancient characteristics but is fast being modernized. The principal attraction of the place is the cathedral which stands on a hill in the northern part of the town. It contains the sarcophagus of its founder, Emperor Henry II., and his wife. Near the cathedral is the bishop's palace. It was Napoleon's headquarters in 1806 and it was from here that he issued the proclamation of war against Prussia.

The same day I continued my journey to Nuremberg where I happened to go to a hotel that was entertaining a company of players among whom were some Chinese. Most of the latter spoke English and one had the British accent to perfection. The strange costumes of the Celestials caused considerable stir among the Germans although in general they are not so quick to make sport of nonconformities in dress as we are in America. In a Paris paper I read yesterday a saying that the fear of ridicule rules the French, which I think is also true of our people But the opposite seems to be the case with the Germans. The most eccentric kind of costumes cause no commotion. Everyone follows his own whims. One day in Cassel I saw an immense fat peasant woman whose dress barely reached to her knees. A cap on her head about as big as your hand helped to make her look as dumpy as the pictures in Tom Hood's "Up the Rhine." I looked around to see if this remarkable figure caused any comment; but no, every one passed along in silence as though that was the regular costume. How far could that woman walk in an American city? In about a minute she would have an uncomfortable troop of street boys hooting at her heels. The country where women and dogs, and horses and cows are harnessed together, cannot have a very delicate perception of the eternal fitness of things. The German writers boast of how from the time of Tacitus they attributed "something divine" (Etwas gœttliches) to them, but I have never yet read anyone lamenting that they make these highly venerated women work like cattle. One cannot help thinking that the Germans, with all their great artistic and musical genius lack a delicate sensibility of the ridiculous and unsuitable.

Even in slow old Europe the relics of the past are disappearing. The cities which twenty-five years ago looked as they did in the sixteenth century, have now the regularity and beauty of modern towns. Even in Augsburg and Lubeck the new is at present so mixed with the old that the antique effect is almost destroyed. Of all the German cities, Nuremberg is the only one which I have seen that presents an unmarred picture of a mediæval town. The solid stone walls with the moat and the picturesque towers and gates, form one of the most remarkable spectacles which one has an opportunity of seeing in Europe. They are certainly among the best preserved antique fortifications extant. They not only serve now as an ornament, but also ward off the inroads of modern iconoclasts. The new villas of the wealthy must be built without the walls. Her gates are even shut against the locomotive, that noisy servant of this century, which has pushed its way through Aurelian's wall at Rome and invaded the resting place of the Cæsars.

All Nuremberg is a museum in which we see relics of the middle ages preserved unimpared. It is entertainment enough to walk up and down the streets and look upon the old churches, the quaint gabled houses and the wonderful fountains. I have been wandering so long among the ruins of other ages that much of the effect was lost on me, but I should think that the feelings of an American would be curious who was transported directly from one of our cities to the antiquated scenes at Nuremberg.

The old City Hall contains a number of pictures and a fresco of the year 1552, representing an execution with a "Fallbeil," or guillotine, which shows that Guillotin was not the first inventor of that horrible machine, although he may have conceived the idea independently. Under the City Hall were the old dungeons, which had an underground communication with the fortress which stands upon an elevation at the northern end of the city. These prisons were the scenes of numberless barbarities which were perpetrated in the name of justice.

The fortress was begun in the eleventh century and continued at different times. In the court yard there is a well which has been drilled through the rock to the astonishing depth of three hundred and thirty-five feet. The custodian lowered a candle, and then by means of a mirror the light was reflected so as to show the water. The subterranean passages from the city hall dungeons open at the bottom of this well, and the prisoners are said to have procured their water from that source.

In one of the towers of the castle there is a large and remarkable collection of instruments of torture, which is one of the most conclusive proofs of the progress of civilization. There one can see all the contrivances for producing pain which a diabolical fancy could invent. There are screws for crushing thumbs, boots for breaking legs, all sorts of pinchers for rending flesh and muscle, the wheel over which the victim's bones were broken, and axes which have deprived hundreds of wretches of their lives. There hangs the blood-stained mantle which the executioner always wore when discharging his office. There are books relating to this terrible subject; one, an autobiography of a legal butcher who numbered his victims by hundreds; another, a code of laws of the last century with an appendix containing engravings and explanations of the manner of conducting the different modes of torture. One picture represents a double execution, where one of the victims a highwayman, who is to be broken on the wheel, is compelled to look on while his companion is slowly disemboweled. When we think that such tortures were often inflicted for mere differences of opinion upon subjects of which no one knows anything for certain; when we remember further that of the hundreds who witnessed the cruelties perhaps none felt the least touch of pity, we may well be astonished at the infernal extremities to which human nature can go. The veriest hyena is a marvel of tenderness compared to such monsters. I feel thankful from the bottom of my heart for two things : first, that I was born in the nineteenth century ; second, that I was born in America. As a Russian officer told Lieutenant F. V. Greene, we are a fortunate people in not having the middle ages at our back.

The custodian of this chamber of horrors one would expect to be a meager skeleton of a man dying slowly of fright from the close contact with these instruments of torture. But no, it is an immense fat old woman, big around as a tub and compelled to use a cane to assist in supporting her accumulation of flesh. She repeats the usual explanations as vivaciously as the keeper of the wild animals at a circus. In moments of leisure she sits down by the headsman's bloody mantle, with the tarnished axes at her feet, and peacefully slumbers and perhaps dreams of a land where there are mountains of sauerkraut and garlic, and rivers of Muenchener beer with other delicacies only appreciated by a Teutonic stomach.

In the Spitalplatz, near the fine new synagogue, is a monument of Hans Sachs, and in a little street adjoining is the house where he livid. He was a "master singer," and lived from 1494 to 1576. In those days verse-making was driven like a trade in guilds. The famous Nuremberg "funnel," which is now proverbial in Germany, was warranted to pour the whole art in one's head within six hours. The members of these poetical guilds generally had another trade to support them, and made verse-making a sort of auxiliary business. Motley says of similar performances in the Netherlands : " To torture the muses to madness; to wiredraw poetry through inextricable coils of difficult rhymes and impossible measures ; to hammer one golden grain of wit into a sheet of infinite platitude ; with frightful ingenuity to construct anagrams and preternatural acrostics ; to dazzle the vulgar eye with tawdry costumes, and to tickle the vulgar ear with virulent personalities, were tendencies which perhaps smacked of the hammer, the yardstick and the pincers, and gave sufficient proof, had proof been necessary, that literature is not one of the mechanical arts, and that poetry cannot be manufactured to a profit by joint stock companies."

Hans Sachs was a shoe maker and seems to have worked at his trade all his life. This did not interfere with his verse making however, for he produced something more than six thousand poetical pieces, among which were two hundred and eight tragedies and comedies. What pigmies our authors are in these days ! One of the French statesmen of the present is said to have found the jolting of an omnibus propitious in translating Homer into meter and I suppose the hammering of sole leather served Sachs' muse in the same way.

Not far from the fortress is the dwelling house of Albert Durer, and near it is a fine statue of him by Ranch. I also visited his grave, at the Johanniskirchhof. He is unquestionably the most famous native of Nuremberg. He visited Italy and the Low Countries and became the royal painter of the German imperial court. One day when he was painting upon a high ladder in the presence of Emperor Maximilian the First, that monarch ordered a nobleman to hold the ladder. He refused saying it was unworthy of one of his rank to serve a painter. Maximilian answered : "I rate such a painter higher than a nobleman, for I can, if I wish, elevate a peasant to a nobleman, but I cannot make such an artist out of a nobleman."

Durer had a terrible shrew for a wife, who made his existence miserable. He tried to run off, but she brought him back. Shakespeare was not then born to tell how to tame her, and the poor artist at last succumbed to his fate. The Bishop of Litchfield wrote, some three centuries ago, that "it is a common jeste, yet trewe in some sense, that there is but one shrewe in all the worlde, and everee man hath her ; and so everee man must be ridd of his wiefe that wolde be ridd of a shrewe." Of course he was nothing but a crusty old priest, and bachelors are recommended not to believe him, but rather follow the Spanish proverb for choosing a wife : " Shut your eyes and commend your soul to God."

From Nuremberg I went to Stuttgart, my home of the previous winter. I was welcomed by my friends in a cordial manner and was heartily glad of an opportunity to rest amid the familiar scenes, after having traveled constantly for six months in Germany, Austria, Italy, Sweden, Finland Russia and Denmark.

CHAPTER XX.

FAREWELL TO STUTTGART.—WEINSBERG'S WOMEN.—HEIDELBERG AND FRANKFORT.—DOWN THE RHINE AGAIN.—AIX-LA-CHAPELLE.—INAUGURATION OF THE GREAT COLOGNE CATHEDRAL.

COLOGNE, Oct. 15th, 1880.

The first part of my two week's visit at Stuttgart was favored with beautiful weather which made the surrounding vine clad hills appear in their finest aspect. But as the day drew near when I was to set off it began to rain long and frequently and brought those disagreeable necessities, mud and fog. Even my last walk through the familiar streets was under an umbrella. But nothing can mar the pleasure with which I think of the dear old capital. I have climbed her hills and looked over her spires, roofs and gardens too often to be ignorant of her beauty. Perhaps I have inherited some patriotic feeling toward Wurtemberg from my nameless ancesters, but be that as it may, I have no place in the Fatherland more dearly at heart than the pleasant valleys and green mantled, ruin crowned hills of the matchless Swabian land.

After bidding farewell to my limited circle of acquaintances, I turned my face toward Heidelberg. As I had three times made the journey by the railway via Bruchsal, I went this time by way of the old free city of Heilbronn which is filled with reminiscences of the Knight of the Iron Hand, Gœtz von Berlichingen, whom Goethe has done so much to immortalize. He was born in 1480 in Wurtemberg and died in 1562. At the siege of Landshut he lost his right hand which he replaced by the iron one that is as famous as the warrior himself. His descendents are still living, one being a major in the Austrian army. The iron hand is said to be still preserved. The Knight's antobiography suggested Goethe's play which however contradicts the historical account in some places.

The rain continued to fall but I am used to that and I made an excursion from Heilbronn to Weinsberg in spite of the weather. The name of the latter place is quite appropriate for it lies in a valley surrounded by luxuriant vineyards. I did not care anything for the town however but immediately inquired the way to the castle. The fellow I asked was quite surprised that I was going up that night. I did not stop to explain why I wanted to visit a ruin during the rain but hurried on up the hill knowing that I had little time to spare before the train would come. At the foot of an elevation stands the residence of the Swabian poet Justinus Kerner who like our Holmes found that the two processes of pill and verse making could be harmoniously pursued by the same person. He died in 1862 and his monument with a bronze portrait medallion stands near his former home which is now occupied by his son who has succeeded his father both as a disciple of the Muses and of Aesculapius.

Passing this house I soon reached the summit of the hill

by a good path. The ruins consist of the fragments of two towers and the scanty remains of the outer wall, but everything is so well arranged that it produces a good impression. This is the old castle Weibertreu or Women's Faithfulness, which has been the theme of many a ballad. It should be the Mecca of all admirers of the gentle sex and I hope it will be put down to my credit that I climbed the hill in the rain.

When the Hohenstaufen Conrad was elected emperor in 1138 the rival house of Guelf felt much injured because they considered that the dignity belonged to them. Their discontent manifested itself in various ways and finally in 1140 Count Guelf of Altdorf marched against Conrad. It came to a battle near Weinsberg which is notable as being the first occasion of the use of those war cries of "Guelf and Ghibiline" which afterwards acquired such a terrible significance in Italy. In the Weinsberg engagement the imperial cause was triumphant and the rebellious town itself was compelled to surrender. Exasperated by its obstinate resistance the emperor determined to give it over to plunder and destruction, but he was gallant enough however to allow the women to depart with their dearest jewels from the doomed city. The gates were opened and the long line moved out, yet great was the astonishment of the monarch when he saw every lady bearing upon her back a husband or lover as her dearest jewel. The courtiers murmured against this interpretation of the mandate but the emperor would not be outdone and spared both men and city. Methinks I hear a growl of skepticism among the bachelors, but it is a fact; if they do not believe it they can read it in the contemporary chronicle of St. Pantaleonis.

The castle was destroyed in 1525. In the early part of the present century even the few fragments that remained seemed about to disappear, but they were taken under the protection of the poet Kerner and secured from further vandalism. The ground was bought by the women of Germany and laid out in the present beautiful style. It was Kerner's plan to build there a women's hall of fame upon the model of the Valhalla which Ludwig I, of Bavaria, built at Ratisbon. The chivalrous project failed for want of means. Among the ruins the faithful women's way is still pointed out. The stones are covered with verses and names of distinguished visitors. Nearly all of the South German poets are represented, as well as the king and queen of Wurtemberg and American Consul Potter, late of Stuttgart.

From Weinsberg I went to Heidelberg the same evening. The following day proved clear and I was so fortunate as to see the classic city at her best. The famous university was not in session. I could therefore do nothing more than look at the building. The city has a magnificent situation on the Neckar between two chains of mountains which are covered with vineyard and forest. It is so closely pressed between the hills and river that it consists of but a couple of long streets which are about two miles in extent. During the university vacation there is little to be seen in the town itself.

After walking about the city I started up the steep path toward the castle. This is the largest and most magnificent ruin in Germany and has been the favorite subject of native poets and painters for ages. What the coliseum is to Italy, the Heidelberg castle is to Germany. The structure is the work of many centuries and presents many variations in style. It is really a number of distinct buildings joined together and partakes both of the character of a palace and fortress so that the visitor may admire its massiveness as well as its beauty. The earliest portion was begun by Count Rudolph at the end of the thirteenth century. The French commander, Count Melac caused the fortifications to be blown up and the palace to be burned in 1689. It was twice struck by lightning which completed the destruction. A rich growth of ivy has covered the ruins. The terrace and towers afford fine views of the Neckar valley. The most curious part of castle is the "blown up tower." The French attempted to demolish it with powder but the masonry was so massive that it was merely split into two parts one half falling into the moat and the other half remained standing.

Of course we descended into the cellar to see the immense wine tun, the famous "Heidelberger Fass." I was with an elderly German couple. The smaller cask first came in view. The lady thought this was the monster and began to invoke the gods and saints in a manner peculiar to Germans. When we finally saw the real tun she cried : "there it is, there it is, mein Gott, mein Gott !" Her husband contented himself with a muffled "Donnerwetter" and then began to examine the wonder. It was constructed in 1664 and holds 236,000 bottles. Opposite it stands a wooden model of the court jester Perkeo who drank daily only about fifteen bottles.

I next ascended the mountain back of the castle which is called the Kœnigsstuhl. It is 1847 feet above the sea and is crowned by a tower which commands an almost boundless view. I met a goodly number of English who came to see the "cawsel." After returning to the city I crossed the old bridge and ascended the opposite hill, passing the inn "Hirschgasse" where the students amuse themselves by slicing each others faces. About half way up the hill one reaches the famous Philosopher's Way which is two miles long and affords fine views of the castle and the Neckar and Rhine Valleys. After seeing this airy and classic path I returned to the city.

I left Heidelberg, Oct. 9th, by the afternoon train for Frankfort. The railroad has been built parallel with the famous "Bergstrasse" which runs along the western side of the Odenwald. The mountains present a varied and beautiful appearance and are crowned by numerous ruined castles. If one were to glide along on the bosom of a majestic river instead of rattling by on a prosy railroad, he would undoubtedly think that the scenery rivaled the Rhine.

The old free city of Frankfort on the Main was founded in the eighth century by Charlemagne. The name of the suburb Sachsenhausen is said to have been derived from a colony of conquered Saxons which that cruel monarch located on the opposite side of the river from Frankfort.

The great Easter and Autumn Fairs had an immense influence in multiplying the wealth of the town. The Golden Bull of Emperor Charles the Fourth appointed Frankfort in 1356 to be the place of election of the sovereigns. The Frankforters worshiped this golden bull as much as the English do their "magna charta."

In the war of '66 Frankfort took the Austrian side and at its close it was swallowed by Bismarck and the Prussians. All South Germany would have likely been gulped into the same insatiate maw, if they had not provided themselves with various impediments to digestion, just as frogs take sticks in their mouths to keep from being devoured by serpents. For instance King Karl of Wurtemberg wisely took unto himself a wife from the Russian tyrant's house. Now if Bismarck had attempted to annex that country the Russian Emperor would have been heard from. That is the way they balance the machine in Europe. If one side of the scale displays signs of going up they fling a woman into it, and, presto! all is even. Verily he that findeth a wife findeth a good thing, especially if he is a neighbor of Bismarck and she has a big brother with lots of soldiers.

One of Frankfort's principal objects of interest is the Stuttgart sculptor Dannecker's marble group of Ariadne one of the best specimens of the later art. Dannecker was a schoolmate of Schiller at the academy of Stuttgart. He afterwards modeled a colossal bust of the poet which is one of his most famous works. The original is in the museum at Stuttgart.

The most interesting historical edifice in Frankfort is the Rœmer or old town hall. It was built about 1406. It stands on a large square called the Rœmerberg which was forbidden ground for a Jew until a century ago. In the second story of the building is the room where the emperors were formerly elected. Its original form is preserved. In front of this is the Kaisersaal where the new emperors dined with the electors and appeared at the windows to the multitude in the square below. The hall has been restored and the walls decorated with paintings of all the emperors. The circumstances connected with an elevation have been immortalized in Goethe's autobiography.

The old bridge, which was the great poet's favorite promenade in his youth, is not far from the square. It was constructed in 1242 and bears a statue of Charlemagne. Near it stands a rooster on a pole. Tradition says the architect vowed that the first living being that crossed the bridge should go to the Devil in exchange for valuable assistance received in spanning the river. The first traveler over the bridge proved nothing but a feathered animal, so the Devil was cheated. Whether the rooster was put up to give proof of the story or the lie was invented to account for the rooster, I am not able to say.

Frankfort is fast losing her old character. She is taking on the appearance of a modern city of wealth. Broad avenues and elegant mansions are succeeding the narrow lanes and dingy houses of the past. Even the Jews' quarter at Frankfort has lost its peculiarities. The famous Judengasse is almost demolished. One must turn now to Prague to see the squalor that once was here. The Jews have not been free a century in Germany but they have already manifested the inherent vigor of their race by attaining some of the highest positions in society. Zealots may adjudge the hottest corners of hell to whom they please, but they are now powerless to bring any of their infernal machines into this world. There is however a good deal of the old feeling in Germany. The Christians hate the Jews and take every opportunity to make it known. Even people who are otherwise quite reasonable, lose their sense when they get on this subject. If one asks whether the Israelites are depraved, treacherous or incompetent, they answer no, but—they have all the best places in the country. I have heard of school boys hating those who were able to surpass them in their sports, but I had thought that men were above such nonsense. We are not perfect over the ocean but I am glad that the American people are great and noble enough not to grudge anyone the legitimate fruits of his toil, whether his grandfather peddled Irish linen or lived off his neighbors and had a handle to his name.

Frankfort had the honor of being the birthplace of Goethe, the greatest genius of Germany. The house in which he was born stands in the Hirschgraben. It has a well to-do appearance though of course antiquated. At present it is the property of a society and contains mementos of the great bard. As it is connected with so many incidents in Goethe's "Dichtung und Wahrheit," it will always remain an object of lasting interest. The house happened to be closed when I was there and I thus missed the pleasure of seeing its interior. I visited the grave of Goethe's mother in the old Peter's Cemetery. She has justly shared the honor of her son even in her grave, for her monument has recently been restored.

I went out farther to the new cemetery which is a beautiful place. Among the others I saw the grave of the celebrated philosopher, Arthur Schopenhauer who died in 1860.

From Frankfort I went to Mayence and embarked on the steamer for Cologne to see the inauguration of the great Cathedral, which has been the labor of so many centuries. As I had two days to spare after my arrival before the celebration would take place I began to study the map to find some convenient excursion. It was raining fearfully, but one grows indifferent to that and if he travel much, the panorama has to move along very fast or the tourist gets weary of the scenes. After searching the chart thoroughly I determined to make a flying trip to Aix-la-Chapelle, some forty-three miles from Cologne.

I took the early train and in a couple of hours reached the ancient coronation city. The ride was wretched enough. The rain was pouring down and a thick fog concealed the country from view. My fellow-passengers were gloomy and silent. When the cars stopped some new-comer would bring in a gust of wind and rain and splash us with his dripping coat and umbrella. There is no sense in these European coaches anyhow. In winter they are as cold as ice, for how can a car be warm when they open the whole side of it at every station? At all seasons everybody inconveniences everybody else when he climbs in and out. Of course if you are a stranger in a strange land you want to sit by the window, and then everyone has to climb over your knees and drag their baggage after them. By the time they have stowed their valises away in the racks, and gotten themselves seated you feel as if an elephant had been walking over you. In Wurtemberg, Russia and Switzerland they have adopted the American style or rather, a feeble imitation of our cars.

Aix-la-Chapelle was the Aquisgranum of the Romans which was founded on account of the warm springs of the neighborhood   It owed its mediaeval importance to Charlemagne who had a palace here and built the chapel from which the name of the city is derived. Thirty-seven emperors were crowned there. The modern town has crooked streets but presents, withal, a well-to-do appearance. It has an air that is not altogether German.

Between the years 796 and 804 Charlemagne erected a chapel near his palace after the style of the church of Saint Vitale, at Ravenna, and it was consecrated by Pope Leo the Third. This structure is still standing and forms a part of the cathedral, a choir in the Gothic style having been added in the fourteenth century. The difference in the architecture of the two parts produces a queer effect. Eginhard, the biographer and according to tradition the son-in-law of Charlemagne, writes thus of the cathedral at that early period : "The minister at Aix-la-Chapelle, which is of extreme beauty, is a monument of his love for the arts, as also of his great piety. After he had it built he caused it to be ornamented with gold and silver, together with windows, lattices and gates of solid brass. He had all the pillars and marble stones used for its construction brought from Rome and Ravenna, as he could not obtain them in any other quarter." All this ancient magnificence has disappeared and the octagonal structure looks quite plain. At present it is being restored and re-adorned.

In the center of the pavement of the original chapel there is a large slab with the inscription " Carolo Magno, " but the great emperor's remains repose in a silver reliquary in the treasury. Charlemagne was born at Aix-la-Chapelle, and died there Jan. 18th, 814. His body was clothed in his imperial robes and placed upon a marble throne in a closed chapel in the cathedral. A golden Bible was laid upon his knees, a pilgrim's scrip wound about and a piece of the original cross placed upon his head. There the stern old Kaiser sat in quiet majesty undisturbed until the year 1,000 when his admirer Otho III., opened the vault and found his body intact. Renewing the garments the emperor resealed the tomb and so it remained until 1165 when Frederick Barbarossa transferred it to a marble sarcophagus. After Charlemagne had been canonized, Frederick II. placed his remains in a silver reliquary in 1215 where they have since reposed in peace. The beadle showed me the tomb of the Emperor Otho III., and the jeweled pulpit and then led me up to the gallery. Here I saw and sat on the marble throne upon which Charlemagne's body rested three hundred and fifty-one years and which was afterwards used at the coronation of the subsequent emperors. I also saw the antique sarcophagus in which Charlemagne's bones were placed from 1165 to 1215. It is of a style similar to those which one sees everywhere in Italy. The sacristan told me that it once contained the remains of Augustus, but sacristans do not always tell the truth and this story is particularly transparent.

October 15th, 1880, will long be remembered by the people of Cologne. The old cathedral after the labor of six centuries and a half had been finally completed and the leading men of the German Empire gathered at Cologne to inaugurate the edifice with appropriate ceremonies. Among those present were Emperor William and Empress Augusta, the Crown Prince and Princess, Prince Wilhelm, Count von Moltke, King Albert of Saxony, the Grand Duke of Baden, and many others.

There were various processions and the crowded heads were greeted with great enthusiasm. Gallant Moltke was cheered again and again. The narrow streets could hardly hold the multitudes. At night the cathedral was illuminated by electric light and the sky was ablaze with brilliant fire works. United Germany rejoiced over the completion of the famous church.

CHAPTER XXI.

FROM COLOGNE UP THE RHINE.—SPIRES.—SESENHEIM.—STRASSBURG.— BASEL.— CONSTANCE— SPENDING THE WINTER AT GENEVA.

GENEVA, Dec. 1st, 1880.

In the midst of the vast Rhine plain, which the tourist views from the summit of the Kaiserstuhl near Heidelberg, stands the old city of Spires, and through the mists the observer sees the towers of its cathedral, the burial place of the Emperors. Here was situated the Augusta Nemetum of the Romans. Here were held many of the diets of the old German empire. Here the princes friendly to the Reformation protested against the resolutions of the congress held by Charles the Fifth in 1529, from which fact the name Protestant was derived. The city, like dozens of others, was plundered by the unprincipled hirelings of his most Christian Majesty, Louis XIV. of France, and there is little left to-day of the historical relics of the past. The place has some thirteen thousand inhabitants but is very quiet. The only attraction is the cathedral, which was founded by Conrad II. in 1030. It was the burial place of the Emperors but the imperial tombs were twice desecrated by the French. The last time was in 1693 by the troops commanded by Hentz. It is a curious fact that the spoliation of the tombs of the French kings at St. Denis was perpetrated by a mob led by a man named Hentz, just one hundred years later. The cathedral was for some time used as a magazine by the French but was finally restored and decorated by Ludwig the First, of Bavaria, the same monarch who raised Munich to one of the chief art centers of the world and made his influence felt throughout all Europe.

The Spires cathedral is particularly rich in frescoes which rank as first class. They are of biblical and ecclesiastical subjects, thirty-two in number, and were executed by Schraudolph between 1845 and 1853. Eight German sovereigns were buried in the church. Their remains are deposited in the crypt beneath the choir, where one can still see the original sarcophagus of Rudolph, of Habsburg, who is the most distinguished of the emperors who rest here. The church contains a good statue of him by Schwanthaler. Rudolph was a powerful administrator of justice and destroyed many a tyrant's castle and hung many a robber knight. He had sense enough, too, not to meddle with Italy, which never could be united with Germany and would have been a useless acquisition even if it had been possible. He compared it to a lion's den, where many traces were visible of those who went in but few of those who came out. In his old age the Emperor was playing chess one day as usual in the castle at Germersheim when his physicians announced that his disease would soon prove mortal. "Well," he cried when the game was done, "up and away to Spires, to the tomb of the kings." In Kerner's ballad he mounts his war horse and rides to his grave. He prays for his people, receives the host and "then all at once the hall grows bright with a supernatural illumination, and in eternal sleep the hero sits there with the peace of heaven upon his countenance."

On the north side of the cathedral is the small Chapel of St. Afra, which was built by Emperor Henry the Fourth. Here the body of that monarch rested unburied for five years upon unconsecrated ground until the ban of excommunication against him was finally removed by Pope Pascal. Poor old Henry had a sad time with the priests. Not only did the proud Gregory VII. keep him barefooted in the snow three days before his gate at Canossa, but his followers on the papal chair incited his son to rebellion and the much afflicted monarch was compelled to abdicate and died of grief.

After spending the morning among these historical scenes I took the train for Strassburg. An hour before reaching the city we passed Sesenheim, the scene of Goethe's intimacy with Friederika Brion. This was in 1770, when the poet was attending the University at Strassburg. Herder had made known to him the beauties of Goldsmith's Vicar of Wakefield when his school-fellow Weyland offered to introduce him to a like amiable family. No sooner said than agreed to. Goethe disguised himself as a poor theological student, and off they galloped "twenty miles away" to the house of the village pastor at Sesenheim, Weyland left the shabbily clad, pretended theologue to discuss the pet subjects of the open-hearted preacher, and went to bring the more interesting members of the family. The mothers and daughters at length arrived, all beautiful, but the appearance of Friederike, the younger, enwrapt the attention of the disguised student. She was dressed in the Alsatian national costume and was gifted with an airy grace combined with an innocent artlessness of manner. For her description I cannot do better than to quote Mr. A. F. Broomhall's excellent lines :

> " Flowing hair and marble brow,
> Waving lashes, drooping low,
> Curtains which were hiding eyes,
> Blue and bright as starry skies;
> Dimpled cheeks and chiseled nose ;
> Budding lips which shamed the rose ;
> Rounded chin and throat of snow ;
> Form from which all graces flow ;
> These are heis—a net of charms,
> Stronger than a giant's arms."

The more Goethe became interested in the new acquaintance the more he became disgusted with his attire. Indeed in the morning he bolted in despair, leaving Weyland to explain matters, but a happy turn enabled him to change his disguise and he returned to the parsonage in the dress of the village landlord's son. A series of surprises followed, the pleasantest being when Friederike found him alone at her favorite resort upon a little knoll. Toward evening the students left to gallop back to Strassburg, but the letters and visits quickly made Goethe Friederike's acknowledged lover. All went well until 1771, when the poet left Strassburg, his dream being ended. "As I reached her my hand from the horse," he writes, "the tears stood in her eyes, and my own spirit was very sad." Their parting is referred by some to their difference in "social condition," but I think it should be ascribed alone to Goethe's eternal thirst for novelty. His connection with Christiane Vulpius shows that he was not disposed to let the views of the public deter him from following his inclination.

Lewes thought Friederike the noblest of the many women whom Goethe loved, and I suppose none will dispute the fact. She never married, for the heart which had been Goethe's, she said, could love no one else. The poet visited her several times in after years. She died in 1813. Goethe has paid her a beautiful tribute in his "Dichtung und Wahrheit," and she has been the subject of many books. Old withered scholars have made pilgrimages to Sesenheim and written an endless amount of sentimentality about the knoll of Friederikens Ruhe. But in later days the romantic spot fell a prey to the cultivator of cabbage and potatoes, until last July when the ground was bought by subscription and a handsome summer-house erected. With the usual speeches of the professors the place was solemnly given over to the village authorities, to be preserved "forever." The knoll is close to the railroad. It looks rather desolate, but the trees are to be replanted.

If any are curious for further details I refer them to the English translation of Dichtung und Wahrheit, which is published in Bohn's Library under the title of Autobiography of Goethe. The narrative begins in the latter part of the tenth book. It must of course be remembered that the translation cannot be expected to be as good as the original. Those who take the trouble to read it will find a nobler character than they meet in novels, and they can have the satisfaction of knowing that this belongs to the true part (Wahrheit) of the story. Perhaps, too, the account will awake an answering feeling, for, as the dainty Austin Dobson says :

> "We shut our heart up, nowadays,
> Like some old music box that plays
> Unfashionable airs that raise derisive pity ;
> Alas a nothing starts the spring ;
> And lo, the sentimental thing
> At once commences quavering
> Its lover's ditty."

Strassburg's cathedral is as famous as the city itself. One may even say that it is the cause of the city being so widely known. The structure was begun in 1179 upon the site of an earlier church, but the work progressed very slowly and is still unfinished. The most famous of its architects was Erwin Von Steinbach in the early part of the fourteenth century. He constructed the facade which is considered the finest part of the cathedral. He is said to have been succeeded by his talented daughter Sabina, although some critics have tried to dissolve the poor girl into a myth. She has a statue at one of the portals, however, and it will take some time to prove that out of existence.

The cathedral of Strassburg was designed to have twin towers, but only one has been finished. In spite of its great height it has a wonderful appearance of airy grace. It was long famous for being the highest spire in the world, but that distinction has passed to other quarters. It now is fourth in rank. The cathedral at Cologne, lately finished, is 524 feet high ; St. Ouen, at Rouen, in France, 492 feet ; St. Nicholas, at Hamburg, 473 feet; and the Strassburg cathedral, 466 feet. The great pyramid of Cheops in now 451 feet high; St. Peter's, at Rome, 435 feet ; St. Paul's, at London, 404 feet ; and the Capitol at Washington, 300 feet.

It was raining hard when I visited the Strassburg cathedral, but I determined to ascend the tower notwithstanding the weather. I climbed as far as the turrets, which are about three hundred and fifty feet above the ground. It is a dizzy height, and when one sees human beings in the streets below, they seem like a realization of Gulliver's Lilliputians. It is possible to go some distance higher, but one requires an especial permit from the city officers, and in wet weather it is like crawling into a cave. My ambition does not seek that kind of glory.

The famous clock is not situated in the tower, as some may suppose, but on the contrary, is in the church itself, in the transept to the left of the high altar. It was constructed between 1838 and 1842, by a Strassburg clock-maker named Schwilgue, and replaced an older and similar piece. On the lowest gallery is the deity which represents the day of the week. Above this an angel strikes the quarters of the hour upon the bell, and a genius at his side reverses his sand glass hourly. Still higher up a skeleton strikes the hours, and figures representing boyhood, youth, manhood and old age strike the quarters successively. Still higher, the apostles move around the figure of Jesus, at noon, and at the same time a large cock upon an adjacent elevation flaps its wings, stretches its neck and crows three times vigorously. The latter is the best part of the show. The clock is calculated to regulate itself for nine hundred and ninety-nine years.

The siege of Strassburg by the Germans lasted from August 11th, 1870, until September 27th. The destruction was awful, but there is nothing visible now to remind one of those terrible days. The fortifications are being extended, and seem unlimited in strength. The city has an appearance midway between French and German. One hears both languages, but all greetings are in French.

After I had spent a day in Strassburg I set out for Basel quite willingly, as the rain continued without interruption. It is a ride of five hours. The mist hid everything from view. I barely caught a glimpse of the castle of the Count of Rappoltstein on the distant hill. The count was the hereditary king of all the musicians and minstrels of the upper Rhine. They paid him a yearly tax and received in return the benefit of his protection. Every year a festival and reunion was held at the castle on the 8th of September, the "Pfeifertag." In 1673 this jurisdiction passed to other hands, and was at length extinguished by the French Revolution. It is a pity that the poets of the present day have not a king to look out for their affairs. I am afraid, however, that his income would be small and his life short if he depended upon them for his revenues.

At Basel I entered Switzerland, the grand old republic. In the suburban village of St. Jacob there is a fine new monument in memory of the 1,300 Swiss who were there cut to pieces by 30,000 French, in 1444. The Cathedral and Rhine bridges are worth seeing, but did not detain me long in the rain. According to Fetridge, Basel people used to keep their clocks an hour ahead of their neighbors. Some say this was done because they were lazier than the rest of the world, in order to keep them up to time. Their descendants are livelier, however, and get along without this stimulus.

In a disagreeable storm of rain I left for Constance. We passed three custom houses on the way, but the examination was as lenient as one could imagine. I stopped at Neuhausen to see the famous Falls of the Rhine. I was disappointed. They say they are finer than Niagara, but that is as if one would claim that candle light is brighter than sunshine. To compare them with St. Anthony's Falls would be nearer the truth. For a franc one can go down to the edge of the torrent and enjoy all the grand effect of the falling waters.

> "Here it comes sparkling,
> And there it lies darkling;
> Now smoking and frothing,
> In tumult and wrath in,
> It hastens along, conflictingly strong,
> Now striking and raging,
> As if a war waging,
> Its caverns and rocks among."

The city of Constance has a beautiful situation by the lake with varied views over water, meadow and mountain. I wandered through the streets, parks and quays and visited the cathedral. Down by the lake stands the Merchants' Hall, in which the famous council was held from 1414 to 1418. That assembly deposed the three anti-popes, John XXII., Gregory II. and Benedict X. and chose another, Martin V. The council has gained an infamous reputation in the eyes of civilization by its treacherous murder of John Huss and Jerome of Prague. The house where the former was arrested is still standing and is marked by a quaint old inscription and a new tablet with his relief portrait. West of the city, in the midst of a large meadow, an immense rock indicates the spot where the two heretics were burned. Huss was murdered July 6th, 1415, and Jerome of Prague, May 30th, 1416. Their ashes were thrown into the Rhine. Their spirits were solemnly given over to the Devil, who was certainly closely related to the givers. Huss and Jerome fell as martyrs to mediæval intolerance, and as such will never be forgotten. They have borne a share in moulding the character of this age and causing us to acknowledge the guiltlessness of honest thought. As Channing says, we are responsible for the uprightness and not for the rightness of our opinions. All hail, then, to Huss and Jerome of of Prague.

> "They never fail who die
> In a great cause. The block may soak their gore;
> Their heads may sodden in the sun; their limbs
> Be strung to city gates and castle walls—
> But still their spirit walks abroad. Though years
> Elapse, and others share as dark a doom,
> They but augment the deep and sweeping thoughts
> Which overpower all others, and conduct
> The world at last to freedom."

It soon became apparent that my hopes for better weather would soon be disappointed, and I took the train for Zurich, via Stein. We ran along the banks of the Rhine which here expands into the broad Untersee. At Stein I took my last look at the old Rhine, and the cars started southward through a rugged country, crossing the Thur by a lofty bridge. At Winterthur I boarded the express from Romanshorn and gossiped with a Vienna gentleman who thought I was a Russian, until we finally rolled into the station at Zurich.

The weather was as bad as possible. I could not see the mountains, not even the Uetliberg. I walked down by the lake and looked at it through the mists, which did not give much satisfaction. After seeing the little churchyard where the physiognomist Lavater is buried, I took the train for Lucerne, via Zug. We passed near the battle-field where Zwingli was killed, October 11th, 1531. A little later we passed along the shore of the Lake of Zug. Neither cars nor stations were heated, and when we reached Lucerne I was almost numb with cold. Under these circumstances I did not care to see anything but the fine Lion Monument. This was erected in 1821, to the memory of the Swiss Guards, who were killed in the defense of the Tuileries in

1792. It represents a dying lion, and was hewn in a sandstone cliff after a model by Thorwaldsen. It is a magnificent work.

In the afternoon I started for Berne by way of Aarburg. We passed the Lake of Sempach and saw the battle-field where the heroic Swiss defeated the Austrian oppressors July 8th, 1386. It was here that Arnold von Winkelried offered up his life for his country. The invaders were clad in armor and with their long lances they easily kept the Confederates at bay. Sixty of the brave mountaineers lay already dead when Arnold rushed forward shouting : "I will open a way for freedom ; comrades, care for my wife and child !" Grasping as many of the enemies' spears as possible he buried them in his own body. The Swiss dashed through this opening and mercilessly slaughtered the knights who were encumbered with their armor. Duke Leopold, of Austria, and four hundred nobles with thousands of their followers perished. The brave Swiss States were saved. To re-apply Dr. Johnson's saying of Marathon I think "the man is little to be envied whose patrotism would not gain force" upon the field of Sempach. One who is devoted to an idea is an uncomfortable neighbor but he alone exhibits his manhood ; all others sneak through life swayed hither and thither by desires and fears, and spend their existence like dogs, hunting for bones and dodging kicks.

Toward evening we arrived at Berne, the capital of the Confederation. The city is bounded on three sides by the river Aar and the environs are very beautiful. One is said to enjoy magnificent views of the Alps from the different elevations in the city. It may be so, but I did not. The streets are bordered on each side by arcades like those at Bologna, in Italy, but they are so clumsily made that they spoil the appearance of the houses.

After seeing the Parliament buildings and the cathedral, I crossed over the Aar to look at Berne's collection of bears. The founder of the city is said to have killed a bear on its present site, and the people have worshiped that animal ever since. You see images and pictures of bears everywhere. If the city erects a statue to a public benefactor, the recipient of such honor must grant a portion of his pedestal to the nation's idol, and man and bear stand side by side. For many years a number of live animals have been kept at public expense. They were carried to France in the time of Napoleon, but were again returned.

In the afternoon I set out for Geneva, my last journey for the season. The scenery along the road is very beautiful. It was dark when we approached Lausanne, but that did not hinder us from enjoying the first view of the Lake of Geneva, whose praises Byron has so finely sung.

In the apartment of the car with me there were two others who were going to Geneva to learn French. Our other fellow-passenger was a German cosmopolitan on his way to Southern France. As usual, he asked me if I was a Russian, as soon as he noticed from my language that I was a foreigner.

About nine o'clock in the evening we reached Geneva, and I felt relieved to think that I was now to throw my old knapsack into a corner and settle down for the winter. My home is near the lake, and this evening, when I go to my window, I can hear the waves breaking over the mole. The Jura and "clear, placid Leman" are my daily sights, and in fine weather the eternal snows of Mont Blanc are visible. This is Calvin's town, and Voltaire's village is but a few miles away.

I said I was glad when I arrived here. Seven months' constant traveling is enough to satisfy almost anyone for one year. If one seeks happiness in wandering, he succeeds no better than than the Spaniards did in their search for the fountain of youth. In Germany I was told that paradise was in Italy ; in Venice they said it was farther down the peninsula ; in Rome and Naples they thought it could be found in the Alps ; in the mountains I was told to look for it in Vienna or Berlin ; in these places I was informed that Eden existed in Scandinavia or Russia ; but I failed to find it ; I traveled pretty fast, but I was told everywhere the next neighbors were in paradise, yet I never could overtake the people in possession. The traveler is like the lover ; he lives at a greater strain than ordinary mortals. His pleasures and pains are volcanic. At times he is carried away with enthusiasm, and again at others he thinks the sun dimmer than a tallow candle and nature seems like a faded fresco. But in spite of all I am persuaded that one derives more real pleasure from good friends and good books than from all these weary wanderings. In prospect or retrospect they seem grand, but it is a delusion. The sun above us we think a prosy thing, but at either side of the horizon it gilds the sky in beauty. Journey toward the golden East or West and they never grow nearer. The present will ever seem mean and the past and future lovely.

One easily preceives the difference in the people as soon as he crosses the Swiss frontier from Germany. Here politics is the universal theme of conversation and even the most ignorant are busily engaged in discussing the current problems of national or local statesmanship. In Germany one never talks on subjects connected with the higher powers except among friends. I have heard the "blood and iron" Bismarck denounced unsparingly but it was "under four eyes," as the Germans say, and when speaking with those who knew that I am an American. What do the people talk about? Well, gossip and scandal, a little, but principally about eatables and drinkables, a regular kitchen debate. The conversation one hears at a country inn makes one imagine the return of those old scholastics, who disputed with each other as to the number of angels who could stand on the point of a needle. The peasants discuss problems almost as ridiculous with as much vehemence as if they were of vital personal interest to themselves. They grow red in the face, scream until they are hoarse and pound the tables with their fists till the glasses dance like corn in a popper, and all about some question which they know nothing about and even if it could be decided would not prove of the least interest or value.

The newspapers of Switzerland are also a vast improvement on the German. They have a more independent spirit and although largely made up of heated discussions on local questions they are more interesting. The Swiss from their mountains look over the political combats of Europe almost as cooly as we do ourselves, and their press, I think, gives as unbiased accounts of contemporary events as is possible at the present day. The German newspapers, which I said were inferior to the Swiss, are in general very unsatisfactory. The English historian said that to become acquainted with a nation it is necessary to read its newspapers. This is only partially true of the Germans. Everyone who has traveled in the country must feel that they are a poor expression of the public opinion except in certain directions. The papers are made up without the least mechanical ingenuity in arrangement and are almost destitute of such aids to the reader as clearly legible head lines. The matter is composed of such things as a panegyric of the powers that be, written with Asiatic servility ; a couple of telegrams ; some stale dispatches copied from a London daily ; an announcement that Bismarck's health is not so bad as is rumored ; a long account of the French war of revenge as a probability of the immediate future, published as a preface to a demand for more soldiers and taxes ; an elaborate denial of the last scare which is put forward with reservation. The "feuilleton" contains a part of an eternally continuing novel divided daily by measure without regard to chapters or sense, also perhaps a little notice about the Yankees and an old joke on an English tourist. My synopsis is long but the papers themselves are very small. Indeed when I show a German an American paper the very sight gives him the headache. A Tribune or Herald would furnish him reading matter for a week.

We Americans have a mistaken notion of the immensity of the knowledge acquired by the German people. We cross the Atlantic expecting to find everyone in the Fatherland a perfect walking encyclopedia and look for nothing else than to be hourly reminded of our profound ignorance. But we deceive ourselves. I do not hesitate to assert that the average American is fully as well informed on current subjects, fully as thoroughly imbued with the spirit of the age as the German. I will even say that the student of our country is little behind one of the same grade in the Fatherland. Whence then comes the fame for knowledge ? From the specialists. There is some truth in the saying that no one reads a book in Germany unless he intends to write another to supercede it. The country's reputation for learning is sustained by the scholars whose indefatigable industry deserves all the praise that is bestowed upon it. The professional savants, who are in great part attached to the universities, form a class which is wanting in our country. Our professors are forced to drudge like slaves and sing the same tune year after year, whereas those of Germany have comparatively light tasks and are continually making independent and progressive investigations.

The Geneva university gives a course of popular lectures during the evenings in winter. They are by different professors on various subjects and are very well attended. Foreigners from the four quarters of the globe go regularly in order to learn the language. The themes are such as the voyage of the "Challenger"; the germs in the air ; papal intrigues in France ; the French Academy ; international arbitration ; but oh ! ghost of Calvin ! the course on modern French actors attracted such crowds that every seat was taken long before the lectures began, and the eulogies of the stage were greeted with tremendous applause.

This popular course is delivered by the professors with

more elegance than they are accustomed to bestow upon their class rooms. In America brilliant ignorance is listened to with more patience than tedious learning but the opposite is the case in Europe. I have heard professors in Germany deliver lectures which were no more interesting than what a school-boy could compile in a short time from an encyclopedia, but they met with approval because their authors were known as learned men. The people do not care about the nature of the repast but they must have the consolation of knowing that the cook has raised all the ingredients.

Geneva is, I suppose, the best known city in Switzerland. It is associated with such famous characters as Calvin, Rousseau and Voltaire, and remembered as a place of refuge of reformers of all nations. Besides this, Americans will not forget the scene of the arbitration on the Alabama Claims, which I believe gave us fifteen millions of dollars.

It is really a finely situated town. Toward the north we see the Jura range with its barren summits. Before us lies the lake, now covered with angry waves which dash against the shore ; now still and smooth, mirroring the snowy peaks of the distant mountains. At times the beautiful tints of the water and the sun-illumined mists along the summits of the Jura give the scene an oriental magnificence, such as we generally think of as peculiar to Italy. Toward the south rise a number of smaller mountains beyond which appear the eternal snows of Mount Blanc.

The Rhone which here flows from the lake divides the city in two unequal parts which are connected by a number of bridges. The finest of these is the magnificent Pont de Mont Blanc which is paved with asphalt and lighted at night by two rows of fine candelabra. Immediately below this bridge is the island of J. J. Rousseau which contains a statue of that philosopher. He was born at Geneva in 1712.

The city in general has a modern appearance, although it is true that in the older parts there are a good many dingy houses and narrow, break-neck lanes. After wandering so long in the old cities of Italy, Germany and other countries, Geneva seemed to me like an American town. The modern additions can boast a great many fine buildings among which are various schools, the university and the magnificent theater, a monument to the downfall of Calvin's regime. The abnormal number of cafes, pensions and hotels in the city show that it is a resort of strangers. The exiled Russian nihilists and German socialists make this their headquarters and the seat of their printing establishments. The Germans come here in great numbers to learn French as it is much more pleasant for them here than in France. Indeed there are so many of them here that it is difficult for one knowing their language to learn French. In almost every shop there is some one who speaks German, and one hears it everywhere on the street.

There are three English churches here: Evangelical Alliance, Anglican and American Episcopal. The latter congregation has a neat little chapel whose corner-stone was laid by Gen. Grant. The Russian residents have erected one of their queer five towered churches here and they seem to be pretty numerous. Across the street from where I live there is a Spanish family on the first floor and a Canadian one on the second. I do not know from what quarter of the globe comes the family on the third. It is plain that strangers are not a rarety in this town and are consequently not lionized as they are in Germany.

A recent number of the Augsburger Abendzeitung contained some interesting statistics on the nationality of the visitors to Switzerland in 1879. There were 700,000 Germans and Austrians ; 280,000 Englishmen ; 200,000 Frenchmen ; 70,000 Russians ; 60,000 Italians ; 60,000 Americans, and 30,000 of other nations, in all 1,400,000, which is just half as many as there are inhabitants. And think too that this army of tourists spend here 200,000,000 francs annually ! It looks as though a mountain was a better investment than a cornfield.

CHAPTER XXII.

I LEAVE GENEVA.—EMBARK AT MARSEILLES FOR EGYPT.—LAND AT ALEXANDRIA AND GO TO CAIRO.—PYRAMIDS AND THE DESERT.

I spent the winter very pleasantly at Geneva. My French teacher was Frau Nawrotil, a teacher who came originally from Vienna and who had lived for years among the French. I devoted myself entirely to the study of French literature and history and read a number of books in German, French and English, which related to the cities I expected to visit during the coming spring and summer.

My room was pleasantly situated in Eaux Vives, a suburb of the city. My landlord was the florist Hiertzeler. His pretty daughter made sport of my French and his roguish son spilled ink over my best books, but that did not occasion any coolness between us. I boarded at restaurants uptown and the long walk gave me all the exercise I needed and kept me in good condition for the hardships of the summer's travels.

In March we had several fine days and in company with several French friends I visited Ferney, Voltaire's home, and and ascended the Saleve mountains which are the peaks nearest Geneva.

I left Geneva, March 26th, 1881, for Marseilles. We had a snow storm just before I started and as my train dashed off toward Lyons the Saleve, Jura and Mount Blanc were white with their wintry covering. I spent the afternoon in seeing the sights at Lyons and started the next morning down the beautiful valley of the Rhone, past the famous cities of Avignon, Nimes and Arles.

As we descended the valley the signs of spring became more and more visible. When we reached Marseilles the trees were covered with blossoms and leaves.

At half past 9 Tuesday morning, March 29th, the steamer Euxene, upon which I embarked, cast loose her moorings at Marseilles, and began her voyage to Alexandria. The weather was cloudy and windy, but not cold. For some hours we hugged the French coast so closely that the towns could be distinguished among the hills. From Toulon we turned into the open sea toward Sardinia. The evening brought us a violent wind and rain, which continued the following day. However, I escaped, as hitherto, the misfortune of getting sea-sick.

Wednesday morning we sighted Corsica and Sardinia, and some time later passed between them through the Strait of Bonifacio. To the right of us lay Garibaldi's home, the little island of Caprera.

Wednesday passed without the occurrence of anything of note. The waves were high and a good many were sick. When I left Geneva I said farewell to the German language, not expecting to hear any more of it for some months to come. I was therefore agreeably surprised to find a Swiss among my fellow-passengers. He went with us only as far as Naples, but I spent a good deal of time in conversing with him, as German comes more natural to me than French. He was very sick, all because he had eaten a bit of fat meat, he said, but that is a delusion to which all sea sick persons are subject. They always ascribe their malady to the last thing they have eaten, but it comes just the same, whether they eat fat or lean.

Thursday morning the Ponza Islands came in sight, and at noon we anchored in the harbor at Naples. Here I bade farewell to the Swiss and to an English fellow-passenger, and, in company with a Frenchman, went ashore to spend the few hours of our stay in the city.

How familiar the old place looked ! The same narrow streets, the same indolent loafers ; the same impudent hackmen, who snap their whips in your faces at every pace and shout their eternal " qui ! qui ! "

We walked the whole length of the grand Strada di Roma to look at its gay shops. Then we returned by the narrow lanes where Neapolitan life is seen untouched by Northern influence. Every one sits at his door to carry on his trade. A mother can conceive of no better place to chase the vermin on her children than at the front door. There she has advantage of the light, and she need feel no scruples of modesty, for all the neighbors are doing the same. And amid all this filth, vermin, beggary and misery, are the people gloomy ? Not in the least. They shout and laugh, and sing like the merriest men in the world.

Leaving the narrow byways we went out to the small but brilliant park to see the moneyed world driving in the Riviera de Chiaji. This is the Bois de Boulogne of Naples, and those versed in local gossip could doubtless tell great tales of the people who dash by in their carriages. At this season of the year the park is thronged with visitors of all nations.

When we returned to the ship at night we could see the flames of the Vesuvius as well as the long stretch of lava which is flowing down the side. At midnight we steamed out of the harbor and turned toward the south. All day Friday we were in sight of the Lipari Islands, among the most prominent of which is the volcanic Stromboli. At dusk we reached the strait between Sicily and the continent, that passage which bore such a gloomy reputation in olden times.

I got out my Homer and read the dismal tales which used to be circulated by the ancient mariners. I read of the terrible goddess Charybdis and of the horrible Scylla, who watched on the opposite shore. "Not a single pilot," says the poet, "who has passed Scylla's cliffs boasts of being spared." And for all that we steamed quietly through the strait without a thought of harm. The Italian shore is an abrupt rock, while the Sicilian is flat near the water. It is remarkable that the old blind poet knew the country so well. After we had passed the strait it grew dark, and the long rows of lamps on one side marked the city of Messina, while on the other were those of Reggio.

Saturday morning nothing was visible but the sea ; but about half-past 10 the Maltese coast appeared directly before us.

At noon we anchored in the fine harbor of La Valetta, the chief city of Malta. The place is protected by formidable forts, and is considered impregnable. Since 1800 the island has been under British sovereignty, and it is the first

English territory I have touched in Europe. It fairly swarms with soldiers and sailors.

Malta plays a great part in history as well as in fable. It was here that Calypso held the wandering Ulysses enchanted. Here St. Paul was shipwrecked when on his way to Rome. The natives tell all kinds of lies about him. I suppose they have the original fire and the snakes which figure in the last chapter of the Acts. At least they have the cave where St. Paul lived during his three months' stay. It is queer that all historical persons lived in caves, but I suppose that it is to be accounted for by the fact that they had an eye to the preservation of their dwellings to be shown to posterity. How thoughtful of them!

Malta passed successively through the hands of the Greeks, Carthagenians, Romans and Barbarians. In 1530 Charles V. presented it to the Knights of the Order of St. John, who retained it until the end of the last century.

La Valetta is built on a number of hills, and its streets have a break neck steepness. The houses are of a yellow color, as though they were often invaded by dust. It is now but the beginning of April, yet the temperature at Malta is as warm as July in Ohio.

The Maltese ladies have a strange sort of head-dress. It consists of a large piece of black silk, which they hold in one hand, while a whalebone keeps it extended around their head like a halo.

Saturday evening we left Malta, steering eastward. There is nothing more remarkable about the Mediterranean than the scarcity of vessels. On the Baltic there is not an hour of the day that several sails are not visible.

At Naples we took on a queer passenger. He is a Pole and a good Roman Catholic, with fiery wrath against the schismatics of his country. He is making a pilgrimage to Palestine, and has been to Rome. He talks no language that anybody on the boat understands, except a few words of German. He is seventy-eight years of age and the father of nineteen children. Where he got the idea of making a pilgrimage I donot know, but he says his family tied him hand and foot to keep him from going, but he went nothwithstanding.

He set out last August with ninety roubles in money, and he always traveled on foot until he reached the sea. He has now not quite fifty cents, but is confident of making his way by begging. There is something great in the confidence with which he goes out into unknown lands. As I was the only one who understood German, he delighted to talk with me, supplementing his limited vocabulary by gestures.

On Wednesday, April 6th, we had left Malta four days and a half behind. The African promontory of Barca, where the famous Cyrena of old once stood, had been visible for a day and then disappeared. We knew that Egypt must be near. The heat was intense, forming a great contrast to the snow of Geneva. At 10:30 A. M., a low line appeared in the southern horizon and the water about us grew muddy. "Voila l'Egypte," cried my French comrade. "Ecco la terra!" quoth the Italian. "Ist das Aegypten?" asked the old Russian pilgrim standing on the bulwarks and straining his aged eyes in the eager effort to see the long desired land.

Our glasses revealed the light-house and the ships in the

harbor at Alexandria. The coast is low like that of Holland and the most conspicuous objects on it are numerous windmills, which also form a prominent feature of the Dutch landscape. Our attention was soon engaged by the arrival of the pilot boat which gave us our first glimpses of Oriental character. One at once conceives a disgust for the effeminate looking natives in their gaudy robes. The pilot was an ugly fellow with a set of prominent yellow teeth which he exhibited constantly without adding to his beauty, especially when he squinted through his long telescope. The captain regaled him with the usual coffee and he soon brought us safely into the harbor.

The engines had scarcely stopped before we were surrounded with boats and as soon as the quarantine officers had made their examination, the Arabs came swarming over the rail like a lot of wolves. A dozen or so of the pirates laid hands on us and it seemed for a time as though our bodies and baggage were to be divided among them. The Frenchman who spoke Arabic made a bargain with one gang to take us ashore for a franc each, whereupon they drove off the others and hustled us into their boat. At the custom house wharf they extorted double fare and after our passports and baggage had been examined we were turned over to the brigands outside. I hired one to carry my valise and started for the Cairo station.

What a strange world this is! I had dreamed of the lovely women of the East with their picturesque attire. Pretty soon we met one. O horrors! The poetry had not mentioned the dirt. She wore a veil over her face below her eyes, and, considering how mortally ugly the upper section was, I rejoiced that she spared us the sight of the other half. As we walked on, the other features of Oriental life appeared. Everywhere were the same picturesque costumes, the same quaint booths for shops that I had so long admired in pictures, but they all had one quality I had neglected in my imagination's dream, and that was the omnipresent dirt.

My guide soon conducted me across the public square in which stands the equestrian statue of Mohammed Ali, the founder of the reigning dynasty. As is well known, pictorial representations of every class were forbidden by Mohammed in his zeal to root out idolatry, and it was with some difficulty that the faithful could be persuaded to permit the erection of Mohammed Ali's statue. But now Cairo has also an equestrian monument and the photographers seem to be well patronized by the richer natives.

When my guide reached the station he generously attempted to extort twice as much from me as he had agreed to take when he started. I referred the matter to two black policemen and after much loud talking in indifferent French and worse Italian, they drove away my persecutor leaving me a victor on the field of battle.

Finding that that the Cairo train did not leave until ten P. M., I deposited my luggage with a station official and started out to see the sights of Alexandria. I first turned my steps southward outside of the city gates and disregarding the doubtful temptations of numerous hovels by the wayside with such signs as "British Bar," and "American Drinks," I continued my course along a dusty road until I reached an Arab cemetery. Upon a hill near by rises in a fine Corinthian pillar of granite one hundred and four feet high, called Pompey's column. It does not take its name from Cæsar's great opponent, but from a Roman prefect of a later date and it was dedicated to Emperor Diocletian. It is thought by some to have once borne a statue of a horse of which the following story is told : When Diocletian had captured rebellious Alexandria he ordered that his soldiers slay the people until the blood reached his horse's knees. His steed however stumbled over a corpse and falling on its knees in blood, the emperor declared his command fulfilled and ordered the carnage to be stopped. The people in gratitude erected a statue to the horse.

An unknown Arab writer of the twelfth century is quoted by Maxime du Camp in his book " Le Nil, " as saying, that Pompey's column belonged to a lot of three hundred, with which the genii built a grand audience chamber for King Solomon. He says the "columns are of red marble, shaded with divers colors, brilliant as the shell of Venus of Arabia the Blessed, polished like a mirror and reflecting images." "Among them there is one which moves and inclines toward the east and west at the moment of the rising and setting of the sun. ,C'est la une chose merveilleuse."

There is one good thing about the old world : they tell a nice story about every spot of interest. I cannot help thinking that if our political campaign liars would turn their inventive genius in this direction, our rocks and woods might soon be alive with fairies, and thick with enchanted castles filled with fair princesses and noble knights waiting for some one to break the spell which holds them fast.

While I was standing gazing at the column a little native

girl came and begged for backsheesh, that miserable word which rings eternally in the traveler's ears everywhere in the Orient. She knew a little English, for the beggars know it pays.

I stopped at one place to buy some oranges of a dealer and he proved to be a native of Athens, Greece, who had spent some years in California and had become an American citizen. He seemed glad to see me and talked some time, but his interest in me vanished when I refused to buy some mining stock which he had on hand as a memento of his American travels. A tourist meets some strange people.

After dark I continued to wander about the streets until train time. The city at night made me half believe I was in Italy, as it was very similar to the older quarters of Naples. The dirt and noise reign supreme in each and the fleas take away one's inclination to stand still or sit down. Homer makes Menalaus say in recounting his adventures to Telemachus:

"There is an isle
Within the billowy sea before you reach
The coast of Egypt,—Pharos is its name,—
At such a distance as a ship could pass
In one whole day with a shrill breeze astern.
A sheltered haven lies within that isle,
Where the good ships go forth with fresh supplies of water."

When Alexander passed through the country he chose that spot for the foundation of the famous seaport which still bears his name. After his death Ptolemy Soter took possession of Egypt and extended and improved Alexandria. He founded the Museum and assembled the great philosophers and scientists which under himself and his successors have rendered the institution famous. He also began the light-house on the island of Pharos, which was then connected with Alexandria by a long causeway, but which is now part of the mainland. This light-house was finished under Ptolemy Philadelphus and was the first one ever built. The name Pharos is perpetuated in the French word for light-house, "Le Phare," and the Italian, "Il Faro." It was at the Museum that the Greek translation of the Old Testament was made by the Seventy. It was there that Euclid, Theocritus, Aristarchus and hundreds of other famous men lived and wrote. But they are gone and not a stone remains to tell where once the Museum and the Serapeum stood.

Alexandria is associated with Cæsar, Cleopatra and Mark Antony; it was honored by the lovely and learned Hypatia; it was disgraced with the interminable brawls of Christians, Jews and Pagans, whom Hadrian calls all "astrologers, interpreters of signs and quacks." In its palmiest days the city had half a million inhabitants. Hadrian wrote: "No man's hands here are idle. At one place glass is manufactured, at another paper, and at another linen. All these busy people seem to carry on some kind of handicraft. Men with gouty feet, blind persons, and even those with gouty hands, all find some occupation." Alexandria was taken by the Arabs A. D. 641, and sank into insignificance. At present it is gaining in prosperity and already numbers more than two hundred thousand inhabitants.

There is perhaps no country in the world which is regarded with such a general feeling of interest as Egypt. It is associated with our first recollections through the Mosaic accounts with which we become familiar in infancy. Historians turn to the valley of the Nile for their earliest records of civilization. Scientists trace the origin of their specialities to the Egyptians, whom the greatest of the Greeks and Romans were glad to claim as their masters. Farmers and mechanics note with interest the queer ways in which their own professions were carried on in that strange country.

The distance from Alexandria to Cairo by rail is one hundred and thirty-one miles. I started by the 10 P. M. train which is due at Cairo about 5 o'clock in the morning. It was with much impatience that I awaited the dawn as the train rolled slowly along. The growing light soon revealed broad fertile fields of golden grain, for wheat is there ripe in April. The country might be easily mistaken for an American prairie, were it not for the palm trees and swarthy natives in blue robes who were going to work in the field with long strings of camels.

The latter were somewhat shabbier looking than those which travel with the circus. Their hair was nearly all worn off and their skin looked as black and nasty as a tarpaulin. They are steady walkers and turn aside for neither man nor beast. Their stomachs are vigorous, being able to digest anything from a bucket of water to a keg of nails. When on the march they have a sort of a jerking and pitching motion which has the same effect upon the uninitiated as the rolling of a ship.

Modern Cairo lies a little north of the site of a city called New Babylon which was founded by Cambyses about 525 B. C. and was garrisoned by a legion during the supremacy of the Romans. Their fortified camp can still be seen. When Khalif Omar's General Amr ibn el-Asi besieged the city he pitched his tent on the site of Cairo. After the capture of the place he ordered his tent to be taken down, but as it was discovered that a pigeon had built its nest upon it, he directed that it should be left standing until the young birds could fly. After the taking of Alexandria he returned to his tent and a city sprang up around it, which from this circumstance was called Fostat which means a tent. The walls of the modern city were commenced when the planet Mars was crossing the meridian. Therefore the Arabs called the place Masr el-Kahir which means Egypt the Victorious. The European name for the city is derived from the adjective. The French Le Kaire and the Italian Il Cairo still preserve the article, but in German and English it has been dropped.

Cairo has about 400,000 inhabitants and is the largest city in Africa. It lies nine miles south of the point where the Nile divides and has been termed by somebody "the most beautiful diamond on the handle of the green fan of the delta."

Like all modern Oriental cities Cairo has two distinct divisions. The one contains the fine villas in European style with their lovely gardens where eastern fertility is aided by western skill; it contains too the shops where European articles are sold and which vary from Parisian elegance to Oriental filth. The other quarter contains the older part of the city where native character is seen uncontaminated by foreign influence.

The center of European Cairo is the Ezbekiyeh Square, a park of some twenty acres, nicely laid out and planted with fine flowers, shrubs and trees, which present a luxuriance of growth and beauty of color which is peculiar to the warmer climates. The principal hotels and shops are around this square and it is the favorite promenade of both natives and foreigners. An Egyptian military band plays there every afternoon.

Louis Pascal, thus describes the tourists on the Ezbekiyeh in his " Le Cange ; Voyage en Egypte: " "One meets there the English traveler with his impossible dress and outlandish hat ; the Frenchman is made known by the mocking smile which wanders over his lips and the unabashed way (sans facon, Ungenirtheit) in which he stares at the women. One recognizes the American by his loud voice, his bad-mannered forwardness, his incessant emission of saliva and the benevolent regard he addresses to his good friends the English."

The Native Quarter begins but a short distance from the Ezbekiyeh. The bazaars at first have a European appearance but a little farther on they are entirely Arabian. One of the first things I did was to purchase a fez at one the shops. This is a red skull cap with a black silk tassel which is worn by everybody from a sultan to a donkey driver. I did not particularly admire that sort of head dress, but I donned it to keep off the beggars which hats in that country are sure to attract. It may flatter one's vanity to have people think he is a nabob, but for an impecunious traveler it is a too expensive opinion to encourage. My fez did not protect me from the rays of the sun but I think it did protect me somewhat from the beggars. I wore it about six weeks and got so well Africanized that when I accidentally met one of my old college professors on the street at Paris he failed to recognize me.

The Bazaars are generally divided according to the nature of the stuffs sold. Thus there are bazaars of shoemakers, jewelers, copper smiths, book binders, woolen merchants and dealers in spices and perfumes. The whole neighborhood of the latter is pregnant with the odors of Araby the Blest. Even the much married Mohammed said : " there are two things in the world which delight me, women and perfumes. These two things rejoice my eyes and render me more fervent in devotion." They both seem to be held now in the same favor among the followers of the prophet.

The bazaars are merely collections of little shops only a few feet deep where the whole stock can be seen at a glance. The merchant sits tailor fashion smoking or casting up his accounts. When a customer comes in he orders coffee and the two quarrel over the price of the goods for hours in the perfect conviction that time is not money.

The Orientals are like children and do not attempt to restrain their passion, consequently they make a great deal of noise, whether they are mad or merry. Nothing can convey any idea of the Babel of noises one hears on the Muski, the principal street of the Arab quarter of Cairo. Here comes a bearded and turbaned native with a long spouted jug on his back, rattling two metal cups and loudly bawling : "Confection, O sugar for a nail, O confection!" He will sell you a sweet drink or trade it to you for nails and old iron. Then come water carriers with big black skins on their backs. Ice they have not, but they have kullehs or porous bottles which make the water of a pleasant temperature. Then there are hawkers of every imaginable article which they cry out in their own peculiar style. Just as you are intent on looking at some shop a muscular fellow in white toga and gold embroidered vest dashes past you swinging a stick and whooping " guarda u-ah ! u-ah ! " Then you know you must squeeze up against the wall for a carriage is coming and the lane is narrow. Every minute you will be run down by a donkey if you don't heed the driver's shrill cry, "she-malak ! " which seems to rhyme with the continual whack of the whip over the beast's back.

A German traveler, Herr Goltz, says : "In the Boulevards of Paris and London Bridge I saw but the shadow, and at Alexandria the prelude only, of the Babel of Cairo, to which the Roman and Venetian carnival is tame and commonplace. These marvelous scenes cannot fail to strike everyone, and particularly the uninitiated new comer, most forcibly. In order to enjoy them thoroughly, one cannot help wishing for eyes behind, as well as before, and for the steady power of forcing one's way possessed by the camel of burden."

On the south-east side of Cairo rises the citadel which commands the city with its cannon, but which is itself subject to the batteries on the higher summits beyond. It is an interesting old pile of irregular shape. The walls were erected in 1166 with stones from the smaller pyramids of Gizeh. It was in the citadel that Mohammed Ali on March 1st, 1811, caused the Mamelukes to be murdered to the number of four hundred and seventy. Amin Bey made his horse spring from the wall into the moat and escaped. They still point out the spot where he took his famous leap.

The Alabaster Mosque of Mohammed Ali which stands within the citadel is one of the most prominent landmarks of Cairo. One hesitates whether to admire most the matchless beauty of the material, when viewed closely, or the exquisite symmetry of form of the mosque when seen from the desert miles away. The shapely dome and the lofty, yet slender and delicately built, minarets have an appearance so full of grace, that it can neither be imagined nor described.

Afer putting straw shoes over my more vulgar northern pedal coverings I passed in and made my first visit to a Mohammedan mosque. The sacristan led the way across the broad outer court into the edifice proper. The floor is carpeted with the thick rugs of native manufacture. In one corner is the tomb of Mohammed Ali, the founder of the reigning house of Egypt and one of the principal promoters of its modern improvement.

The minarets are the most striking feature of Arabian architecture and are the first objects visible in approaching a city. They are lofty, slender towers, having an outside gallery near the top where the muezzin stand when they call the faithful to prayer. Their chants are the most characteristic sounds of a Mohammedan town. They are said to be generally blind men in order that their elevated position may not give them too much knowledge of what is going on in the harems below.

When Mohammed made his night journey to Jerusalem and to the seventh heaven, tradition says he received from God fifty daily prayers to be recited by the faithful. In coming out of the Almighty's sanctum the prophet met Moses, who, on hearing the news, told the young apostle of his ill success with the stiff necked Jews and prevailed on him to go back and ask the Lord for a diminution of his task. This was repeated a number of times until he had reduced the demand to five prayers a day, but still Moses was not satisfied. Thinkest thou to exact five prayers daily from thy people? By Allah! I have had experience with the children of Israel and such a demand is vain : return therefore and entreat still further mitigation of the task." "No," replied Mohammed, "I have already asked indulgence until I am ashamed." So the faithful ever since have had five prayers a day.

The women in the Orient are not religious. The men seem to think religion their monopoly and do not encourage their wives to attend to the ordinances of the prophet. In the east the men, while in the west the women are the most willing victims of superstition. The Koran counts a woman but half a man and requires the testimony of two women to counter-balance that of one man. "The hair is long, but the mind is short," says an ungallant proverb of the east.

Within the citadel is the well of Joseph, into which he was put by his wicked brothers. It is 280 feet deep and is cut through solid limestone rock. It was made under the rule of one Joseph, five or six centuries ago. As it was called Joseph's well it had to be identified with the famous one of old. That is the way they make legends.

My guide through the city was a native of Cairo who had lived with an English family at Suez and had made a voyage to India. He spoke tolerably good English and was friendly. He wore a long variegated robe which reached almost to his red low cut shoes. On his head he had a red fez round which was wound a long white scarf thus forming a turban. The colors of turbans vary. Green is worn only by the descendants of the prophet and the Mecca pilgrims. Mohammed himself wore a turban, for he said " the turbans were worn by the angels, and in arranging it he let one end hang down between his' shoulders, which he said was the way they wore it."

I sat for some time with my guide Hasan at a street cafe drinking native coffee and watching the passing people. Oriental coffee is made by putting the ground coffee and the sugar into a brass cup which has a long handle and, after pouring hot water in, letting it boil a few minutes. Usually only enough is made at a time to fill a tiny cup not more than a third the size of ours. Only the top can be drank as the bottom is full of grounds. The natives frequent the cafes in great numbers. They all smoke cigarettes or water pipes.

The tombs of the Khalifs, which lie in the desert north-east of the citadel, form the most picturesque sight near Cairo. They were once richly endowed tomb-mosques of Egyptian sultans. But their revenues have been confiscated and they are going to ruin. Their domes are magnificently shaped, their minarets pleasing, and the half fallen condition of their structures in the midst of the barren desert awakens a feeling of awe mingled with admiration. Between these tombs and the city is a range of hills of sand from whose summit a remarkable view is obtained. Far as the eye can reach toward the east and west lies the cheerless desert, emblem of eternity, whose treacherous sands baffle the skill of man. Beyond the narrow valley of the Nile rise the pyramids, monuments of a forgotten age, whose hoary sides scorn the attacks of time and the human race. They have seen many generations of men till the fertile valley and pass into oblivion. At our feet we see the great city of Cairo with its varied races of men. Behind us are tombs of sovereigns whose power has not availed in keeping their burial mosques from ruin. Few scenes in the world indicate in such a marked manner the transitoriness of fame and fortune.

Some Arab children came to me to beg and interrupted my reverie. They usually say "Backsheesh, yah Khawageh!" which means "O Sir! a gift!" The dusky imps on this occasion abbreviated their request to "Backsheesh, hog, hog!" which to English ears has no complimentary sound.

In the eastern quarter of the city near the bazaar of the bookbinders is a mosque now used for a University. It has over ten thousand students whose energies are devoted to committing to memory the Koran and a lot of old books based upon it. Their learning is useless and antiquated. Mohammedism like all other religions successfully inculcates an indifference to death, but it is fatal to the development of the human mind. Doubt and criticism like the grinding of a diamond have a destructive result if driven to extreme, but they are all that give value to the crude material which would otherwise be worthless. It is sad that western religions have placed errors in doctrine on a lower scale than the most heinous crimes, but how much they are surpassed by Mohammedism will be apparent from the following: Ibn Batutah, a traveler from Tangiers, visited Mecca in the fourteenth century. He relates that "one day a lawyer named Aboul Abbas fell into the gross error of saying that Hosein, son of Ali, left no posterity. The emir of Medina, justly enraged, wanted kill to him. Yielding to intercession however he contented himself with his banishment from the city. They say for all that he sent some one after him to assassinate him ; and it is certain that no one has since heard any tidings of him." The writer concludes with the pious wish that we may all be delivered from such damnable errors.

The Dervishes are interesting to the European traveler. I went one Friday afternoon to see them, visiting first the dancing dervishes. These are men of various ages dressed in a close fitting vest and a short skirt. They close their eyes, stretch out their arms, and revolve on their left foot by propelling themselves with the right one. Their motion is regulated by soft strains of music from a gallery and in their revolutions they display a surprising skill and grace.

The howling dervishes are not of so pleasant a character. A row of men with long hair stand before their leader and rapidly move their bodies backwards and forwards to a wailing chant. At one moment their faces touch their knees and their hair reaches the ground. At the next they bend back with their disheveled locks flying out behind them. These ecstatic movements are often continued until they fall into convulsions. To a European nothing can be more disgusting, or contain less of devotion.

The Khedive of Egypt has a palace at Shubra, a village two miles and a half north of Cairo and it is connected with the city by a broad avenue bordered by stately sycamores and lebbek trees. This is the favorite drive of wealthy natives and foreigners. The aristocratic ladies of the harem imitate those of Constantinople in wearing a thin veil over the lower part of the face which gratifies their vanity by showing their beauty and at the same time has the appearance of conforming with the law of the prophet. The ladies ride in covered carriages with half drawn blinds. Before them are generally two out-runners in gay attire whose business it is to warn the people in the narrow street that a carriage is coming.

Although these European vehicles are now quite common in Alexandria, Cairo and other cities of the Delta the genuine Egyptian means of conveyance is the donkey. These useful animals serve as beasts of burden as well as for the transportation of passengers. They are to be seen everywhere in and about Cairo. No matter how secluded the lane may be you traverse afoot, at every corner a number of boys will bar your path by backing their donkeys up in front of you and energetically rehearsing their good qualities. At any time, though it be at the dead of night, by shouting "hammar!"—donkey boys—you will immediately be surrounded by a lot of them.

The donkey drivers of Cairo are a bright set of fellows who have all the shrewdness of New York newsboys and bootblacks. They know something of the three European languages current in Egypt, but they seem most deeply versed in bad English. It is a poor driver who cannot back his donkey up against you and say "you want ride? Good donkey, sar!" A French traveler relates that on his journey up the Nile one of his companions who had just been ashore told him that he had learned at least one Arab word and that was donkey, "qui veut dire un ane." He was surprised to hear that the natives of Upper Egypt had been teaching him English unawares.

My first donkey-back excursion was to Heliopolis. The rider has nothing to do but sit on the animal as it is guided by the boy who runs behind, whipping and shouting at the top of his voice. I carried an umbrella to shelter me from the sun and the donkey was constantly kept in a gallop by the swift footed and noisy boy behind.

Five miles north of Cairo is the Virgin's Tree, under which the Virgin, Joseph and Jesus rested on their flight to Egypt. When Empress Eugenie of France visited Egypt at the inauguration of the Suez canal the Khedive presented her the Virgin's Tree and it is now surrounded by a beautiful garden. Truth however compels me to say that the present tree is only two centuries old. The Virgin may have rested under some tree somewhere, so I suppose they may as well say this is the one as any other.

In the neighborhood of this spot the first experiments were made in growing cotton which has since been so widely cultivated in Egypt, especially during the American war. The country as I rode along was beautiful. The wheat was just of a golden hue, but the other vegetation was green and luxuriant.

Some distance north of the Virgin's Tree is the site of Heliopolis the famous city of the sun. There the richly endowed temple of the god Ra once was situated. There too were the famous schools which were visited by Herodotus, Plato and many other famous Greeks. The peasant now plows and reaps on the site of the once populous city, perfectly oblivious of the countless thousands who there lived and died and returned to dust. So completely has Heliopolis passed from existence that there seems some truth in Shelley's lines :

A STUDENT'S VIEWS ABROAD. 373

> "There's not one atom of yon earth
> But once was living man;
> Nor the minutest drop of rain,
> That hangeth in its thinnest cloud,
>   But flowed in human veins;
>   And from the burning plains
>   Where Lybian monsters yell,
>   From the most gloomy glens
>   Of Greenland's sunless clime,
>   To where the golden fields
>   Of fertile England spread
>   Their harvest to the day,
>   Thou canst not find one spot
>   Whereon no city stood."

All that remains now of Heliopolis is the red granite obelisk which still stands in the plain sixty-six feet high. It is the second oldest monument of the kind that is known and has seen many millions of men come and go since Herodotus and Plato.

My second donkey excursion was to the great pyramids of Gizeh, which are the most famous monuments of Egypt and among the oldest buildings in the world. At three o'clock in the morning I found a donkey and started. We soon left the lights of the city behind and crossing the great iron bridge over the Nile, plunged into the pitchy darkness. Of course the donkey driver, who was an ugly old Arab, demanded a fee when we were out in a dark place, but on meeting a prompt refusal he did not press matters. The Khedive has built a good straight road to the pyramids and has planted trees along the sides, making a nice drive. As it grew light and we began to meet the peasants on the road I had frequent applications for backsheesh. By the time I reached the end of my ride I had quite a following of beggars.

The pyramids have been the wonder of thousands of

years. We possess the account of Herodotus' visit to them B. C. 454, and since that time they have been described by travelers of all ages and nearly all nations. Their object has been the problem for which numberless solutions have been presented.

The Arabs say that the pyramids were constructed by the chief of the fairies before the creation of Adam.

The tradition of the Druses says that they are the work of God himself and that the book of the record of human actions is kept within them.

Others call them the graneries of Joseph.

Dr. Clark said Joseph was buried in the pyramid of Cheops.

The Copts think the pyramids served the Pharoahs as thrones while reviewing their troops.

Some modern writers have thought they were built to prevent the encroachment of the sand upon the fertile land.

Procter's idea that they were constructed for astronomical purposes is the latest.

The almost universally accepted explanation of the origin of the pyramids is that set forth by the learned Prussian Doctor Lepsius, the most famous living Egyptologist : "Each king began to build his pyramid when he ascended the throne. He began it on a small scale, in order that if a short reign should be in store for him his tomb might be a completed one. As years rolled on, however, he continued enlarging it by the addition of outer coatings of stone, until he felt that his career was drawing to a close. If he died before the work was completed the last coating was then finished and the size of the monument was accordingly proportioned to the length of the builder's reign ; so that, had the progress of these structures always been uniform, it would have almost been possible to ascertain the length of each king's reign from the incrustations of his pyramid, in the same way as the age of a tree is determined by the number of concentric rings in its trunk."

The age of the pyramids is placed variously by different Egyptologists. Lepsius thinks they are five thousand years old, while Mariette reckoned it at six thousand.

The Bedouins of the desert consider it their birthright to guide the visitors at the pyramids. As the morning was foggy I selected a couple of the Arabs and went to see the Sphinx. Its long body is buried in sand but the head is erect and the face wears the same smile as thousands of years ago, although vandal sheykhs and mamelukes have badly mutilated its countenance.

We next went inside of the great pyramid. It is a pretty difficult task, as the passage is narrow, low and rough. Farther on it becomes better, but where the ascent begins the stones are so slippery that one can only keep on his feet by holding to his barefooted guides. After much scrambling we managed to reach the King's Chamber which contains the remnant of a sarcophapus but its royal owner has long since disappeared. The immense blocks of stone appear as closely joined to-day as they did thousands of years ago. The temperature of the interior of the pyramid is 79 degrees which some people find stifling but it did not affect me uncomfortably.

After again reaching the open air and resting some we ascended the pyramid. A Bedouin caught hold of each of my hands and leaping nimbly from step to step dragged me after them. They soon had me out of breath in spite of my frequent requests to go slow : "Pian piano : chi va piano, va sano."

The view from the summit is grand. It embraces the desert, the wondrous valley of the Nile and the brilliant city of the Caliphs. The impression it makes on the mind remains after hundreds of others have vanished.

The guide asked me to carve my name on the stone but I refused to perpetuate the Lutz tribe in such a vandal way. Then one fellow offered for a consideration to run down the side of the great pyramid and up another and come back in twenty minutes. Not wishing to be accessory to his murder I again refused. We then began the descent, which I found harder than going up. The guides are of little use and one must jump down from one step to another with the sight of the precipice to embarrass him. It was nearly a week before I recovered from stiffness caused by this descent. All the way up and down the Bedouins kept begging of me, but I assured them I was a poor devil and pointed them to a couple of Englishmen who were just driving up the hill as fatter victims. They thought I was an Italian which does not say much for their knowledge of that language. When I paid them they bade me "Addio, signore," with pretty good grace for an Italian was not expected to be such a spendthrift as an Englishman.

My last excursion from Cairo was up the Nile to visit the site of Memphis and the pyramids of Sakkara. I set out on the Upper Egypt railway which is designed to extend to Thebes and is already running as far as Siut.

The cars ran slowly through the green, fertile fields, having the desert on one side with its somber tombs of antiquity and on the other side the sparkling Nile with its lively assortment of sailing craft. The dust was almost intolerable on that rainless road and soon covered the passengers with white. The natives wear long mantels like sheets in which they wrap themselves and effectually keep off the dust. All we poor Europeans could do was to turn up our coat collars and shut our eyes.

Through the driving dust we frequently caught glimpses of the natives working at the eternal task of drawing water in shaduf buckets and of the blindfolded oxen going round and round turning the sakiyeh water wheels which elevate earthen jars attached to an endless band.

I left the train at Bedrashen station, my ticket containing the name in Arabic and French. I was soon surrounded by donkey drivers and, on mounting what I thought the best donkey, was hurried over to the village where the boy bought some candles. He then whipped the donkey to a brisk gallop and we scudded along an enbankment through groves of palms and past crowds of peasants in their blue gowns.

In a hollow about half way between the river and the desert lies the famous colossal statue of Ramses II., the great Sesostris of the Greeks, supposed by some to be the Pharoah who oppressed the Israelites. The statue is mutilated but the features are uninjured and exhibit excellent workmanship. The royal effigy was originally about forty-two feet high. All around it are the scanty remains of the famed and populous city of Memphis, which Herodotus says was founded by Menes, the first king of Egypt, whose reign is estimated by Lepsius to have been B. C. 3,892, and by Mariette, B. C. 5,004. A few scattered heaps of rubbish which rise above the golden grain were all I saw of the metropolis. The ancient Egyptians gave little attention to the ornamentation or the solidity of their dwellings which they called temporary quarters, while they termed their tombs eternal houses and built and adorned them with the greatest care. We are wiser than they and if we are only comfortable while living, we will not be over fastidious about our tombs.

My driver kept the donkey at a brisk gallop and we soon reached the village of Sakkara which lies almost at the limit of the fertile land. From there we turned northward along the edge of the desert and soon were among the pyramids and sand covered tombs.

We passed close by the famous step-pyramid which is so called because there are four terraces between the base and the summit which give it a peculiar appearance when seen from a distance. Some authorities consider this pyramid the work of a member of the first dynasty, the one founded by Menes, which would make it the oldest structure in the world.

At the house of the well known Egyptologist M. Mariette I dismounted and guided by two Arabs descended into the vaults where sacred bulls of Apis were interred by the superstitious Egyptians thirty-five hundred years ago. The part we visited contains a long arched passage with a row of cells or chapels on each side in which stand the gigantic granite sarcophagi. All of these are now empty but in 1851

M. Mariette discovered one chamber still walled up, which was in the same condition as it was left thirty-seven hundred years ago. The finger marks of the mason were still visible in the mortar and the prints of naked feet were seen on the sand within the vault. "Such discoveries," says M. Mariette, "produce impressions compared with which everything else sinks into insignificance and which one constantly desires to renew."

I climbed into one of the immense sarcophagi. They measure thirteen feet in length, seven feet in width and eleven feet in height, and weigh at least sixty-five tons. It is sad that mankind went to such pains to immortalize a quadruped.

From the Apis vaults we proceeded to the still more interesting tomb of Ti, who was a high officer at the Egyptian court five or six thousand years ago. The world would be little concerned about Ti or his royal master if the tomb of the former had not been adorned and preserved as it is. The walls are covered with delicately sculptured bas-reliefs which are appropriately painted. The scenes represent the every day life at the home of Ti before the dawn of history. The designs are remarkably good and impress one more than anything else could that humanity was much the same in those days as it is now. Among the things represented are the slaughter of cattle, feeding of poultry, sailing of a boat, reaping and threshing of grain, building of boats, sowing, plowing and hunting. Think of seeing photographs of a people who were ancient when Greece was young!

From these interesting monuments of primaeval art we returned across the sand past innumerable ruins, half buried tombs and crumbling pyramids. The fertile soil only extends as far as the annual flood rises and one can stand with one foot on the fruitful land of the valley and the other on the blighting sand of the barren desert.

My donkey was kept at a gallop by the energetic boy and we reached the railway station by noon. As the Cairo train did not come along until toward evening, I walked over to the bank of the Nile. The river presented a lively scene as boats were sailing past almost constantly. After a bath in the historic stream, I returned through the palm groves to the station and began the dusty ride to Cairo. The sun was just setting as we passed the great pyramids of Gizeh, and for a moment it was just behind the largest one making it glow like massive gold, one of those glorious sights the tourist never forgets.

CHAPTER XXIII.

VOYAGE FROM EGYPT TO PALESTINE.—THE SUEZ CANAL.—
LANDING AT JOPPA.—JERUSALEM AND BETHLEHEM.—
THE HOLY FIRE.

JERUSALEM, April 29th, 1880.

Another all night ride by rail brought me from Cairo back to Alexandria where I looked for a steamer to Palestine. Having determined to go by the Russian vessel which left the following day, I employed the intermediate time in reviewing the limited sights of the town. When I first arrived in Egypt, Alexandria seemed to me quite Oriental, but now I was fresh from the glories of the capital, whose praises the story teller so enthusiastically proclaims : " He who hath not seen Cairo, hath not seen the world ; its soil is good ; its Nile is a wonder ; its women are like the black-eyed virgins of Paradise ; its houses are palaces; and its air is soft, its odor surpassing that of aloes wood and cheering the heart." In comparison with such Oriental splendor, Alexandria is a wretched imitation of a European town.

On Easter Sunday I went on board the Russian steamer and at the appointed hour we left the harbor. We had a slight rain during the night, and the following morning we ran into Port Said, the northern entrance to the Suez Canal. Large steamers were coming and going all day while we lay at anchor and the Arabs had various articles for sale which were brought from India. The great canal is one hundred miles long, twenty-six feet deep and from sixty-five to one hundred and twenty yards wide at the surface. It was begun in 1858 and finished in 1869 and cost about ninety-five million dollars. In 1880 two thousand vessels passed through the canal. The net receipts make five or six per cent. on the capital invested and the traffic increases every year.

We had a rough voyage from Alexandria and when we left Port Said again in the evening we found the waves still running pretty high. During the night we had another rain. The majority of the passengers were seasick.

The next morning at day break we were in sight of land and we stood at the rail and hailed with satisfaction the beautiful sunrise as its golden rays gradually illuminated the blue Judean hills.

As we drew near the shore the town of Joppa became distinguishable and seemed of rare beauty. It stands on a conical hill surrounded with magnificent groves of orange trees. Alas, that one should go ashore and walk through its nasty streets!

Joppa has no harbor, unless the dangerous reef which protects small vessels be called one. Our steamer anchored about half a mile from shore and immediately drifted around so that the heavy rollers gave her a broadside. Dirty Russian pilgrims with their pans and buckets and gayly dressed Arabs with their carpets and bed clothes tumbled about in delightful confusion. A great many could not resist the temptation, as the boys say, to "heave up Jonah," as though their being on the very spot where the historic whale threw up the Jew, lent a new vim to their sea sickness. Just as the ship gave a tremendous lurch, I saw one Arab roll heels over head down the hatchway, followed pell mell by his bundles and boxes.

The native boatmen swarmed over the rail shrieking like a lot of pirates and a half dozen of them laid violent hands on each passenger and his baggage and endeavored to carry them in as many different ways.

The boats were of large size, and were gathered around the foot of the companion ladder, which went up and down with the roll of the vessel, at one moment high up from the water and at the next coming down with a splash, threatening to swamp the frail barks beneath. The Russian pilgrims would creep timorously down the ladder, invoking the whole calendar of saints, and being afraid to leap into the boats when the roll brought them close up, they were unceremoniously kicked in by the Arabs. The roar of the sea, the curses of the sailors, the shouts of the natives and the prayers and howls of the pilgrims made a din indescribable.

The waves washed over the sides of the boats every minute and we saw one that had capsized on the way out and was being paddled back by the natives up to their knees in the water. We got safely over the reef and clambered up the narrow, slippery wharf in a drizzling rain.

Without knowing where I was going, I went with some well dressed Russians to the rooms of the consulate. An official soon came around to arrange for transporting them to Jerusalem. As he spoke some Italian I asked him to take me with the rest, to which he agreed.

After a great deal of delay a carriage road was finally constructed from Joppa to Jerusalem a few years ago, and the travelers are now taken over in rough spring wagons of Russian manufacture, which were first introduced by the German Temple Colonists. I occupied the front seat with the driver, who was a broad faced Swabian whose familiar South German accent sounded out of keeping with the Oriental surroundings.

The Temple Colonists are a sect whose chief peculiarity consists in holding it their duty to settle in the Holy Land. They owe their origin to a movement in Stuttgart in 1858 which foun d adherents in all Germany and in parts of the United States. The American colonists were a failure, but the Germans are now in a fairly prosperous condition. There are about three hundred near Jerusalem and about the same number near Joppa. A recent number of the New York Zeitung boasts that a German brewery, a tavern and beer house are flourishing before the gates of Jerusalem.

We drove away from Joppa about three in the afternoon past the beautiful orange groves with their golden fruit and cactus hedges. A ride of several hours across the plain brought us to Ramleh, a town which was repeatedly won and lost by the crusaders, which contains a tall tower as a relic of those stirring times.

I spent the night comfortably at the picturesque German hotel, which was filled with Englishmen, one of whom was just retuning from a tour around the globe.

At daylight the next morning we continued our ride, soon reaching the hilly country. We halted at Bab-el-Wady for dinner and then entered the mountains in earnest. From one of the highest points we had a grand view of the whole far famed plain of Sharon, bordered on the west by the blue

Mediterranean. All around us were the bleak, limestone mountains which were here and there crowned with decayed villages, the robber strongholds of other days. The grades were so steep and the wagon road so winding that we often left the carriage and out-distanced it afoot. After going up and down what seemed to be an endless number of hills we finally approached the holy city. The traveler who arrives from the north or south may rave about his first impressions, but those who come up from Joppa have no opportunity to be sentimental. They can see nothing until they are nearly at the city gate, and before they have time to appreciate the situation they are besieged by beggars and porters innumerable. They only have opportunity to see a wall enclosing what the distance might transform into a myriad of domes but which in the close view resemble the tops of so many country bake ovens.

For centuries unnumbered pilgrims have wept with joy at sight of the promised land, but in these later days Jerusalem and Bethlehem are merely way stations on the tourist's route and are chiefly remembered for their beggarly accommodations for the traveler. The ideal element is all but vanished. I am not sure but that it is unsatisfactory to visit Palestine. Room is found in the holy writ to tell how the patriarchs girded up their loins and went hither and thither, how shepherds strove with each other, and endless other trifling details of everyday life which are surrounded in our minds with a halo of glory. It jars painfully on our natures to visit this land which we consider so near the heaven of our dreams and find that its hills resemble the hills of our native soil, only more barren, and in the holy city meet with degraded beings, animated by the basest passions that move mankind. In Palestine the traveler may say with a peculiar feeling :

> There was a time when meadow, grove and stream,
> The earth and every common sight
> To me did seem,
> Appareled in celestial light,
> The glory and the freshness of a dream
> It is not now as it has been of yore :—
> Turn whithersoe'er I may
> By night or day,
> The things which I have seen, I now can see no more!"

As the Greek Church uses the old calendar, which is twelve days behind ours, they celebrated their Easter April 24th. The first ceremonies began on Thursday in the Church of the Holy Sepulcher. They set up a sort of scaffold in the piazza before the church, and then thirteen of them gave a representation of the last supper in a very realistic style which recalls the old mystery plays of Europe.

The church covers the spot which has been considered the genuine tomb of Jesus since the time of Constantine, but many doubt its verity, especially as so many other legends are told in regard to the place. One is surprised to find it in the midst of the city when the Bible narrative leads one to look for it beyond the walls. Upon entering the church we pass the Turkish guards who are sitting crosslegged in one corner and endeavoring to pass the time by smoking and drinking coffee. Then we reach the slab where Christ's body was anointed, which is surrounded by immense candelabra. Pilgrims are constantly kissing the stone. Farther on is the spot where the women stood while the anointing was taking place. Before us is the dome under which is the Chapel of the Holy Sepulcher.

It is a large, marble-covered structure, entirely above ground. The outer chapel is that of the angels, and contains a part of the stone they rolled away. Then we enter the tomb itself, which is small, and contains an altar, upon which the body rested. The pilgrims of all nations crawl in upon their hands and knees and cover the place with kisses. When the chapel is illuminated with its hundred lamps upon the exterior it makes a magnificent appearance. I went around last night to see it, and had the misfortune to be locked in the church. It seemed rather a gloomy prospect to spend the night there with the chanting monks, but a Greek priest helped me to squeeze through the loop-hole in the door, while two Arabs upon the outside pulled me by the feet.

Opposite the sepulcher is the Catholicon or Greek Chapel, which is the richest in the church. In the middle of it is a fragment of a column which, according to the priests, marks the center of the world ! It was an interesting sight to see this chapel crowded with the rough old Russian pilgrims, each holding a lighted candle. Their wrinkled faces and eyes dim with age were all aglow with joy. They seemed to have attained their ideal of happiness. The other parts of the church contain chapels to various saints, and one to commemorate the finding of the "true cross." By the side of the stone of the anointing a flight of stairs ascends to a chapel that marks the site of Mt. Calvary. The places where the true crosses stood can still be observed. Beneath is the Chapel of Adam, who was buried there and brought to life by the blood of Christ, which flowed through a cleft in the rock upon his head. Melchisedeck is buried around here some place too. The priests have made one grand effort to embrace within the walls of this church, every prominent incident recorded in the Bible, and the result is one of the most startling medley of legends imaginable.

This, then, is the scene of the Easter ceremonies. Friday evening there is a sort of a service, but Saturday is the great day, for then takes place the miracle of the sending down of the holy fire. Early in the morning the vicinity of the sepulcher begins to be crowded with pilgrims from all parts of the Orient, each holding a bunch of tapers to be lighted with the heavenly fire. By noon all the galleries and temporary scaffoldings are full, as well as all the area available upon the ground.

I took my stand a short distance from the sepulcher, in one corner where I could see the crowd very well. When all seemed packed to its utmost capacity, a band of swarthy, bare-footed pilgrims would dash up with a grand war-whoop, push all before them, climb up the columns, and were only stopped by the whips of the Turkish soldiers. Then the band would form a circle and execute a war dance, flourishing their candles aloft and clapping their hands.

Then a couple would climb upon the others' shoulders and perform the dance at that height. They continually chanted monotonously at the top of their voices: "O Jews! O Jews! your feasts are the feasts of monkeys, but the Lord hath redeemed us! This is the sepulcher of the Lord," etc. Pretty soon another mob would dash up and the first would be pushed aside for a moment. Then they would rally and have a fight, and the Turkish soldiers would run up and whack them over the head right and left with their whips. I have always despised the Turks, but this time I was astonished at their moderation. If I had been in their position, I would have laid on a good deal harder.

These chants, war dances and skirmishes began at noon and continued three hours. The holy fire usually descends at 2 o'clock, but either for want of sufficient fervor in prayer or some other cause it did not arrive until 3 o'clock. The lamps were extinguished and a procession of the clergy moved around the church while the patriarch was within the sepulcher. At length the holy fire came down (from the patriarch's match box, I suppose) and was passed out to the pilgrims, some of whom pay large sums to the priests to be the first to light their tapers. In a few minutes thousands of candles are in a blaze and the church is completely illuminated. It is really a fine sight. The people in the galleries let down candles upon strings and draw up the fire. The pilgrims pass their candles over their faces and into their bosoms. They say it does not burn, but I saw one fellow's coat and another's hair in a blaze. After the tapers have burned a few minutes they are extinguished and carried to all parts of the Orient to be used on solemn occasions.

Such is the great miracle of the holy fire which attracts so many visitors. It is astonishing that more accidents do not happen to such a frenzied multitude. This time a temporary scaffolding fell, but as far as I can learn no one was seriously hurt. The mothers go there with their babes in their arms ; for what do a few lives count when we are to get the holy fire ? In 1834, when the church was crowded with some 6,000 people, a riot broke out, the Turkish guards, thinking they were attacked, used their weapons, and 300 perished in the press.

I took a long walk this morning in the plain north of the city. As the walls on the other sides stand upon the brink of deep gorges the hostile armies of every period have carried on the operations of the siege upon this plain. It is sparsely covered with olive trees and contains many ruins and tombs. A few modern houses are also springing up and the only steam engine I have seen in Jerusalem is located near Demascus Gate which is the entrance upon the north side.

About two miles from the city are the Tombs of the Judges, which though not genuine are certainly very old. They seem to be used now as a shelter for the goats which are at pasture on the neighboring hills and it is no agreeable task to climb around in them. I saw some Arabs bathing in the water that had been collected on the floor of another tomb. Rather queer use human burial grounds are put to! The tombs of the kings are nearer the city and are larger. They are supposed to be the tombs of Queen Helena of Adiabene and her descendants who are mentioned by Josephus. The most prominent mountain toward the north is the Neby Samwil which is believed to be the place where Samuel was born and where he was buried. The buildings upon it can be seen from every elevated point in the vicinity of Jerusalem.

Near the Damascus Gate is a tomb called that of Jeremiah and he is said to have written his Lamentations there. Opposite to it is an opening under the city wall which leads to an extensive subterraneous quarry. I went in some distance this morning but being alone and having but a small piece of a candle I did not care to venture too far from the entrance.

A short walk toward the east brings one to the valley of Jehosaphat through which the brook Kedron would flow if there was any water to flow. After crossing the valley we reach the tomb of the Virgin and her parents which is a subterraneous chapel to which one descends by a long flight of steps. Near by is the traditional site of the martyrdom of St. Stephen.

A little farther toward the south is the Latin Garden of Gethsemane, which is enclosed by a wall and contains seven ancient olive trees. The Greek Garden of Gethsemane is farther up the hill. The road to the summit of the Mount of Olives ascends between them. A person with ordinary sense may well doubt the traditions which locate every scene in the Bible, but he can feel certain that Jesus often came to this very hillside with his disciples to converse of the duties of man as well as of the hollowness of that religion whose proud temple he saw rising on the hill opposite.

The Mount of Olives still bears numbers of the trees which give it the name but there were doubtless many more in the name of Christ. The summit commands not only the finest view of Jerusalem but also of the Jordan Valley, the Dead Sea and Mount Nebo. The mysterious lake of salt seems but a short distance away and the vegetation on the banks of the Jordan can be clearly distinguished, but a ride of nine hours through a desert region is necessary to reach them, and the Dead Sea lies 3,900 feet below level of the Mount of Olives. As I have not been able to make this excursion I have gone often to enjoy the view. If this portion of the country was not immensely better in Moses' time his glimpses of the promised land from Mt. Nebo could not have been very encouraging. There are nothing but yellow hills without the faintest sign of vegetation.

Descending the eastern slope of the hill we soon reach the miserable village of Bethany where Jesus so often retired from the strife of Jerusalem. It is about an hour's walk from the city and being out of sight and hearing of the capital it afforded a resting place more like those Jesus had enjoyed upon the shores of the Lake of Tiberias. The modern village is, as I have said, a miserable place and is peopled entirely by Mohammedans. It contains a ruined tower of ancient date and a hole in the ground which inventive credulity has dubbed the tomb of Lazarus. Attended by a couple of Arab boys with candles I descended into the cave by the break-neck stairs and was rewarded by seeing nothing—that is nothing but a prosy cavern lined with masonry.

I returned to the city by the main road which passes a spring which is a welcome sight in this parched country. The slope of the Mount of Olives next to Jerusalem is covered with thousands and thousands of Jewish graves which are marked merely by rough slabs of stone. The Israelites come from all parts of the world that their ashes may repose in the sacred soil. What obstinate fanaticism! say some. What touching devotion! say others.

At the bottom of the ravine opposite the temple plateau there are four rock tombs which tradition calls those of Absalom, Jehosaphat, St. James and Zachariah. The one supposed to belong to Absalom is surrounded by a heap of small stones, for the Jews pelt the tomb in passing as a mark of their disapproval of the conduct of the ungrateful son of David.

Farther down the course of the Kedron is the fountain of the Virgin, so called because tradition says she washed Jesus' clothes here. It is deep down in the rock and is reached by descending some thirty steps. I arrived at it the other morning at the same time with a lot of Russian pilgrims who came to bathe in the holy fount. When I returned a couple of hours later I found only two natives in the water and after they had finished and some Siloan women had filled their vessels I concluded to take a plunge too. The water is of an agreeable temperature and forms a large basin near the source about four feet deep. As the water is constantly being renewed it is one of the finest bath tubs imaginable. A tunneled channel connects it with the pool of Siloah which is situated farther down the ravine. After I had come out of the water a Musselman came down and went in saying his prayers. A prayer may be a good accompaniment for a bath but I think a cake of soap would be a better one.

Opposite the fountain is the village of Siloam which is built among the rocks so as to be scarcely distinguishable from the cliff itself. Some distance farther on at the junction of the valleys of Kedron and Hinnom is Job's Well which is connected with the history of another rebellious son of David. In spite of the fact that considerable water issues from these two fountains it is not sufficient to form a rivulet in the valley. The thirsty soil absorbs the water from the pool of Siloah within a hundred yards of its outlet. The gardens there, however, are very fertile.

From Job's Well the valley of Hinnom branches off toward the west. It is full of tombs which were formerly inhabited by the early Christian hermits. Among them is the traditional site of the field of blood purchased with Judas' bribe. This is the valley of Gehenna which the Jews considered synonomous with hell.

From the south-western corner of the city the road leads off past the German colony to Bethlehem. It passes through an extensive plain and then ascends a hill where there is a fountain whose summit commands a view both of Jerusalem and of Bethlehem. It then descends past the traditional tomb of Rachel and soon reaches the village—in all a walk of two hours and I went down and back quite comfortably in a morning. Bethlehem is the finest looking place I have seen in Palestine. No houses are better built and the artisans seem busy everywhere. In contradiction to the Biblical account the spot where Jesus was born is shown in a cave. It is marked by a large stone and is surrounded by lamps. The church above it is very old and was the scene of Baldwin's coronation as King of Jerusalem.

CHAPTER XXIV.

MOONLIGHT RIDE FROM JERUSALEM TO THE SEA.—ALONG THE COAST OF ASIA.—SITE OF ANCIENT TROY.—CONSTANTINOPLE.—ATHENS.—BACK IN FRANCE.

———

PARIS, June 3d, 1881.

I took leave of Jerusalem just four weeks ago last Monday. After a farewell ascent of the Mount of Olives and a last visit to the Holy Sepulcher I engaged a place upon the carriage to Joppa. The vehicle was to set off at two o'clock P. M. but in true Oriental style it went three hours behind time. We rolled off through the crowds of picturesquely attired Jews and dirty Russian pilgrims and just had time for a hurried glimpse of the walls of the holy city before it disappeared from view.

My traveling companions were Spanish Jews, descendants of those expelled by the fanatical policy of Ferdinand and Isabella. They still retain their language, though it is said to be a bad dialect. The driver was a Russian Jew who spoke German also. Like all Russian peasants he was a jack of all trades and master of none except driving horses. Being a fiery young blood and a hired servant he did not spare his animals but dashed up and down the hills in a way that would have done credit to Jehu. We had not gone far before it grew dark and the impressions produced by riding over these historical mountains in the moonlight are of such a wild romantic character that they will not soon be forgotten. Crack, crack, went the driver's whip every minute and the little Arab horses dashed down the steep slopes at a full gallop. How fast the familiar places went by! That dark village on the hill to the left was already the famous old robbers' nest of Abu Gosh. We ran up the hills and plunged down into the dusky ravines scattering the herds of cattle and sheep in every direction and leaving their angry drivers cursing our Jew with the hottest oaths in Mohammedan vocabulary. Eight o'clock and Bab-el-Wady where custom compelled even our Jehu to rest till midnight. A bite of lunch and a nap on the seat and then we were off again faster than ever for our Jew just ran down some loaded donkeys and seemed to fear pursuit. Two o'clock and Ramleh! We drive through the narrow streets to the stable to change horses. Soon an angry German woman appears with an immense lantern and gives our Jehu an awful scolding for driving one of the animals to death. At four o'clock we were off once more and at six we reached the orange orchards at Joppa which were loaded with the delicious fruit, known as one of the best qualites in the world.

I had scarcely reached the quay with my baggage when the Russian steamer appeared in the offing. One company of pirates who were going out to meet it agreed to take me along and I was soon on deck.

The following morning we ran into the port of Beyrout. It is the finest looking city I had seen thus far in the Orient. The bright colored houses with their luxuriant gardens rise one above another forming a magnificent scene while toward the east is the lofty Mount Lebanon with its snowy peaks. The streets of the city are better and the shops cleaner than most places in the Orient but they have too much of a European look for one seeking picturesqueness in its native filth. Our steamer lay all day in the harbor and as it was extraordinarily hot the snow on Mount Lebanon had a rather tantalizing appearance. Toward evening however some boys brought some of it on board and we had the pleasure of eating as well as seeing it.

As an example of the curious people we meet in traveling let me mention that one of the native boatmen who brought us aboard at Beyrout, had been at New York and another had been a fireman on a rebel blockade runner. The latter said those were good times in those days; they got forty-five dollars every trip, even though it were but ten hours.

The following day we stopped at Tripoli, an ancient looking city at the foot of some snow covered mountains. It was taken by the crusaders but at present it seems a rather sluggish place. I was so tired of seeing dirty Oriental streets that I did not go ashore.

We stopped a short time during the night at Latakia and the next day at noon reached Alexandretta, a small place named after the great conqueror, which however has no share in his fame. It lies in the extreme corner of the Mediterranean upon the gulf surrounded with mountains, which would be beautiful were they not so desolate. The port derives its chief importance from its being on the route to Aleppo and Bagdad. Here I gained two companions who helped considerably in lightening the tedium of the voyage. One was a Greek fur merchant who has been traveling in

Asia and Europe for forty years. The other was a German Russian who was returning from India and the far East. He did not give a very flattering account of Bagdad, that ancient capital of the caliphs which we associate involuntarily with the glories of the Arabian Nights. The two travelers spent forty-five days upon a Euphrates steamer. As the coal ran out they were obliged to stop and send the crew ashore to cut wood whenever they had the opportunity.

After leaving Alexandretta we ran along the coast having the snow covered peaks of the Cilician mountains always in view. We stopped at a little port called Messina which is near ancient Tarsus. I little thought when I first made my acquaintance with this region in the narrative of Xenophon that I was once to see the very mountains through which the hopeful army of Cyrus passed.

The following day the coast of Asia was visible on one side and the island of Cyprus upon the other. Then we passed Rhodes where the old colossus once stood astride the harbor. The town is surrounded by walls and has a decidedly antique appearance. At dark we passed Patmos and during the night Samos. Early the next morning we anchored off Chios which was recently overtaken by the terrible earthquake. We could not detect any traces of the disaster from the ship, but one of the men who had been ashore said the walls of the houses were in a very shattered condition. The calamity seems to have paralyzed commerce for we halted but a few minutes and then left for Smyrna which we reached in the afternoon. The sight of the neat streets and bright shops of this city were particularly refreshing to me. Let those rave over Oriental picturesqueness who wish but for my part I prefer European cleanliness and comfort. We staid two days at Smyrna and I spent them pleasantly in the city and in rambling over the hills by the castle enjoying the fine views. The situation of Smyrna is one of singular beauty.

We left one evening and the next morning at daybreak we were between the continent and Tenedos, that little island behind which the Greeks hid when they conducted the siege of Troy. And there before me was the veritable spot where the angry heroes and the wooden horse played their parts. Later we passed the narrow Hellespont where the haughty Persians crossed to invade Greece. Then came the sea of Marmora and finally the Turkish capital itself with its palaces, gardens and mosques.

"Stamboul!"

"Constantinople!"

The Turk and Frank alike cried out with joy at the sight of the minarets of the famous capital as the steamer swiftly bore us nearer and nearer to the city of the Sultan. The white capped waves of the Sea of Marmora danced gayly in the perfect sunshine of the May morning and every passenger on the crowded vessel watched the brightly colored outlines of Constantinople as they became visible amid their setting of somber cypress trees across the waters.

"Vedi Constantinopoli e poi mori, see Constantinople and then die!" exclaims the enthusiast in the heat of his admiration for the scene which lay before us. For ages its beauties have inspired poets and word painters and yet all have felt speech inadequate to describe its transcendent glory. The atmosphere has a warmth and mildness peculiar to itself.

The color of the hills, the trees, the water, the sky and even the buildings seem to be of a richer tint than that of any other clime. It is a place of all others to awaken those dreamy fancies that are so in keeping with Oriental character.

We were hardly given time to fully admire the scene presented to our eyes before the steamer's prow rounded the Seraglio point and anchor was dropped in the mud at the mouth of the Golden Horn. The chains were scarcely unwound from their windlass, before the steamers's deck was crowded with boatmen.

"Want a boat, sir?" was demanded in all languages.

I engaged for a guide a Polish Jew who could speak German and we were soon over the steamer's side and in the caique, or boat. We were not a hundred feet from the steamer before we were stopped by some Turkish soldiers who examined our passports and then permitted us to pass on to the tumble-down custom house. The examination of our baggage was speedily completed and we began our rambling over the city. The streets are narrow, winding, badly paved and dirty. The romance of Constantinople is all in the distance. The illusion is rudely dispelled by a nearer view. The majority of its buildings are uninteresting or positively ugly.

The Golden Horn is a river-like inlet whose shape suggests its name and it forms a harbor capable of floating over a thousand ships. Kinglake says:

"Nowhere else does a sea come so close to a city as to the Mohammedan capital. There are no pebbly shores, no sand bars, no slimy river bed, no black canals, no locks nor docks to divide the very heart of the place from the deep waters. If being in the noisiest part of Stamboul, you would stroll to the quiet side of the way, amid those cypresses opposite, you will cross the fathomless Bosphorus ; if you would go from your hotel to the bazaars, you must pass by the bright blue pathway of the Golden Horn, that can carry a thousand sail of the line; you are accustomed to the gondolas that glide among the palaces of St. Mark ; but here in Stamboul it is a hundred and twenty gun ship that meets you in the streets. Venice strains out from the steadfast line, and in old times would send forth the chief of the state to woo and to wed the reluctant sea ; but the stormy bride of the Doge is the bowing slave of the Sultan. She comes to his feet with the treasures of the world ; she bears him from palace to palace ; by some unfailing witchcraft she entices the breeze to follow her and fan the pale cheek of her lord ; she lifts his armed navies to the very gates of his garden ; she watches the walls of his serail ; she stifles the intrigues of his ministers ; she quiets the scandals of his court ; she extinguishes his rivals, and hushes his naughty wives all one by one ; so vast are the wonders of the deep."

Across the Golden Horn is the famous Karakeue bridge of boats upon which can be seen every nationality of the world. It is the best place on earth to study the costumes of the various people of the globe. No peculiarity of dress can there attract the least attention because all are common. It is the point of contact for all mankind.

From the bridge a line of horse cars runs through the heart of the city and brings some of the ideas of the present century into direct contact with the relics of the buried centurles. My guide and I sipped Turkish coffee at a native restaurant opposite the mosque of St. Sophia, resting from our tramp and watching the motley throng on the street.

The mosque of St. Sophia is one of the great churches of the world. It is the principal sight of Constantinople. The original church was founded by Constantine the Great and the present edifice was begun in 532. The history says: "Anthemius of Tralles and Isidorus of Miletus were the architects employed by the Emperor Justinian, at whose command the enterprise was commenced. No fewer than 10,000 workmen are said to have been engaged under the direction of 100 master builders, and when the work was completed it cost the imperial treasury about $5,000,000. The principal material of the walls was brick, but the whole interior was lined with costly marble, and to add to its splendors the temples of the ancient gods at Heliopolis, and Ephesus, at Delos and Baalbec, at Athens and Cyzicus, were robbed of their columns. To render the dome as light as possible it was constructed of pumice stone and Rhodian bricks, and to secure the building from the ravages of fire no wood was employed except for the doors."

Since 1453, when Constantinople was captured by the Turks under Sultan Mohammed, the church has been used as a mosque. Four minarets of tall and graceful proportions now rise far above the shapely dome and from the galleries near their top the muezzin summon the faithful to prayer.

St. Sophia is now accessible to the Infidel and my guide and I paid it a visit. At the door we pulled on clumsy slippers over our shoes, which is the way the Frank visitors are permitted to comply with the Mohammedan requirement of removing the shoes upon entering a mosque. One of the Faithful with an eye to backsheesh conducted us over the building and as we stepped around among the praying and kneeling Turks he pointed out the remarkable objects of interest. Our Vandal friend with the turban even picked some stones from the mosaics on the walls and gave them to us as souvenirs.

The Sublime Porte or gateway to the Sultan's palace at Seraglio point, is near the mosque of St. Sophia. The name is used as synonymous with the imperial government but the gateway is far from sublime.

We visited the hippodrome square which was the center of life in ancient Greek times. At the war department we saw dummies dressed in the costumes worn by Turkish soldiers during the past four hundred years. Many of them are fierce looking and calculated to inspire terror on the raids which the Turks formerly made into western Europe. They would not be fit for anything but a dime museum now. We visited an immense subterranean reservoir and found some men twisting long lengths of rope in the half lighted caverns which gave them plenty of room for their labors. We took a stroll through the bazaars which are the commercial center of the modern city. The shops are not as Oriental in appearance as those of Syria and Egypt but the wares are more varied. The shopmen display truly western zeal in making sales.

We continued our walk through the miserably paved and narrow streets, meeting everywhere the ugly yellow dogs which are the recognized inhabitants of the streets. Unnumbered stories are told of the traits of these canine scavengers of the great city and of the considerate regard in which they are held by the people. Strangers wonder that the Sultan does not have the whole breed dumped into limpid waters of the swiftly flowing, classic Bosphorus.

We crossed the bridge of boats over the Golden Horn and strolled through the streets of Galata and Pera which are inhabited by the foreign element and built up in western style. To one returning from Asia the streets of Pera have an almost Parisian appearance.

At sundown my caique carried me to the French steamer "Amerique" which lay at anchor opposite the Seraglio and as the evening shadows grew darker we steamed out into the sea of Marmora and watched the domes and minarets of St. Sophia and her sister mosques fade away in the night.

The next morning we made several stops on the Sea of Marmora and the Dardannelles and then reached the open sea. Early the following day we sighted the famous peak of Mt. Athos and its sister promotories. Finally we anchored off Salonika half a mile from shore and remained several days. I did not go ashore as I felt little interest in the place. We noted the unusual area covered by the cemeteries with their tombstones and cypresses. At night we stripped off and took a plunge in the sea.

Coming down the bay from Salonika we had inspiring views of Mt. Olympus. The snowy peaks appeared amid beautiful banks of clouds. We stopped some time at Volo where we found multitudes of Turkish soldiers and some men-of-war called hither by the boundary troubles with the Greeks.

We left Volo one evening and passed the famous field of

Thermopylae at night. We paused briefly at Laurium and took on a large shipment of lead in bars. It was encouraging to see a flourishing industry in ancient Greece.

After leaving Laurium we passed the beautiful ruin of an ancient temple standing on a lofty peak by the sea. We then approached the ancient harbor of Piraeus and saw the city of Athens in the distance with the famous ruins on the Acropolis distinctly visible.

The harbor was full of men-of-war and merchant vessels, both steam and sail. The Greek boundary disputes had made the little kingdom alive with military.

It was about noon when we anchored in the harbor of Piraeus and were told that we would have till evening on shore. We quickly made a bargain with a boatman and set foot on the classic soil of Greece. I was accompanied by a Roumanian medical student who spoke German.

Piraeus looks like a poor Italian town and has nothing to interest the tourist except its surroundings. The lovely blue sea and sky, the mountains in the distance and the memory of the great past together suggest thoughts of lasting interest.

We found the way to the railway station and were soon rolling along the plain of Attica toward Athens. A railroad in Greece seems odd indeed. We passed near the site of the ancient town walls which were built to join Athens and its harbor at Piraeus. We crossed the old highway and the nearly dry bed of the Cephissus. An olive grove engaged our minds for a while and then the ruins of ancient Athens became the sole object of our attention.

We left the train at the station at the foot of Hermes street and immediately began our ramble among the ancient landmarks. It seems queer enough to arrive at Athens by rail but on every hand we saw modern civilization pushing its way into the home of the people who are the real founders of its development. Greece taught Rome and Rome taught the modern world.

We walked along Hermes street turning aside once to see the ruins of the Stoa of Hadrian, one of the many magnificent creations of that Emperor. At the end of Hermes street is the palace of King George which is much like the palaces of the petty princes of Germany.

We then turned southward toward the Acropolis and passed through the well preserved gate of Hadrian and soon saw the sixteen columns which remain of the once magnificent temple of Jupiter. Near this point is the bed of the famous brook Ilissus and the spring Callirrhoe.

Proceeding toward the Acropolis we passed the monument of Lysicrates and a confused array of ruins along the base of the citadel hill. We climbed to the top of the Areopagus which was once the seat of the highest judicial tribunal at Athens. From thence we passed the Propylaea and entered the Acropolis, one of the most famous places on earth. Amid the bewildering mass of ruins rise the Parthenon and Erechtheum two of the most interesting relics which have come down to us from the ancient world.

In the halcyon days of Athens every citizen felt a just pride in the beauty of statue, painting and architecture displayed in this famous citadel. Even now the sensations of the student of history are grand, who stands among these ruins and traces the outlines of the once magnificent buildings and mentally restores the statues and paintings to their places. He can feel something of the pride which animated the breast of the Athenian of old when he stood among these triumphs of true taste and gazed on the city, the plain of Attica, the familiar mountains and the bright blue Aegean sea.

Not far from the Acropolis is the Temple of Theseus, standing on an elevated plateau. It is the best preserved edifice of ancient Athens and owes its present condition to the fact that it was used as a Christian church during the middle ages and thus rescued from desecration.

The Tower of the Winds and a few other scattered ruins are to be seen here and there in the city. In many places parts of ancient buildings have been incorporated in modern edifices.

After seeing the principal points of interest we went to the post-office and I received a large stack of letters and papers which had accumulated for me. As we came out of the office a number of little Greek boys ran after me to beg the United States stamps from my letters and papers. I was surprised to see that the stamp collecting mania had reached even Greece.

Towards evening we returned to Piraeus by rail and rejoined our friends on the French steamer, which soon commenced its voyage to Marseilles.

Modern Greece seems at present to be unfairly treated by the civilized world. If you pick up a book of travel you generally find all the bad points of Greek character referred to and the little kingdom seems to be a special object of ridicule and contempt The city of Athens is sneered at as an imitation of a third class western city and its improvements are treated with scorn.

Sixty years ago Europe and America were intensely interested in the future of the Greek nation which was then engaged in a heroic struggle against the Turks for independence. Never was a similar war for liberty waged with more courage, more devotion, or more perseverance. The bravery of all classes of the Greek people in that memorable struggle challenged the admiration of the world. It is no wonder that the lovers of freedom in every quarter of the globe came to regard the modern Greeks as the peers of their famous ancestors and expected Athens to assume a place hardly surpassed by that maintained in its golden age.

After the independence of Greece was recognized its people turned their attention to the problems of peace. A nation that had been oppressed for a thousand years sought to manage its own affairs. It could hardly be expected that they should escape financial and industrial difficulties. Complications arose in its government. A change took place in the sentiment of Europe. It became the fashion to ridicule the new kingdom and proclaim its people degenerate descendents of a great nation. Greece was compared with England, with France, or with Germany, and naturally enough the comparison showed the new nation in a bad light. Take, for instance, Edmond About's "Grece Contemporaine." The witty author draws a startling picture of the short comings of the Greeks. You would hardly believe that such a worthless people really waged such a heroic war for independence. You finish the Frenchman's sarcastic book with a feeling of sorrow. Yet when you think the matter over you cannot help regarding About's position as extremely unfair.

Modern Greece is not to be measured by France, by England or by Germany. The Greeks are the descendents of an oppressed people. They should be compared with the Roumanians, with the Servians, or with the Bulgarians. The Greeks are children of the Levant. Compared with any other people who have experienced the horrors of Turkish bondage the Greeks appear well indeed. I had a fair opportunity to judge the Greeks something as they should be judged. I had been for weeks among the Egyptians, Syrians and Turks. To me the strides in progress visible at Athens seemed worthy of the highest admiration. Far from leaving Greece disappointed, I felt encouraged at the condition of the little kingdom. We may not be able to maintain the enthusiasm felt for Greece by our fathers during the war for independence but I am sure we should not share the contemptuous opinions which have been current in the last few years.

CHAPTER XXV.

IN FRANCE AGAIN.—PARIS.—ACROSS THE CHANNEL.—LONDON.—STRATFORD.—AYR.—GLASGOW.—EDINBURGH.—ABBOTSFORD.—LIVERPOOL.—IRELAND.—VOYAGE HOME.

The voyage from Greece to Marseilles was without incident. We made a stop at Naples and had another view of that city. At Marseilles I received another lot of letters and newspapers. I took a draft to the "Credit Lyonnais" to have it cashed and was astonished to hear that they had failed to receive the necessary instructions from the Paris bank. As I only had about six dollars when I landed from the steamer, it began to look as though I would have to turn tramp in earnest. After waiting several days the difficulty was happily cleared up and I received my money.

From Marseilles I made the trip to Paris by the night express and early on the morning of June 1st I left the "Gare de Lyon" to get my first impressions of the great capital. The broad boulevards and the well built houses gave early proof of the wealth and beauty of the metropolis. From the station I went to the Place de la Bastille, the site of the famous fortress which was taken by the insurgents July 14th, 1789, on which date the great revolution began. In the center of the square rises the July Column erected to the memory of the martyrs of 1830.

From the Place de la Bastille I went down the Rue Rivoli, long the principal street of Paris, and saw the Hotel de Ville, the Louvre and the Tuileries, all famous for many memorable events.

Beyond the Tuileries Gardens is the Place de la Concorde, where the guillotine stood during the reign of terror. Louis XVI., Marie Antoinette, Charlotte Corday, Danton, Robespierre and St. Just are among the victims of the place who in all numbered about 2,800. In the center of the square now stands an Egyptian obelisk and on every side are signs of wealth, beauty and culture.

Toward the west stretch the Champs Elysees, bordered on each side with palaces and terminated by the grand triumphal arch of the armies of Napoleon I.

I crossed the Seine to the parliament buildings and the Hotel des Invalides where I saw the magnificent tomb of Napoleon I. Opposite the Louvre is the famous Academy and back of it is the Latin Quarter. Still farther is the Luxembourg palace with its art treasures. Toward the east are the Pantheon and the Sarbonne. On an island in the Seine is the grand cathedral of Notre Dame.

I found a couple of pleasant rooms in the Latin Quarter. I then secured my heavy baggage which I had shipped direct from Geneva. For the first time in two months I felt at home. I was so thoroughly bronzed by the sun that when I met an old friend on the street he failed to recognize me. I settled down to rest after the long tour in the Levant and viewed the sights of Paris leisurely. One day I would make a little excursion up or down the Seine on the little steamers. Another day I would spend in the galleries among the treasures of art. While a third I would wander among the tombs of the famous dead at Pere Lachaise. I made trips to Versailles, Vincennes, St. Denis and St. Cloud. At the cafes I had ample opportunity to study the various phases of Parisian life, while the libraries afforded means of informing myself thoroughly of the past.

The charms of life in Paris are great. The resourses of the city for gayety or study are equally good. No one can wonder that the Parisians think life away from Paris hardly worth living. I spent a month in the great city and thoroughly enjoyed every minute of the time.

At the end of June I started for London. I first went to Rouen, which contains some of the most beautiful Gothic churches in existence. Rouen is also famous as the place where Joan of Arc was burned at the stake in 1431. I spent the night at Dieppe, which is quite a popular watering place and early the next morning took the steamer for Newhaven. The voyage across the channel was pleasant but a good many of the passengers suffered from sea sickness. I escaped that misery as usual.

From Newhaven to London is a short ride. I left the train at Victoria station and soon found comfortable quarters for a three weeks' stay. London seems very dingy and dirty after seeing Paris.

I started from my quarters in the morning. Walking down Victoria street I came to Westminster Abbey which contains the ashes of more famous Englishmen than any other spot in England. The sensations of the student may be imagined when he stands at the graves of so many famous men and women. The thoughts inspired by such scenes are not easily forgotten.

Beyond the Abbey is Westminster Hall, famous for the greatest trials in English history. Connected with it are the Houses of Parliament, an immense Gothic structure. I went through the great assembly halls but Parliament was not in session.

From Westminster steamers run every few minutes to London Bridge, from which it is but a short walk to the Tower. There can be seen the crown jewels of countless value. There are the dungeons which have been occupied by many famous victims who were led out to the neighboring hill for execution. The Tower is suggestive of many mournful memories. It is one of those places which make one glad that he lives in the nineteenth century.

Returning towards the center of the city I came to St. Paul's cathedral, one of the largest and most magnificent churches in the world. Beyond St. Paul's are Fleet street and the Strand.

On the second of July I was coming down Cheapside, when I was startled and horrified to hear the newsboys crying an extra, "all about the assassination of President Garfield." While in Europe I had been used to hearing every week or so that this or that sovereign had narrowly escaped assassination but I never dreamed that any American President's life would be endangered in a time of profound peace. The evening papers contained but a very brief telegram concerning Guiteau's infamous act and the Sunday papers had nothing more. It was not till Monday that the details of the crime were published. From this time until I sailed, news from the dying President became the absorbing item of interest.

I left London on a late night train on the Great Western railway, passed the school towns of Harrow and Rugby and stopped at Coventry in the early morning. Taking another train I was soon at Kenilworth viewing the ruins of the castle which the pen of Sir Walter Scott has made forever famous. The crumbling walls are picturesque and their history makes them doubly interesting. The castle was built in the twelfth century and in 1565 was presented by Queen Elizabeth to her favorite, the Earl of Leicester. The latter's prodigality embellished and enlarged the castle and his receptions of the Queen attained an Oriental magnificence.

From Kenilworth it is a short ride to Stratford-on-Avon, the birthplace of Shakespeare, the greatest genius the world has seen. The house in which the poet was born contains many interesting relics and the church which covers his mortal remains stands by the river Avon where the trees, the sparkling stream and the fragrant fields make a charming sight.

From Stratford I traveled direct to Scotland passing Birmingham and Carlisle. I alighted at Ayr and paid a visit to the birthplace of Robert Burns. The two bridges of Ayr, Alloway Kirk, the Burns monument and Tam O'Shanter's bridge are among the many sights in that neighborhood which are made places of pilgrimage on account of their connection with the history of the bard.

I went from Ayr to Glasgow and then to Edinburgh, one of the most interesting and most beautiful cities in Europe. The monuments and public buildings which embellish Edinburgh give it a grand appearance. From the castle the view of the city and the Frith of Forth is one that becomes forever fixed in the traveler's memory.

Holyrood palace on account of its association with the mournful history of Queen Mary Stuart is one of the most interesting spots in Edinburgh. The city also contains many places which are identified with Scotland's statesmen, warriors and men of letters.

From Edinburgh I went to Melrose, saw the famous abbey and Abbotsford which is crowded with relics of Sir Walter Scott, and visited the grave of the great novelist at the picturesque ruin of Dryburgh abbey.

I went from Melrose to Liverpool where I embarked for Belfast. I spent a week on the banks of Lough Neagh amid the green fields of Ireland. I then returned to Liverpool and took passage for New York on the "Egypt," of the National line. We steamed down the Mersey in the evening and stopped a short time at Queenstown next day. When the shores of Ireland disappeared below the horizon that night the Irish emigrants were making the air musical with their songs. They turned hopefully to the New World and remembered nothing but the bright side of the home they had left.

The voyage to New York was uneventful and everybody seemed overjoyed when we sighted Sandy Hook. On the evening of August 18th, 1881, I reached home, having been absent two years lacking ten days.

I left home alone and in the two years that I spent in the Old World I never had any other companionship than the fellow travelers I chanced to meet for the day. Of course I missed many pleasures which agreeable companionship would have afforded and passed many lonesome hours which I could have avoided had I been accompanied by some other student of kindred turn of mind. On the other hand the lack of companionship compelled me to talk with the people I happened to be with and forced me to always be in immediate contact with the inhabitants of the country through which I was traveling.

THE END.

www.ingramcontent.com/pod-product-compliance
Lightning Source LLC
Chambersburg PA
CBHW032144010526
44111CB00035B/1044